THE LORD BLESSES ME

THE LORD BLESSES ME

CENTER CELEBRATIONS
OF GOD'S WORD
FOR CHILDREN AND
YOUNG FAMILIES

BY DICK HILLIARD

ILLUSTRATED BY
GEORGE COLLOPY

RESOURCE PUBLICATIONS, Saratoga, CA

Nihil Obstat: Rev. Martin Greenlaw

Imprimatur: John R. Quinn
        Archbishop of San Francisco

The Nihil Obstat and Imprimatur declare that this book is considered to be free from doctrinal or moral error. The content of this book is not intended to replace the official liturgy of the Church but rather complement and lead into it.

ACKNOWLEDGEMENTS
Except where noted, the Scripture quotations in this publication are from the Today's English Version Bible-Old Testament: Copyright © American Bible Society 1976, New Testament: Copyright © American Bible Society 1966, 1971, 1976. Used by permission. Text of Luke 2:16-20 is from the NEW AMERICAN BIBLE, © 1970 by The Confraternity of Christian Doctrine, Inc., Washington, D.C. Used by permission of the copyright owner. English translation of the Apostle's Creed by the International Consultation on English Texts.

Cover Design by George Collopy

Printing: 8   7   6   5   4   3

Library of Congress Catalog Card Number: 78-61308

ISBN: 0-89390-005-2

Published by Resource Publications.
Editorial and Business Office Mailing Address: PO Box 444, Saratoga, CA 95070

Printed and bound in the United States of America.

FOR:
JOE AND SHARON
KATHY
CARL AND TERRY
AND FATHER MATT
THROUGH WHOM
THE LORD
FIRST MADE KNOWN
THIS BLESSING

CONTENTS

Foreward 9
Author's Preface 11

Introduction

From Liturgy to LIGHTERGEE 13
The Center Celebration Concept 16
   The Greeting Center 16
   The Word Center 16
   The Praise Center 17
   The Creation Center 19
   The Sharing Center 19
   The Witness Center 19
Who Participates in Center Celebrations 20
Celebrations in the Religious Education Classroom 20
Parish Program Celebrations 20
Celebrations in the Family Home 21
Guidelines for Beginners 22
How to Use These Celebrations 24
Footnotes to the Introduction 25

Center Celebrations

A First Celebration 26
THE ADVENT SEASON
Songs for Celebrating the Advent Season 29
Introduction to the Advent Season 29
First Sunday of Advent, Year A 30
Second Sunday of Advent, Year A 34
Third Sunday of Advent, Year A 38
Fourth Sunday of Advent, Year A 42
First Sunday of Advent, Year B 46
Second Sunday of Advent, Year B 50
Third Sunday of Advent, Year B 52
Fourth Sunday of Advent, Year B 56
First Sunday of Advent, Year C 58
Second Sunday of Advent, Year C 62
Third Sunday of Advent, Year C 64
Fourth Sunday of Advent, Year C 68
THE CHRISTMAS SEASON
Songs for Celebrating the Christmas Season . . 71
Introduction to the Christmas Season 71
Christmas Vigil, Year A, B, C 72
In the Octave of Christmas, Holy Family Sunday,
Year A 76
In the Octave of Christmas, Holy Family Sunday,
Year B 78
In the Octave of Christmas, Holy Family Sunday,
Year C 80
The Octave of Christmas, Solemnity of Mary,
Year A, B, C 82
Second Sunday after Christmas, Epiphany, Year
A, B, C, ... 84
Third Sunday after Christmas, Baptism of the
Lord, Year A, B, C 86

THE LENTEN SEASON
Songs for Celebrating the Lenten Season 89
Introduction to the Lenten Season 89
Ash Wednesday, Year A, B, C 90
First Sunday of Lent, Year A 92
Second Sunday of Lent, Year A 94
Third Sunday of Lent, Year A 96
Fourth Sunday of Lent, Year A 100
Fifth Sunday of Lent, Year A 102
First Sunday of Lent, Year B 104
Second Sunday of Lent, Year B 106
Third Sunday of Lent, Year B 108
Fourth Sunday of Lent, Year B 110
Fifth Sunday of Lent, Year B 112
First Sunday of Lent, Year C 114
Second Sunday of Lent, Year C 116
Third Sunday of Lent, Year C 118
Fourth Sunday of Lent, Year C 120
Fifth Sunday of Lent, Year C 122
Passion (Palm) Sunday, Year A, B, C 124
THE EASTER TRIDUUM
Songs for Celebrating the Easter Triduum . . . 127
Introduction to the Easter Triduum 127
Holy Thursday, Year A, B, C 128
Good Friday, Year A, B, C 132
The Resurrection of the Lord, The Easter Vigil,
Year A, B, C 136
The Resurrection of the Lord, Easter Sunday, Year
A, B, C 140
SUPPLEMENTAL CELEBRATION
Songs for Celebrating Pentecost 142
Pentecost Sunday 142

Appendices

Calendar Table of Liturgical Seasons and Feasts 145
Glossary 146
The Kidsletter 148

Indices

Index of Creation Center Activities 149
Index of Food Recipes 149
Index of Games for Celebration 149
Index of Puppet Shows Based on Scriptural Tales 149
Index of Short Stories 149
Index of Songs and Refrains 149
Index of Stories and Familiar Personalities of
Scripture 150
Index of Traditional and Cultural Customs . . . 150
Index of Traditional Prayers Adapted for Use
With Children 150
Index of Themes 150
Index of Theme Titles 151

Foreward

Ring around the rosie,
A pocket full of posies
Ashes, ashes,
We all fall down.

Can you recall chanting this familiar childhood rhyme and playing the circle game that accompanies it? As in Humpty Dumpty and his famous fall, this rhyme celebrated youthful frivolity in one breath and human fragility and death in the next. It may appear unusual to preface a book on the enlivening of children's celebrations with talk of death; yet this childhood game introduces ritual in its simplest form, parodying nature and imitating life. The ritual song of ashes and posies, of life and death articulates a universal human experience illuminated for Christians by the gospel, by the paschal event of the Lord Jesus and by the sacramental rites which express the Easter mystery.

The life process implied by the chant: "Ashes, ashes, we all fall down," begins with growing up. Growing up means falling from a primal innocence that no one of us adults escapes. Life is not all dances and flowers. Playing house differs from managing a home and a family. Shooting an imaginary rifle at make-believe enemies is not the same as training for war. The ancients marked this fall from innocence with rites of passage. Facing the fall, facing Eve's challenge to Adam, confronting the reality of life and death with its attending excitement leads human beings to ritualize, to make tangible their beliefs, to engage in mythic imagination and, paradoxically, to become more childlike. Perhaps the rhymes and riddles associated with childhood are not child's play after all, but an indication of a natural flair for ritual making in all of us from the very beginning.

We adults who wander around in the world of early childhood education must rid ourselves of romantic notions that childhood is a time free from all fears, anxieties and tensions and remind ourselves again and again that children are people, whole and complete, who experience the world differently but no less really than we adults. They deserve more than a pocket full of candy-coated truths and moralisms from us. They deserve a chance to express themselves and to do so in a supportive, prayerful and educational atmosphere.

This is what Dick Hilliard provides in his thoughtful and imaginative resources. *The Lord Blesses Me* ritualizes childhood moments within Christian family and classroom settings. Dick Hilliard understands how a child experiences the world and bases his approach on current pedagogical techniques. He also understands that helping children learn the how's and why's of worship can make sense only if there exists an adult community of faith of which the children can be a part.

Special liturgy should be seen in the context of the whole worshipping community. The Eucharist requires an adult commitment, for worship "in spirit and truth" cannot be separated from how one lives a mature faith daily. The liturgical cult signs forth in praise what an adult Christian community claims to be at all times. Elementary age children need to be readied for rites like the Eucharist long after their First Communions. Dick Hilliard's work presents one man's efforts to bring children to such a readiness through simple, prayerful, gospel related experiences.

The Lord Blesses Me calls children to pray as children and invites catechists to prepare their children for the loss of innocence and to plant seeds, challenging them to recover and reclaim as adults the sense of innocence that Jesus found and praised in his own rough-hewn band of disciples:

"I bless you, Father, Lord of heaven, for what you have hidden from the learned and clever, you have revealed to the merest children." (Lk 10:21)

Jack Miffleton
Oakland, CA 1978

9

Author's Preface

Remember the days of years gone by when a young man would walk through the gates of seminary grounds and remain within the building's hallowed halls with but a few encounters with the "outside" before his ordination day? When I first walked the paths and roads of St. Patrick's College as a seminarian in 1971, I could not help but realize that I was an heir among a new generation of men preparing for the priesthood. My inheritance was a program of priestly formation marked by unprecedented freedom, a freedom made possible by the vision and trust of the Sulpician Fathers and the bishops of the dioceses in northern California.

My years in the seminary have been marked with a freedom to be involved "outside," in what today we have come to regard as the "pastoral ministry." That this freedom was made possible is the brilliant insight of seminarians and seminary faculties from years gone by. That this book is in print is the miraculous benefit of the seminary programs of my day.

If my writing in this book has any hint of pious piffle, romantic meanderings or ideological rantings, then I have not been true to the teaching tongue of Father Dick Basso, SS, who first encouraged my involvement in liturgical celebration with children. With but a morsel of his enthusiasm for Christian celebration, I embarked on a new venture in seminary training and landed on the doorstep of my first pastoral frontier, St. Julie's Parish in San Jose, California. I was drawn through the rectory doors by a magnet of enthusiasm for human celebration, Father Matt Sullivan. With his unceasing interest and benediction, Joe and Sharon Hein, Kathy Tobin, Sr. Pat Helin and I managed to create a paraliturgical program for the youngsters of St. Julie's. It developed with the aid of Carl and Terry Bialorucki and other faithful parents into the present concept of Center Celebrations. I am indebted to these outstanding parish leaders and to the worshipping community of St. Julie's Parish which has done so much to broaden my understanding of what priestly ministry can and should be, and whose long encouragement helped give birth to the ideas in this book.

When I prepared to leave my pastoral assignment at St. Julie's, my sister, Sr. Maureen Hilliard, SND, insisted that I prepare an article, based on our paraliturgical program, for publication. Her insistence proved to be valuable as it was readily accepted by *Modern Liturgy's* Bill Burns, an incredibly courageous publisher with prophetic foresight. While my article remained in his files pending publication, Bill summoned me to his office to explore the possibility of expanding the article into a full-length book. Soon the creative liturgists of *Modern Liturgy's* Editorial Board bravely accepted a proposal for such a publication project.

During the summer before my last year of seminary training, my parents cleared their garage so that I might begin the project of condensing my notes and writing this edition. Their patience during this endeavor cannot be ignored and their support will never be forgotten. My mother's efficiency as a secretary helped prepare my manuscript for publication. Her work was truly love made visible.

As I began to present the Center Celebration concept to teachers, parents and others interested in the liturgical maturation of young people, I was not aware that it would grow as the mustard seed of the Gospel parable. My sister-in-law, Beverly Hilliard, must be credited as the first to nest in the classroom branches of the Center Celebration program. Her ingenuity and dedication to Christian education served me well in her adaptation of the concept at St. Pius School, Redwood City, California, and in her critique of my writing.

Dr. Eileen Freeman provided a scholarly review of my use of biblical passages and helped me rid the text of sexist and clericalist language. Rev. Mr. Dennis Browne, my learned classmate, proved his professional writing ability in his editing and preparation of my manuscript. Rev. Doug Adams helped me broaden the scope of this book with his insightful ecumenical suggestions. Marilyn Neri's success as a Director of Religious Education and her devotion as a parent ensured the book's appeal in both religious education programs and family homes. And Joe and Sharon Hein invested their experience with the Center Celebration concept in reviewing my manuscript and produced numerous practical suggestions.

The observant eye of Sr. Helen Marie Gilsdorf, SM, preserved the text from typographical error. And the artistic mind of George Collopy is expressed eloquently, simply and provocatively in his illustrations. Their work is an immense contribution to the appearance of the book.

Few people ever achieve their due recognition in their own lifetime. Jack Miffleton is one of such a few. His talent and creativity in the realm of celebration with children is regarded with high esteem throughout the nation. It is rightly so! His assistance to me in preparing this book is deeply treasured and is further evidence of his unquestioned concern for the liturgical needs of all children. His own conviction and vision of children's celebration helped me perceive this present task from the start and has allowed me to write the following paragraphs with my own firmness of intention.

This book should be thought of as a resource of ideas for getting you started on your development of Center Celebrations with young children. It is full of suggestions for activites to be celebrated with young children growing in their appreciation for God's Word and the liturgical life of the Church.

At the outset, it should be emphasized that the Center Celebrations which are planned and described in this book are not blueprints. That is, they are not restricted units which do not allow for flexibility and adaptation. On the contrary, they are celebrations which should be considered as possible Center Celebrations by parents, teachers, and other leaders of children.

Occasionally all the activities of a particular celebration will be appropriate for your situation. Great! Celebrate, then, with your participants, using as guidelines these written descriptions and directions.

Sometimes, however, one or more activities will not be suited to your circumstances. In these cases, I hope you will freely adapt or change the activity to something which will let you be more comfortable with your participants. You know your participants best. It is my hope that these Center Celebrations will be guidelines and resources, rather than directives or blueprints for your celebrations.

As you begin, then, to celebrate with young children and as you continue to pray with them in response to God's Word, may your Center Celebrations bring to the lips of children the words of Mary,

> *My heart praises the Lord;*
>   *my soul is glad because of*
>   *his lowly servant!*
> *From now on all people will*
>   *call me blessed,*
>   *because of the great things*
>   *the Mighty God has done for me.*
>   *(Luke 1:46-49)*

Indeed, may each of us believe in our hearts and proclaim with gladness, "The Lord blesses me!"

Dick Hilliard
Menlo Park, CA
February 2, 1978
Feast of the Presentation

Introduction

From Liturgy to LIGHTERGEE

The need for children's liturgies is obvious to those who live and work with young people. Children are not capable of thinking and acting as adults. Thus, their religious profession, indeed their identity as a Christian, and their expression in prayer and worship should be those of children.

The Christian community has taken children seriously from its earliest times. In fact, the Roman Church's nearly exclusive concentration on the child as the object of religious education has marked its history for centuries. It should be no surprise, then, that the Church has broadened its concern for the religious growth and experience of the young and focused much of its present energies upon improving the climate of liturgical formation among children.

With the publication in 1973 of the *Directory For Masses With Children* by the Sacred Congregation for Divine Worship, the post-conciliar liturgical renewal of the Catholic Church gave prominent attention to the re-examination of ways in which we priests, parents and educators present the signs and symbols of the eucharistic celebration to young children. For the Church in North America, the *Directory* implicitly recognized the previous calls of such children's liturgists as Virginia Sloyan, Gabe Huck, Sr. Elizabeth Blandford, Sr. Janet Marie Bucher, Jack Miffleton, Rev. Carey Landry and others to adapt the pattern of adult Catholic worship to a level of understanding which could be genuinely grasped by children celebrating the Mass. The spirit of the *Directory* has endorsed the many excellent volumes of resources for children's Masses which have since been published for use in the American Church, for which we priests, parents, educators and children must surely be grateful.

It would seem, however, that the *Directory's* emphasis lies solely with the concern for improving eucharistic celebrations with children, as its full title implies. But on the contrary, a careful examination of the text reveals that the interest of the Church is not merely in renewal of children's eucharistic celebrations *per se*, but reaches far beyond this need by summoning "all who have a part in the formation of children" to evaluate preparatory eucharistic catechesis by which young people are introduced to the eucharistic celebration of the faithful assembly.[2]

Let us not relegate this summons of the *Directory* to the religious education classroom nor to the catechist who accepts the community's responsibility for preparing its younger members for First Communion. No, this would too readily suggest that catechesis is only a schooling event. Catechesis is much more than this. Catechesis is not just to be provided through the implementation of lesson plans, but is to be experienced by association with the Christian family in every social situation. That's the celebration of life in which every Christian must take part! As the *Directory* notes, "Various kinds of celebrations may also play a major role in the liturgical formation of children and in their preparation for the Church's liturgical life. By the very fact of celebration children come easily to appreciate some liturgical elements.[3]

Essential to the child's preparation for the Church's liturgical life, the source and the summit of all its activity,[4] is the experience of a worshipping community. Community is at the heart of Christian education not simply as a concept to be taught but as a reality to be lived.[5]

In its Pastoral Message on Catholic Education, the National Conference of Catholic Bishops wrote, "As God's plan unfolds in the life of an individual Christian, he grows in awareness that, as a child of God, he does not live in isolation from others. From the moment of Baptism he becomes a member of a new and larger family, the Christian community."[6] Bearing in mind that, as members of the Christian community, all are called to participate actively in the liturgical prayer of the Church, proper eucharistic catechesis, indeed all of religious education, must therefore involve the child in his/her faith community and in that community's liturgy.[7]

Center Celebrations were developed out of concern of one small Christian community for the liturgical formation and eucharistic catechesis of its children. The faithful community of St. Julie's Parish in San Jose, California, recognized and affirmed what children's liturgists had been saying since the church's liturgical renewal had been stimulated by the bishops at Vatican Council II. Their analysis of a child's participation in the Sunday celebration of the adult Christian community might be typified in just one ugly word: PROBLEMS!

P - Prayer is experienced by the young child at Mass as nothing more than a monotonous dialogue between priest and assembly. Liturgical prayer could be nothing more than the mere repetition of memorized or verbalized verses.

R - Readings from scriptures are rarely, if ever, made intelligible to a young child attending Sunday Mass. Rather than fostering an appreciation for the Word of God, the readings serve only to instil in the child dissatisfaction with the Gospel message.

O - Obligation to attend Sunday Mass is understood by the young child as the penalty placed upon everyone having the misfortune to be born of Catholic parents. The environment of Sunday worship does little to create a realization of obligation as the promise one makes to the community with whom one chooses to profess the faith.

B - Boredom with liturgical ritual quickly leads to apathy. When apathy toward liturgical celebration encompasses any Christian's outlook, particularly the child's, then the greatest obstacle to fostering the Gospel message in the hearts of people is created.

L - Locations for liturgical action are frequently situated outside of a child's line of sight. The very physical size of children prevents their giving active attention to something so distant as a sanctuary, which cannot be seen between the bodies of towering adults.

E - Encouragement to let children be children during liturgical celebrations is so foreign to the parish experience of Sunday Mass that children quickly come to think of reprimands and punishments for their conduct as by-products of the Sunday obligation. This is hardly the atmosphere one would hope to create for the teaching which lies at the core of Christian doctrine: love God and love your neighbor as yourself!

M - Mystery becomes the perplexing frustration of the child who cannot yet fully grasp the meaning of the liturgy's prayers, readings and purpose. For years we've been giving the wrong answers to the child's query, "What happens at Mass?"

S - Sermons can be the most tedious moments for the child unwillingly caught up in the mysterious ritual of Christian eucharist. This occasion for unfolding the mystery of the celebration is the homiletic device of the preacher, but the continued neglect of priests for speaking in words and signs which are understood by children adds to the already mounting resentment in the young person.

What the St. Julie community discovered had been determined by other similar communities long before. It was this widespread experience which led the Church to officially speak out in its *Directory for Masses With Children.* It feared, as did its communities throughout the world, that the PROBLEMS children experienced would soon lead to a lack of affection for sacred worship as might be described in

A Kid's OHde To Liturgy
Liturgy.
You mean liturGEE.
Oh GEE, do I have to go to liturgy?
GEE whiz. There's nothing to do at liturgy!
Liturgy.
That means God's stuff. Prayer and stuff.
GEE whiz. There's something stuffy about liturgy.
GEE, don't make me go to liturgy.

Liturgy.
I mean liturGEE.
Oh GEE, I had to go to liturgy.
GEE whiz. There's a mystery to liturgy.
Liturgy.
That means grown-up stuff. Talk and stuff.
GEE whiz. Don't stuff liturgy at me!
GEE, did I have to go to liturgy?

Liturgy.
I mean lit-ur-GEE!
Oh GEE, did you see me at liturgy?
GEE whiz. No other kid was at liturgy.
Liturgy.
That's your stuff. Church and stuff.
GEE whiz. I'm stuffed full of liturgy.
GEE, I just won't go to liturgy.

So the St. Julie community created Center Celebrations to answer the call for Eucharistic catechesis "directed to the child's active, conscious, and authentic participation"[8] in the liturgical life of the Church. As non-sacramental liturgies, Center Celebrations engaged young children in a genuine participation in the liturgy of the Church, not by explaining the meaning of ceremonies, but by preparing children for communal prayer, for a correct understanding of our creeds, for listening to the Word of God, and for an authentic response in service to the Gospel message: all those things necessary for a true liturgical life.[9] In the very act of celebrating together outside of the eucharistic setting, children came to recognize that their own expression of themselves was at the heart of liturgy, as might be characterized in

Another Kid's OHde to Liturgy
Liturgy
You mean liturgy for me
GEE, that's LIGHTurgy?
No, LIGHTurGEE!
Liturgy.
That means kids' stuff. Fun and stuff.
GEE, LIGHTurGEE! Fun stuff for me.
LIGHT I said. There's somethin' funny about liturgy.

Liturgy.
You got it, LIGHTurGEE.
A LIGHTer GEE than I thought.
Ain't nothin' heavy about LIGHTurGEE.
Liturgy.
That means fun stuff. God's stuff.
GEE whiz. Stuff me full of LIGHTurGEE.
LIGHT I said. I wanna go to liturgy.

Liturgy.
I mean just for me.
LIGHTly now, my own liturgy.
GEE whiz, it's fun to go to liturgy.
Liturgy.
That means celebratin' stuff. Life's stuff.
GEE whiz. Life is what is LIGHTurGEE.
LIGHT I say. I'm gonna go to liturgy.

In fact, over a long period of catechetical Center Celebrations, children came to recognize a similarity between the eucharistic liturgy and the liturgies they loved to call their own. Their attitudes toward Sunday Mass gradually shifted from resentment to what might be called

A Kid's Final OHde to Liturgy
Liturgy.
Who says litERgy?
There's somethin' better than LIGHTur GEE?
Liturgy.
You don't mean lightERgee? That's tough!
GEE that's tough to do. For me and you?
ER, you say we're goin' to a LIGHTERgee?
Liturgy.
You and me at LIGHTERgee?
Liturgy.
ER it's a lighterGEE?
There's somethin' happenin' to LIGHTurGEE!
Liturgy.
That means you and me and all that stuff?
Golly GEE. Look what's happenin' to LIGHTurGEE.
ER, I'd like to say we're goin' to a liturgy.
Liturgy.
Everybody's at LIGHTERGEE.
ER, that's a GEE for you and me.
C'mon, let's go to LIGHTERGEE.
Liturgy.
That means us and God and prayer and stuff.
GEEsus too! Spirited stuff at LIGHTERGEE.
Er, what happened to liturGEE?

The Center Celebration Concept

At the time of the evolution of the Center Celebration concept, an innovative approach to elementary education was sweeping its way into nearly every school district in the United States. Concerned for the individual progress of each student, teachers established "learning center" areas in their classrooms where students would assemble to complete assignments according to their own pace and capacity for learning. It was not surprising, then, for a young child to walk into an elementary grade and find different learning centers for math, reading, social studies, vocabulary skills and many other fundamental subjects.

Because authentic liturgical celebration is a summary expression of the experience of life, it should at once be both the summit of human interaction and its source. For the young child, life's experience might be described in three general, distinct yet overlapping, areas: family interaction, school life, and play time. Combining these three aspects of a child's life experience, Center Celebrations join playful activities with a "family" atmosphere and place these within a learning center format, all in response to the concern for proper eucharistic catechesis.

Imagine one large confined area for celebration within which five smaller areas are designated for specific kinds of activities which would allow children to celebrate freely in a way which is distinctly childlike, yet genuinely both religious and liturgical. These areas are known as "centers"; hence, the concept of Center Celebrations. The centers are given titles which represent the general kinds of activities which would be celebrated: The Greeting Center, The Word Center, The Praise Center, The Creation Center, The Sharing Center. These centers seek to foster the human values which are found in the eucharistic celebration: the activity of the community, exchange of greetings, capacity to listen and to seek and grant pardon, expression of gratitude, experience of symbolic actions, a meal of friendship, and festive celebration.[10]

Adults, those fully initiated into the Christian community, should be the leaders of these Center Celebrations, often sharing responsibility not only for the planning and preparation of these liturgies, but also for the implementation and supervision of the children participating in the many different events of each celebration. To familiarize the leaders with the specific purpose of each center and the activities which give body to the purpose, let us examine more closely each of the five physical centers within the celebration area. We will also examine a sixth center, the Witness Center, which aims to send the theme and message of the celebration in the heart of each participant following every Center Celebration.

GREETING CENTER

Among the human values which the *Directory* lists as necessary to eucharistic celebration are the "activity of community" and the "exchange of greetings." As a means of placing these values in the lives of children, the Greeting Center has been formulated as the area which is ordinarily chosen for the initial activity of each Center Celebration. Here the participants gather for their liturgy, becoming acquainted with one another, sharing the events of their lives, welcoming new participants into their liturgical community, and listening to the leader's introduction to the theme of the celebration for which they have assembled.

The Introductory Rite of the Mass serves to awaken the congregation to the reality that they have come together as a community. This, quite simply, is the purpose of the Greeting Center. It is where the participants are given the opportunity to prepare for the activities of the subsequent centers, to sing and to set the mood for the liturgical event for which they are gathered.

Just as the entrance hymn of the eucharistic liturgy enables the congregation to become aware that they are a community, so also does an opening song at the Greeting Center help participants to sense their unity, and common purpose. Throughout this text, each Greeting Center activity begins with a suggested opening song, except for a few rare instances when an uncommon mood must be set.

After the opening song, each celebration might begin with the Sign of the Cross, a familiar Christian symbol which simply states the common purpose which has called the community together — their shared faith.

An appropriate place for the Greeting Center area is near the entrance to the celebration room. It could be simply decorated with colors or signs which suggest the theme of the day's reading from the Word of God.

Usually the Greeting Center activities suggested in the texts of the celebrations are designed to reveal the theme of God's Word which is to be proclaimed during the time together. These activities are intended not only to place the participants in the spirit of the Word's message, but also to call upon their own life experiences which could give light and meaning to the message.

Ideally the Greeting Center activity should be "brief, bright, and joyful," opening the participants to one another and to God's Word.[11]

WORD CENTER

At the heart of our Christian faith is the Word of God. It is no wonder, then, that the liturgical assembly of the faithful places strong emphasis upon the proclamation of the Word of God. The Liturgy of the Word invites us to show our reverence for the Scripture and for its essential message when it is proclaimed by the Christian community.

In its instruction on eucharistic catechesis through liturgical celebration, the *Directory* clearly indicates that "Depending on the capacity of the children, the Word of

God should have a greater and greater place in these celebrations."[12] It is in response to this directive that the Word Center has become the focal activity area in Center Celebrations.

Note, however, sensitivity in the *Directory* to the "capacity" of children for hearing the Word of God. The works of Ronald Goldman and John Peatling represent the more important studies which have been made to ascertain the child's capacity to understand the Scriptures.[13] Goldman sought responses from children to the question, "What kind of book is the Bible?" Their answers could be organized into three categories related to age.

> The young children (ages 6 to 9) tended to describe the Book in terms of its physical properties (i.e., size, color, print, etc.). The slightly older children (ages 10 and 11) tended to describe the Bible in terms of its external use (i.e., a Book that is used in worship, read by the vicar, etc.). At this age insights into the Bible as being a venerated Book begin to appear. In later childhood (ages 12 and 13) the Bible is described in terms of its teaching quality. It is seen as a book which is helpful in directing people's personal lives. It is only in the middle and late teens that the Bible is seen as a summation of mankind's spiritual experience as he or she meets God in history.[14]

The implication of these findings is that some biblical stories are more easily adapted to certain age levels than to others. The *Directory* is written with this important fact in mind and states in its chapter on "Masses With Children in Which Only a Few Adults Participate" that "if all the readings assigned to the day seem to be unsuited to the capacity of the children, it is permissable to choose readings or a reading either from the *Lectionary for Mass* or directly from the bible."[15] It later clarifies, however, that "In the choice of readings the criterion to be followed is the quality rather than the quantity of the texts from scriptures. In itself, a shorter reading is not always more suited to children than a lengthy reading. Everything depends upon the spiritual advantage which the reading can offer to children."[16]

The Center Celebrations described in this book follow the Sundays of the Church's liturgical seasons and are, therefore, based on the readings assigned for each Sunday in the *Lectionary for Mass*. Care has been taken, however, to suggest only those readings from the Lectionary's assignments which are apporprate to the capacity of children according to the criterion set down by the *Directory*.

Thus, the Word Center is the place for proclaiming the essential message of the Center Celebration from the Word of God written and announced in Scripture. Leaders of these celebrations should reverently display the Bible in an appropriate setting at the Word Center so that children can associate the proclamation of the Word with the sacred book in which it is written.

The location of the Word Center within the Center Celebration area should be prominent. Give it the focal emphasis which the Word of God deserves.

Included in this book are complete passages of the suggested readings. The Good News Bible translation by the American Bible Society has been selected for its simple English written in words that are suited to the understanding of children.[17]

The Word Center activities described in this book will take a variety of forms that permit children to make biblical readings their own so that they may come more and more to appreciate the value of God's Word, as the *Directory* recommends.[18] Puppet shows, dramatic interpretations, spontaneous role playing, flannel board illustrations, songs and storytelling will frequently give shape to the proclamation of God's Word at the Word Center.

Leaders of Word Center activities must carefully balance enjoyment of and response to the stories and readings of scripture with a genuine reverence for the proclamation of the Word of God. Their sincere invitations to allow children to fully respond to God's Word[19] should be combined with their own skills as storyteller[20] and their own appreciation for the Word of God in the liturgy and in the life of the believer.

Often older children can be selected as readers of God's Word during Center Celebrations. In this way they not only develop an appreciation for God's Word in their lives and in the liturgy, but they also come to cherish the liturgical ministry of the reader. With smaller children, some of the bible readings included in this book should be shortened or freely adapted to their ability to listen.

PRAISE CENTER

The Praise Center has been developed to foster and promote among young children not only an appreciation for the importance of prayer in the Christian life, but to provide the instruction and the experience necessary to make prayer an integral component of their growth in faith.

The Church has always been a praying people united in Christ. This fact is evidenced from the earliest of Apostolic times ("They went as a body to the Temple every day but met in their houses for the breaking of bread; they shared their food gladly and generously; they praised God and were looked up to by everyone." Acts 2:46-47). Thus, the faith of the Church community is marked by its insistence on frequent and regular communal worship, the pinnacle of its prayer.

In the recent study commissioned by the Office of Research, Policy and Program Development of the United

States Catholic Conference Department of Education, it was discovered that

> children between the ages of 5 and 7 tended to have a very vague concept of prayer. They linked the concept to God in the sense that they realized that prayers are addressed to God but were unable to comprehend the meaning of the concept of prayer itself. In the second stage (ages 7 to 9) prayer was conceived as a verbal or physical activity. It could be differentiated from other activities but on the whole it was external and concrete lacking any cognitive or affective significance. In the third stage (ages 10 to 12) prayer was regarded as an integral activity derived from personal conviction and belief. At this stage prayer emerged as a true communication between the child and God.[21]

Granted, then, that the intent of the Praise Center is to foster a spirit of prayer, which the Church has held as a fundamental precept throughout its heritage, caution should be taken by the leaders of children's celebrations that realistic expectations of the child's capacity for prayer be determined by stages related to age. One should not expect a first grader, therefore, to eagerly respond to the invitation to pray with the community. Nor should the fourth grader be expected to explain the affective nature of prayer, though the child of ages 10 to 12 can be expected to experience genuine affection for the Father in various modes of prayer. Similarly, second and third graders should not be denied the experience of prayer simply because it is often recognized by them as but another form of human communication devoid of deeply spiritual commitment.

Growth in prayer is a process which demands instruction and experience. As a child matures in his/her awareness of the meaning and centrality of prayer in the Christian life, so also should the techniques of instruction and the opportunities for experience in prayer be developed for them by their educators and religious leaders. Praise Center activities, at home or in the classroom, led by parents and teaching adults who value prayer, will provide both the instruction and the experience.

Christian people can pray together as a community when they share some common prayers. It will be important to the prayerful maturation of the children with whom these center celebrations are conducted that some of the Church's great prayers be understood, prayed frequently and sometimes even memorized. Among these are the Sign of the Cross, the Lord's Prayer, the Hail Mary, the Apostle's Creed, and Acts of Contrition, Faith, Hope and Love.[22] Many of the so-called "common prayers" are included as specified Praise Center activities during different celebrations. The leaders of the center celebrations should freely make use of common prayers during all celebrations, even if they are not specifically included among the suggested instructions for a particular center activity.

But there is more to prayer than memorized formulas. Talking with God spontaneously and familiarly, and listening to him, is prayer.[23] Many of the Praise Center activities seek to cultivate these additional aspects of communal and personal prayer. With the leader as the exemplar of a multitude of praying styles, children will come to recognize and experience prayer in song, dance, bodily movement, silence and listening, greetings and petitions, through expressions of praise, pardon and thanksgiving, and by symbolic actions. Even informal prayer, suited to the child's age and capacity, should be frequently explained and encouraged. Unique forms of prayerful communal expression are occasionally suggested in the texts of these center celebrations. Among these are Chain Prayers, Movement Prayers, Repetition Prayers and Secret Message Prayers. Each of these forms of praying attempts to promote the young child's appreciation for prayer in the setting of the worshipping community of believers. (While these forms are explained in greater detail throughout the text, a summary description of each is given in the Glossary.)

Thus, the Praise Center affords the celebrating participants an opportunity to respond to the Word of God proclaimed during the center celebration through quiet reflection, spoken acclamation or bodily movement. Its activities seek to instruct in prayer while presenting a prayerful event.

The leader should not hesitate to perform the suggested activities. Often, a short private "rehearsal" of some activities will be necessary before the actual celebrations. During the actual celebration of the Praise Center activities, leaders should encourage the active participation of everyone assembled. With the shy participant, support and encouragement from the leader will be necessary. With the more boisterous, the leader must be gentle, yet firm. With all learners of prayer, those responsible for their growth should be loving, concerned and interested in leading them gradually on to a more mature prayer according to their age and capacity. By fidelity and conviction, leaders of these Center Celebrations will be laying the foundation for the growth of young children towards the most sophisticated forms of prayer — meditation, contemplation, and union with God.

As the participants grow accustomed to the nature of prayer and the variety of Praise Center activities, leaders should frequently invite different participants to pray spontaneously, in their own words, with the assembly. An attitude of respect should be fostered for one another at all times, especially when children are learning to pray as leaders. Care for the prayerful growth of every participant will keep the embarrassing word spoken by one youngster praying aloud from becoming a moment of silliness for all.

If some Praise Center activity described in this book does not seem to be appropriate to your situation or to the maturity of your participants, freely adapt it or change it to an event which encourages the active involvement of all the participants. You know your family or class or group best. The suggested activities should be guidelines for you in helping your participants pray and celebrate effectively.

It is at the Praise Center that the young participants come to celebrate not only effectively, but genuinely. "To celebrate genuinely with children," writes Janaan Manternach, "is to pray with them in an unforgettable way.[24]

CREATION CENTER

Children learn by experiencing what they are being taught, by doing and seeing and touching and making, not by figuring out in their heads what they are being taught. Children remember what they do more than what they hear. For this reason the Creation Center has been introduced to Center Celebrations as a setting for activities which bring the proclamation of God's Word to some tangible, active form in the celebration for young people.

Based on the theme of the Center Celebrations, the Creation Center usually provides space for some artistic activity which will either be used directly during other center activities or which might be made for a lasting reminder of the theme's message. All of the activities are suited to the abilities of young children, but should always be supervised by the adult leaders. Each Creation Center activity described in this book presumes that certain materials have been made available by the leaders. These materials are listed separately in each Creation Center activity description.

Younger children like to see a finished example of what they are going to make. Whenever possible, it is good to prepare a "final product" in advance of the celebration activities to be exhibited as a model.

As the Creation Center projects accumulate after several celebrations, children might enjoy compiling a scrapbook of their art for future review and recalling of Center Celebration themes and memories.

Art is the binding force that unites a child's experiences and sensations. It can become an outward manifestation of a very personal religious experience.[25] Thus, Creation Center activities allow the participants to "create" their own symbols, or to interpret other symbols in liturgical celebration. In this way they are afforded an appreciation for yet another essential human value which the writers of the Directory have recognized in the eucharistic celebration: the experience of symbolic actions.

SHARING CENTER

The Sharing Center is ordinarily the last "stop" before dismissal. It is here that the leaders should repeat what has been done and said in the preceding center activities so that the participants might be inspired to live the Gospel by service to God and others.

The Sharing Center has been created to answer two remaining needs which the Directory has determined should be met in eucharistic catechesis and liturgical formation. The Sharing Center provides for a meal of friendship[26] and invites a response to the Gospel in the daily lives of the children.[27]

To meet the need for a life-response to the Gospel, the Sharing Center is a place to draw all the activities which have preceded it into a simple summary statement or group discussion. It is here that the leader must express the connection between the liturgy and life.

In our eucharistic celebrations, the homily often serves to connect the message of God's Word with the lives of its listeners. Sharing Center activities allow the participants to express their own responses to God's Word through events which make the Gospel message meaningful to their young lives.

The Sharing Center also provides an opportunity for leaders to acquaint the young participants with the value which forms the heart of the eucharistic liturgy: a meal of friendship. Simple refreshments, when appropriately provided at the Sharing Center, are signs characteristic of festive human celebration and will offer a catechetical experience of close association in sharing a meal in response to the proclamation of God's Word.

Included in every Sharing Center activity is the giving of what has come to be called "The Witness Center" activity assignment.

WITNESS CENTER

These assignments are simple, concrete actions which the participants are encouraged to perform in response to the Word of God proclaimed through service or "witness" to others. These assignments are described at the conclusion of each Center Celebration included in this book. Their purpose is to enable the participants to respond to what "all liturgical and eucharistic formation should be directed toward: a greater and greater response to the Gospel in the daily life of the children."[28]

Witness Center activities should frequently be the topic of discussion in subsequent Center Celebrations during the initial Greeting Center activity. In this way the value of witness and service to the Gospel message is made accountable in the lives of the young who are themselves not capable of such responsible action.

Who Participates In Center Celebrations?

Center Celebrations are created for young children of elementary school age. Because of their primary purpose as eucharistic preparation, these celebrations are more closely suited to children who are still growing in their appreciation for the Eucharist. Both those who are preparing to participate fully in the Eucharist by receiving First Communion and those who have been initiated already into the faithful communion of the Eucharist can benefit from these Center Celebrations.

Younger children will ordinarily be the participants in Center Celebrations. But they need not be the only participants. Older children, too, will benefit by sharing in these activities with younger children and adult leaders. In fact, when given the opportunity to lead the young ones in some of the center activities, older children grow in their appreciation for the ministry of liturgical leadership.

Center Celebrations with children are most effective in three distinct situations: in the religious education classroom; in parish programs for children's celebrations; and in the family home. Each of these settings will contribute to the religious growth and liturgical formation of the young, yet each will have its own advantages and peculiarities!

Celebrations in the Religious Education Classroom

A "religious education classroom" can be a vague term. Here it is meant to describe two different types of educational structures in the Catholic Church. The one is the parochial Catholic school. The other is the parish CCD class. Let us look first at the Catholic school setting.

Center Celebrations find effective implementation in the primary grade classrooms of Catholic elementary schools as part of the regular religious education program of the institution. Teachers entrusted with preparing children in grades 1, 2 and 3 for reception of First Communion find the Center Celebration concept particularly helpful in leading young people to participate authentically in the parish community's Mass.

Teachers can prepare for Center Celebrations in their schools in a number of ways. One obvious method would be to select one day each week to use the time allotted to regular religion class for a Center Celebration based on Sunday's Mass readings. Celebrations can be conducted right in the classroom by moving desks to the room's sides, providing open space for movement and center locations. In this way children quickly come to realize that celebration is at the heart of religious formation.

Some schools find it more convenient to designate a special classroom just for Center Celebrations to be used by all grades and teachers on a rotation basis. In this way children not only appreciate celebration as part of religious formation, but they also recognize its unique and distinctive contribution to one's religious experience and expression.

CCD classes sometimes find it more difficult to replace weekly lesson plans with Center Celebrations based on Sunday Mass readings. Instead, teachers of classes which meet only once a week should freely adapt the Center Celebration concept as a format for class lessons. That's right, make every classtime a celebration! In this way children become more eager to respond to the message of religious education when they are encouraged to make that message their own celebration. By their nature, Center Celebrations are didactic and include many of the elements of an ordinary religious class: revelation of truth in God's Word, instruction and creative response.

Ideally, classroom groupings for Center Celebrations should not exceed 15-20 participants. When situations necessitate larger numbers, caution should be taken that there are several adults present to help lead the different center activities. Needs vary according to different circumstances, but as a norm, there should be one adult leader for every 5-7 participants in a Center Celebration.

Many parishes and schools have found it very rewarding to encourage high school students to be leaders of younger children in Center Celebration activities. This arrangement not only meets the needs of the young, but also actively involves teenagers in the catechetical and liturgical areas of parish life.

Parish Program Celebrations

Many parishes have already initiated innovative programs to meet the liturgical needs of young children. Special Masses and para-liturgical celebrations are just two of the various ways in which some parishes have begun to celebrate with children.

Center Celebrations are ideal for the parish in which liturgies for younger children are already an emphasis, or for parishes where they are about to be emphasized. Parent-Teacher collaboration in preparing young children for the Eucharist can meet its realization in Center Celebrations where parents and teachers coordinate and lead celebrations as supplementary, yet essential, elements of formalized religious instruction.

In parishes where "Family Programs" constitute the child's experience of religious education, coordinators will find Center Celebrations particularly helpful as liturgical events for the participants.

Some parishes also find it especially helpful to use some center activities in programs where it is common to separate younger children from the adult community during the Liturgy of the Word at Sunday Mass.[29] Time may not allow for an entire Center Celebration in such circumstances, but the Word, Praise or Creation Center activities described in this book have proven to be helpful aids in revealing the message of God's Word during these Sunday celebrations.

In any of these kinds of programs, the parish church, sacristy or hall could easily serve as the location for the Center Celebrations, which should be conducted by adults or young adults responsible for the catechetical formation of young children. Again, the size of such groupings should be restricted for easy management and proper supervision while celebrating.

Celebrations in the Family Home

It is carefully noted in the *Directory For Masses With Children* that "the Christian family has the greatest role in teaching the Christian and human values" which lie at the heart of eucharistic catechesis. It continues, "By reason of the responsibility freely accepted at the baptism of their children, parents are bound in conscience to teach them gradually to pray. Thus by praying daily with their children, even from their early years, they will easily begin to sing and to pray in the liturgical community."[30]

It is particularly fitting, therefore, that Center Celebrations have found their way into the very homes of families concerned with the eucharistic catechesis of their young. Weekly home celebrations of the Sunday readings often afford the family the unique opportunity and advantage of growing more closely together in their appreciation for the Word of God and for liturgical celebration. In families where one of the children is preparing to make First Communion, Center Celebrations can be an especially touching way of making that preparation truly a family affair.

It was the conclusion of the USCC Department of Education's study on the Religion of Children that "It is the family which is the primary agent of religious instruction."[31] Center Celebrations provide a simple format in which religious education can take shape in the prayerful adventure of family life. When mother and father take seriously their responsibility as Christian parents, they provide natural leadership for Center Celebrations within the home. Children, too, can become more involved in the preparation of Center Celebrations as they become more accustomed to the format.

Different rooms in the house can serve as appropriate centers for these celebrations. For example, the entrance hall could be the Greeting Center, the dining room could be the Word Center, the living room would become the Praise Center, the kitchen could serve as the Creation Center, and the family room could provide the area for the Sharing Center. Different members of the family can take responsibility for the preparation of the separate center activities.

Each family should determine a regular weekly time for celebrating together. Be it Saturday or Sunday evening, or Sunday afternoon, it should be a regular time during which the entire family can assemble to pray and hear God's Word.

ENTRANCE HALL

DINING ROOM

LIVING ROOM

KITCHEN

FAMILY ROOM

Guidelines for Beginners

Anyone just beginning to celebrate with young children will find it helpful to understand the general capacity which each different age level has for celebration. Each represents a noticeable degree of personal maturation and demands corresponding adult awareness of needs and expectations.

Although the Center Celebrations in this book are not intended for use with preschoolers, occasionally a little child will be a part of some celebrations. It is important to realize that the preschool years are marked by rapid fluctuations, between overdependence and independence, between competence and ineptitude, between affection and sudden destructiveness. For a young child, however, apparent acts of aggression may be more an exploration than an outburst of hostility.

In the young child's eyes, his/her parents are the source of all wisdom and virtue, but during the preschool years children's horizons broaden to include people outside their immediate families.

The preschool child also learns to distinguish between "make believe" and reality. Developing thinking skills give rise to new powers of imagination. Preschoolers enjoy dramatic play and the taking on of roles and the acting out of themes. Their descriptions of events and narratives of activities are often rambling and loose-jointed and include endless detail.

Most four-year-olds are very much creatures of the moment, whereas by age five many children can engage in planned projects and activities. A good leader of preschoolers will leave room for surprises and improvisation and spontaneity.

School-age children will be the ordinary participants of Center Celebrations. It is helpful to remember that they spend much of their time in the company of peers, from whom they learn firsthand about social structures, about in-groups and out-groups, about leaders and followers, about loyalties and heroes or heroines. They differ from preschoolers in that they are less egocentric and more able to view themselves with objectivity. They begin to see themselves in terms of labels society applies to them — male or female, white or black or brown or yellow, rich or poor, smart or dumb — and all that these connote.

Early in the school years, children's concepts of rules and morals are conceived and accepted as given: they are timeless and unchangeable. Late in the school years, children can grasp the fact that rules are arrived at by general agreement and serve only to define conduct in an orderly way.

Certain individual children — usually the best-looking, the biggest, the strongest, the brightest or most energetic — acquire a great deal of popularity and, with it, some power of leadership. However, children of school-age are in many respects hard-headed pragmatists, and when it comes to engaging in particular activities, they look for leadership in those children competent in that activity.

In general, boys tend to be doers and girls talkers. Boys tend to be oriented to things, with a special emphasis on things mechanical, and girls to people and social relations.

What follows is a summary exerpt of James Notebaart's "Liturgy With Children" which appeared in *Modern Liturgy* magazine, 1:7 (October 1974).[32] It is an excellent and sensitive statement about the children for whom Center Celebrations are developed.

First Grade

We don't have to become children to think in their patterns. To grasp this is critical at the first grade level. If you fake interest, they will know. The first grader has a very short attention span at the beginning of the day and at the beginning of the year. Take advantage of the time from 10:00-11:30 am. During the year you can gradually lengthen your prayer time.

When you are calling children to prayer, let them know what you are going to do. Tell them firmly if they misbehave. The leader of prayer has a great control over their attention and behavior.

The sense of touch will play an important part, so liturgies can be quite tactile. At this age children will want to act things out, but they will need a lot of direction from the leader. Children at this age are just beginning to understand rhythm and beat and tone.

Topics of prayer are frequently family, hurting, helping, being a brother or sister. Many of these themes can be brought out by stories that are told by the leader or by the children themselves. They also like to repeat prayers.

Second Grade

In many respects, second graders are similar to first graders. Their attention span is somewhat longer. Group acting is more coordinated and the children need less direction.

Third Grade

Children may understand the active elements better than they do the verbal thrust. So capitalize on what they are to *do* in liturgy.

Fourth Grade

A fourth grader feels that he or she is pretty much an adult and sometimes doesn't like all that kid stuff performed the year before. Yet while they separate themselves from the past grades they are often still very much children.

Participation in planning becomes important because fourth graders really will speak their preferences. Topical liturgies often work quite well.

Fifth and Sixth Grades

Fifth and Sixth Grades are demarcation lines in the children's lives. At this time the relationship they have with the leader of prayer is critical. They should know the leader and they should feel comfortable in the presence of the leader.

At this time as well they are becoming more aware of the changes within them. There are many activities which will embarrass them. Be sensitive to their own self-consciousness.

A Hint for Disciplining and Giving Directions

A key element in celebration with children is the leader's willingness to allow youngsters to be uninhibited and free to express themselves not only in prepared songs and dances or in planned activities, but also in actions which arise spontaneously. Sometimes, however, small incidents become distracting events and require appropriate discipline from the leader.

Children do not always readily accept correction for their behavior when voiced in front of other young ones. But teachers and parish leaders can employ a helpful tool when correcting little children — a puppet! Children quickly respond to the appearance of a puppet and heed its pronouncements without questioning.

When children are in need of being quieted, or when told to sit, stand, or move, even a parent can let a puppet do the talking. Puppets can be used to make announcements, introduce new participants and visitors or give instructions for such activities as are described in the Creation Centers.

Marionettes, glove puppets, even dolls or a ventriloquist's dummy can be used effectively in celebration with children. Young people love puppets and give them their quick and enthusiastic attention.

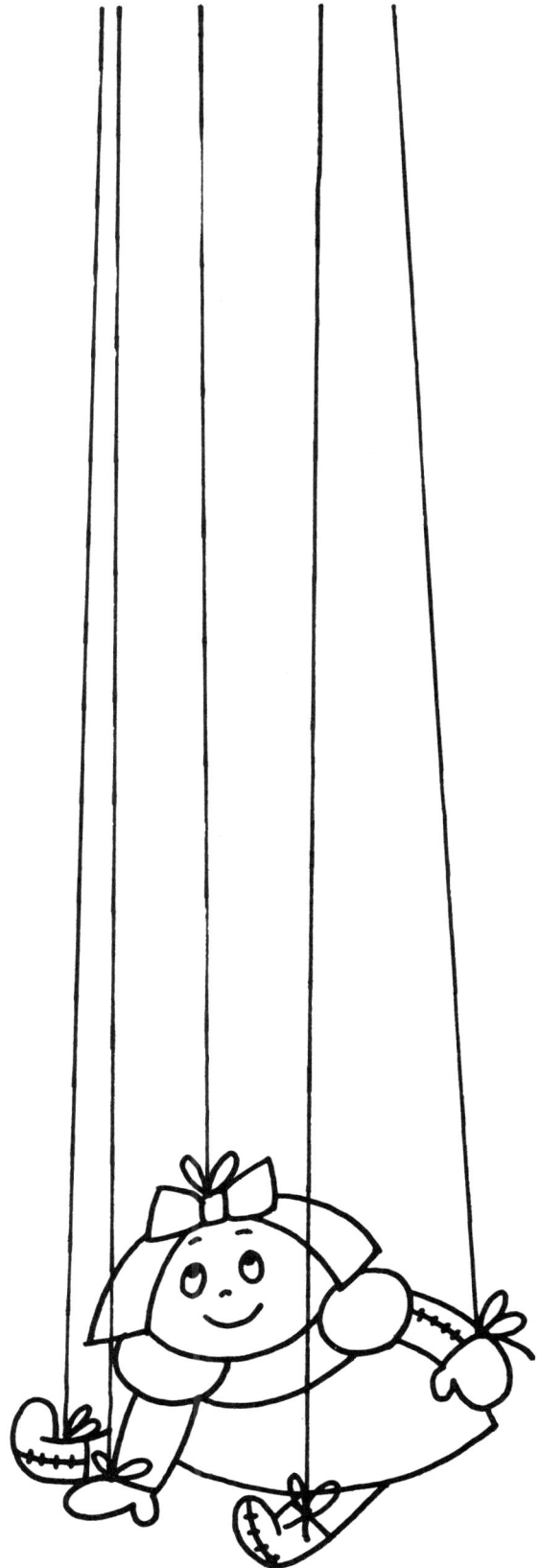

How To Use These Celebrations

In its first chapter of the *Directory*, the Sacred Congregation for Divine Worship has concluded that, "as the capacity of children develops, celebrations of the Word of God in the strict sense should be held frequently, especially during Advent and Lent."[33] In response to this seeming request, the Center Celebrations described in this book have as their base the readings suggested in the *Lectionary for Mass* for the Sundays of Advent and Lent and the special days which follow these liturgical seasons.

In compliance with the Vatican II Council's directive that at Mass "the treasures of the bible should be opened up more lavishly," the *Lectionary for Mass* provides a more and varied reading of Sacred Scripture on Sundays and feasts by arranging the texts in a three-year cycle. Thus the same text is read only once every fourth year. Each year is designated A, B, or C. (Refer to Table 1 in the appendix for determining the cycle of readings to be used during each school calendar year).

The Church's liturgical year begins with the First Sunday of Advent which comes at the close of each regular calendar year. For this reason, the Advent Season is the first set of celebrations described in this book.

Each Center Celebration begins with a heading indicating the Sunday or feast of the season for each year (e.g., "First Sunday of Advent, Year A"). Directly underneath the heading is the title given to the particular celebration. Directly underneath this title is a listing of the readings assigned in the Lectionary for proclamation at Mass. (The complete citation of scripture is ordinarily listed, except for the psalm responsorial which is not cited by verse, but only by Psalm number.)

To the right of this list of readings is a listing of the readings or passages which have been chosen for celebration from the *Lectionary* assignment. In most cases, only one or two of the readings assigned are to be a part of the suggested activities. Often the readings have been shortened. Sometimes readings have been expanded to capture the fuller sense of the passage, or readings altogether different from those assigned have been added to the celebration.

Each celebration then begins with an introductory statement of theme with certain hints for celebrating. Often special caution or direction is given for the different setting for which these Center Celebrations are designed: in the Religious Education Classroom; for Parish Programs; and in the Family Home.

Then each center activity descriptions begins. It must be noted that there is not a set sequence of center activities. Although most will begin with a Greeting Center activity and conclude with a Witness Center activity assignment at the Sharing Center, the Word, Creation and Praise Center activities will rotate in sequence depending on the theme and events of each celebration. Here, too, the leaders will want to freely adapt the suggested sequence of activities to best suit their circumstances.

The music and songs suggested for most activities are included in the accompanying songbook, "My Heart Is Happy." These are also available on cassette or album recordings. Other songs from Resource Publications and *Modern Liturgy* magazine are suggested for use in a listing at the beginning of each seasonal section.

Song plays an important role in celebration with children because of their "special affinity for music."[34] If the leaders can play such instruments as the guitar or piano, this would be ideal. The playing of cassette or album recordings are usually as effective during celebration activities.

Due to the different capacities of children, it will not always be suitable to sing every song which is suggested. Here, too, the leaders must feel free to choose songs which are familiar to young children while always attempting to add new songs to their repertoire.

Included at the start of this book is an introductory celebration which could be helpful in acquainting young children and families with the Center Celebration concept and format.

Footnotes

1. A translation prepared by the International Committee on English in the Liturgy is available from the Publications Office, United States Catholic Conference, 1312 Massachusetts Avenue, NW, Washington, DC, 20005.

2. Consult the *Directory*'s chapter on "Introduction of Children to the Eucharistic Celebration," numbers 8 through 15 inclusive.

3. *Directory for Masses With Children*, #13.

4. The core of the Church's official teaching on the liturgy is found in its Constitution on the Sacred Liturgy of the Documents of Vatican II, where it is written, "The liturgy is the summit toward which the activity of the Church is directed; at the same time it is the fountain from which all her power flows (#10)."

5. National Conference of Catholic Bishops, *To Teach As Jesus Did, A Pastoral Message on Catholic Education* (November 1972), #23.

6. *Ibid.*, #22.

7. NCCB, *Basic Teachings for Catholic Religious Education* (January 11, 1973), p. 3.

8. *Directory for Masses With Children*, #12.

9. Sacred Congregation for the Clergy, *General Catechetical Directory* (Washington: USCC, April 22, 1972), #25.

10. *Directory for Masses With Children*, #9.

11. Rev. James Dallen, "The Mass Today" in *The New Library of Pastoral Liturgy*, vol. 3, Dan F. Onley ed., (Phoenix: North American Liturgy Resources, 1976), p. 6.

12. *Directory for Masses With Children*, #14.

13. Cf. Ronald Goldman, *Religious Thinking from Childhood to Adolescence*, (London: Routledge, 1964), and John H. Peatling, "The Impact of the Word of Ronald Goldman: A Prospect," in *Religious Education*, 33 (1968), pp. 449-456.

14. Hart M. Nelsen, Raymond H. Potvin and Joseph Shields, *The Religion of Children*, Office of Research, Policy and Program Development, Department of Education, (Washington: USCC, 1977), p. 10.

15. *Directory for Masses With Children*, #43.

16. *Ibid.*, #44.

17. The *Directory* allows for and recommends the use of biblical translations "which may already exist for the catechesis of children and which are accepted by the competent authority (#45)."

18. *Directory for Masses With Children*, #46.

19. Cf. Bob and Margaret Miller, IHM, "Children Listen With Their Whole Bodies," *Modern Liturgy*, 4:6 (September/October 1977), pp. 8-9.

20. Cf. Ann M. Friedman, "Tips For Tellers of Tales," and Robert Bela Wilhelm, "The Liturgist As Story Teller," *Modern Litrugy*, 3:8 (November/December 1976).

21. Nelson, et al., *The Religion of Children*, p. 9.

22. *General Catechetical Directory*, #22 and #25.

23. *Basic Teachings for Catholic Religious Education*, p. 3.

24. Janaan Manternach, "Once Upon A Time," *Modern Liturgy*, 4:6 (September/October 1977), pp. 4-5.

25. Thea Eroes, *Handbook of Art Activities*, (Los Angeles: William H. Sadlier, Inc., 1971), p. 6.

26. *Directory for Masses With Children*, #9.

27. *Ibid.*, #15.

28. *Ibid.*

29. In its chapter on "Masses with Adults in Which Children Also Participate," the *Directory for Masses With Children* states, "It will perhaps be appropriate...to celebrate the liturgy of the word, including a homily, with the children in a separate area that is not too far removed. Then, before the eucharistic liturgy begins, the children are led to the place where the adults have meanwhile been celebrating their own liturgy of the word. (#17)."

30. *Directory for Masses With Children*, #10.

31. Nelson, et al., *The Religion of Children*, p. 35.

32. Before August 1976, *Modern Liturgy* was known as *Folk Mass and Modern Liturgy*.

33. *Directory for Masses With Children*, #14.

34. *Ibid.*, #30.

GETTING TO KNOW YOU

Genesis 2:4-7, 18-20

This celebration is prepared as an introduction to the format and types of activities which are conducted during Center Celebrations. It will be important for all the participants to get acquainted with one another, if necessary, as well as to become acquainted with the celebration room and its many centers.

Before the celebration, prepare a listing of the participants' names. Cut the list into strips so that each name is on a small piece of paper, and place the paper strips in a hat or can for use at the Creation Center.

GREETING CENTER

Materials Needed: a dictionary of names.

When the participants have arrived for this first celebration, begin by singing "Howdy Friends," allowing each to announce his/her name, in turn, as the song is sung by all.

After singing, let each participant explain the meaning of his/her name, such as:

    Benedict - one who is blessed
    Donna - a lady
    Nathan - a gift
    Deborah - a bee
    Margaret - a pearl
    Thomas - a twin

It might be helpful to have a dictionary handy with a section on the meaning of names to help some of the participants. If some names are not readily explainable, let it be a research project for the participants during the coming week.

Then simply explain that every time a Center Celebration begins, everyone should gather at the Greeting Center. Why? To greet each other! Ask the participants to suggest different types of greeting, such as:

    saying "Hello!"
    shaking hands
    kissing
    waving
    wishing "Peace!"

Let them demonstrate their suggestions as they are given.

WORD CENTER

Materials Needed: a bible, a stand or table for the bible.

Ask the participants to define "word." Help them realize that a "word" is something we use to identify persons and things. A "word" is a name for something.

Then show the participants the Bible. Ask them to identify the Bible. It is a book that contains many words that we cherish and respect. The Bible contains the many words which identify God and his care for human beings and all of creation. Let them know that the Bible is a holy book that we respect because it contains many of God's words, the words he has spoken through people long before us.

At the Word Center we will always hear the words of God in stories and tales from the Bible. (The Bible should be placed in a special position at the Word Center to emphasize our respect for the source from which we proclaim God's Word.)

Then ask one of the participants to read this passage from the Bible:

Genesis 2:4-7, 18-20

When the Lord God made the universe, there were no plants on the earth and no seeds had sprouted, because he had not sent any rain, and there was no one to cultivate the land; but water would come up from beneath the surface and water the ground.

Then the Lord God took some soil from the ground and formed a man out of it; he breathed life-giving breath into his nostrils and the man began to live.

Then the Lord God said, "It is not good for the man to live alone. I will make a suitable companion to help him." So he took some soil from the ground and formed all the animals and all the birds. Then he brought them to the man to see what he would name them; and that is how they all got their names. So the man named all the birds and all the animals.

Then ask the participants to close their eyes and think of their favorite animal. After a few moments ask them to think of the sound which their favorite animal makes. Then let each participant, in turn, make the sound of the favorite animal. After each sound, the other participants should try to guess the animal's identity by saying the animal's name, such as:

    roar - a lion
    chirp - a robin
    honk - a duck
    meow - a cat
    bark - a dog

See how much fun it is to give names to God's creation!

HONK!

PRAISE CENTER

When the participants have moved to the Praise Center, ask them if God has a name, too. Let them suggest different names for God, if they can, such as:

Creator
Lord
Father
Yahweh
Master
Shepherd
King

(Let their suggestions be their own. Don't suggest any titles or names which are too sophisticated for the participants' capacity for understanding. Also, remember that we only speak of God by way of analogy, that is, God is like a father or mother or lord to us.)

You might then ask, "When should we use God's names?" There will be many kinds of responses to discuss. Help the participants to realize that when we pray we should use God's names.

Then sing "Call My Name."

Continue in words such as these:

God wants us to call his name whenever we pray. When we pray we should give him praise and thanksgiving. Whenever we gather at the Praise Center, we will call on God's name and give him thanks and praise for all that He does for us.

Conclude by addressing God in the words which Jesus gave us:

Our Father...(see page 91).

CREATION CENTER

Name Tags

Materials Needed: a hat or can; construction paper; scissors; crayons or marking pens; paper punch; and yarn pieces.

In a hat or can should be placed paper slips with each participant's name. Let each participant draw a name from the hat or can.

Then let each make a name tag for the person whose name was drawn. Use crayons or marking pens on construction paper cut 3" X 5".

Punch two holes at the name tag's top and thread a three-foot-long piece of yarn through the holes. Tie the ends to form a hanger.

As the participants create their name tags, simply announce that whenever they gather at the Creation Center they will create something very special.

SHARING CENTER

Assemble at the Sharing Center, each participant holding the name tag he/she has created.

Teach the song, "Who Am I In God's Eye?"

When the participants have learned the song, sing it again while each places the name tag he/she made over the head of the person for whom it was made. Indeed, we are very special persons!

The Sharing Center is a place to share some ideas about the celebration activities. Let the participants share their answers to these questions:

What idea did you learn at the Greeting Center?
– we all have names
– our names have meanings

What idea did you learn at the Word Center?
– God lets us give names to all of creation

What idea did you learn at the Praise Center?
– He asks us to call His name

Then give the Witness Center activity assignment and conclude with a verse of "Call My Name" if time allows.

WITNESS CENTER

Each participant should be instructed to find out the meaning of the word "Christian." Ask them to bring an answer written on a piece of paper to their next Center Celebration.

At your next Center Celebration, let your Greeting Center activity include the participants' findings about the meaning of "Christian" — it is a name used to describe those who believe in Christ!

See Appendix III, "The Kidsletter," for additional suggestions for this Center Celebration.

THE LORD BLESSES ME

Mary's hymn of praise to the Lord for choosing her to bear the savior is at the heart of this happy song. Children will come to cherish the words of the Magnificat from Luke's gospel when they sing this melody. It should be used for celebrations of vocation, blessing and thanksgiving to the Lord and on feasts of Mary, the Blessed Mother.
the Magnificat for children

Dick Hilliard
arr. Rev. John H. Olivier, S.S.

My heart is hap-py in God, my Sav-ior. My heart sings with thanks to God.____ My heart is filled with love for the Fa-ther, for He has come to me.____

1. The Lord has smiled up-on me.____
2. He is all-pow - er - ful.____
3. The Lord ___ is ___ my God.____

1. The one He loves, a small poor one.____ From now on ev'ry-
2. He ___ has done great things for me.____ "Ho - ly is ___ His
3. He does mar-vel ous things for me.____ He has filled my

1. one will know:____ the Lord bless-es me!____
2. name", I sing.____ The Lord bless-es me!____
3. life with good.____ The Lord bless-es me!____

Songs For Celebrating The Advent Season

Title/Composer	Modern Liturgy Vol:No	Gather 'Round Page	Gather 'Round, Too! Page	The Lord Blesses Me Page	My Heart is Happy
ADVENT SONG JoAnn Brown	4:6	84			
THE ADVENT WREATH SONG Dick Hilliard				61	
COME OUT OF EGYPT W. F. Jabusch	2:6	8			
DO YOU KNOW? Dick Hilliard					X
FATHER, CARE Dick Hilliard			44		
JOHN THE BAPTIST Sr. Helen Marie Gilsdorf	2:6	7			
THE LORD BLESSES ME! Dick Hilliard	4:6	89		28	X
THE LORD IS COMING Angel Tucciarone	4:6	86			
NOAH'S SONG Dick Hilliard					X
THE OLD ARK Nancy Marsters	3:8	54			
PREPARE! THE LORD IS NEAR Sr. M. Angelita Amann	1:8	52			
PREPARE YE THE WAY Jeff Johnson	2:6	6			
REJOICE! BE GLAD! Dick Hilliard					X
SEE HOW THE VIRGIN WAITS W. F. Jabusch	2:8	19			
WAIT FOR THE SAVIOR Dick Hilliard					X
WAKE UP! WAKE UP! Dick Hilliard					X
WE HAVE A KING W. F. Jabusch	2:8	18			

Introduction to the Advent Season

The season of Advent is one of the most deeply cherished times in the Christian calendar. It provides an occasion for Christian people to reconsider the saving event of the Lord Jesus' coming among men and women. In addition to recalling to our minds the first coming of God's Son, Advent prepares us for our celebration of the feast of Christmas by focusing our attention upon the second coming of Christ. Advent is, then, the Church's season of joyful and spiritual expectation.[1]

The celebrations which have been included for the Advent Season are liturgies of God's Word redisovering the events of religious expectation among the Israelite people who awaited the Lord's coming as man on earth. With the recent trend toward commercialization of Christmas, this deeper meaning of Advent is easily lost amid the wrappings of advertising and public "holiday." Give these celebrations which follow your searching heart and discover with the children with whom you celebrate the message of salvation in the Lord.

Our Christian heritage and ethnic traditions give us many different ways to celebrate our preparation for Christmas Day. These Center Celebrations combine customs from many nations with Christian symbolism and provide a ceremonial expression of Advent in signs which are appropriate for contemporary understanding. The celebrations of the four Sundays of Advent for Year A take four cultural customs (Advent Calendar, Jesse Tree, Prophet Puppets, and Christmas Cards) and place them within a Christian liturgical context. The celebrations for the Advent Sundays of Year B focus upon four favorite personalities of the Christmas story (God the Father, John the Baptist, Isaiah, the angel Gabriel). And the centuries-old celebration of lighting the Advent Wreath is combined with simple contemporary signs in ritualizing the four Sundays of Advent in Year C.

May your Advent Season be joyful and spiritual and lead you to realize the Lord's blessings in your life!

THE LORD COMES TO US

Isaiah 2:1-5
Psalm 122
Romans 13:11-14
Matthew 24:37-44   Matthew 24:37-44

Helping young children to prepare for the religious significance of Christmas is difficult because they live in the highly commercialized world of our day.

The activities of this Center Celebration should encourage children and families to make every day of Advent a prayerful preparation for our celebration of the Lord's coming among us at Christmas. While the passage of Matthew's gospel chosen for this first Sunday of Advent is really a lesson about the final judgement, its meaning is applied to our Advent season of preparing a way for the Lord's presence in the world.

*For Parish Programs
and in the Religious Education Classroom*

Because of the Creation and Witness Center activities, this celebration should be shared during the last meeting before the first Sunday of Advent or the first day of December.

In the Family Home

Celebrate these activities on the first Sunday of Advent and look forward to each following day of the season as suggested in the Witness Center activity.

GREETING CENTER

Materials Needed: black cape and mask for an adult

Allow the participants to get acquainted, if necessary, by singing ''Howdy Friends,'' or sing any favorite Advent song, such as ''Rejoice! Be Glad!''

Hide-and-Go-Seek Game

Begin this Advent celebration by allowing the participants to elect someone to be ''it'' for a quick version of ''Hide-And-Go-Seek.'' Set boundaries for possible hiding places and allow the game to start. Soon after the seeker begins his/her search, one of the adults, dressed in black cape and mask, should secretly gather up as many of the ''hiders'' as possible without the seeker's knowing. Then the masked captor should try to kidnap the seeker on his/her travels.

When this short episode is completed, gather the participants together again at the Greeting Center and lead a discussion including answers to these questions:

1. How do you play ''Hide-And-Go-Seek?''
2. Did we play it correctly?
3. Were you expecting a masked captor?
4. How did you react to the unexpected intruder?

WORD CENTER

Invite the participants to tell the Old Testament story of Noah and the Ark (see Genesis 7 and 8 in your bible). Help them highlight the aspects of the lack of preparation among Noah's people and God's wish to save them and the animals from the harm of the flood. If time would allow, you could sing "Noah's Song" or "The Old Ark." Then, have one of the participants read this teaching from Matthew's gospel:

Matthew 24:37-44

The coming of the Son of Man will be like what happened in the time of Noah. In the days before the flood, people ate and drank, men and women married, up to the very day Noah went into the boat; yet they did not realize what was happening until the flood came and swept them all away. That is how it will be when the Son of Man comes. At that time two men will be working in a field: one will be taken away, the other will be left behind. Two women will be at a mill grinding meal: one will be taken away, the other will be left behind. Watch out, then, because you do not know what day our Lord will come. If the owner of a house knew the time when the thief would come, you can be sure that he would stay awake and not let the thief break into his house. So then, you also must always be ready, because the Son of Man will come at an hour when you are not expecting him.

Lead a discussion about the reading emphasizing that we must be prepared for the Lord's coming at the end of time and at all moments of our lives. We cannot be busy doing other things as people were in the time of Noah and we should not be taken by surprise when the Lord comes as we were when playing our version of "Hide-And-Go-Seek." Remind the children that before the first Christmas in Bethlehem, the Hebrew people had to prepare for the Lord's coming.

Sing "Wake up, Wake Up," a song about being ready for the Lord's coming.

PRAISE CENTER

Talk with the participants about Christmas. It is a time when we celebrate the Lord's coming. What, then, is this season of Advent all about? It is a time for us to wake up and prepare for the Lord's coming at Christmas, because at Christmas we celebrate Immanuel, God-with-us.

We know that Christ is with us today because of the first Christmas many centuries ago. But our celebration of Christmas each year allows us to pray in thanksgiving for God's presence in our Lord Jesus. Advent, then, should be a time for us to reflect upon the ways in which God truly is with us in our lives so when Christmas Day comes, we are really prepared to give thanks for Immanuel, God-with-us.

Lead the participants in a Litany of Thanksgiving, allowing each to contribute an ending to this prayer phrase:

Thank you, Lord, for coming to us...

After every two or three responses, sing the refrain to "Wake Up, Wake Up" or a verse of "The Lord Is Comin'."

A sample litany might be:

Thank you, Lord, for coming to us in our friends.

Thank you, Lord, for coming to us in times of joy.

refrain:

Thank you, Lord, for coming to us and helping us say "I'm sorry."

Thank you, Lord, for coming to us in the care of our parents.

refrain:

CREATION CENTER

Advent Calendars

The Advent calendar is a favorite custom among many peoples. However it is used and celebrated, it is intended to be a daily reminder to us that we should prepare ourselves through good deeds and prayer for our celebration of the Lord's coming at Christmas. Because there are varied ways of constructing an Advent calendar, three methods are suggested here, each for a particular setting. Whichever is chosen, it should be adapted to the understanding and ability of the participants.

For Classroom Celebrations

Materials Needed: paper to cover classroom board; 5 x 7 index cards or paper; marking pens; paper punches; straight pins.

This particular way of constructing and celebrating the Advent calendar is best used in a classroom setting where the children will meet every day as Christmas comes closer.

Designate one of the bulletin boards for the class Advent calendar. Cover it with bright colored paper and a heading which reads, "The Lord Comes To Us..."

Distribute a 5 x 7 index card (or a similar-sized piece of paper) to each child. Punch a hole at the top middle of the shorter edge. On the front side, each child should write a large number (coordinated by the teacher) from 1 to 25 for the days of December leading to Christmas. On the reverse side, each child should write a completion to the phrase, "The Lord Comes To Us..." Without the other participants seeing the completed phrases, each should hang his/her card on the bulletin board (the hole hanging on a straight pin) in consecutive order from December 1 to December 25.

For Parish Celebrations

Materials Needed: 3 x 5 cards or paper; scissors, if necessary; paper punches; crayons or marking pens; pieces of yarn.

When the participants will not be together on a daily basis, individual Advent calendars can be constructed for personal celebration at home.

Distribute 26 3 x 5 index cards, or enough paper to be cut into 26 equal rectangles, to each participant. Let everyone punch a single hole at the middle of the shorter side of each card near the edge.

With crayons or marking pens, let each participant number each card's bottom half, beginning the stack with "1" and finishing with "25," for the Advent days of December. On the top card print the words, "The Lord Comes To Us..."

Then have the children repeat the many phrases they mentioned in their prayer at the Praise Center. These phrases should be written, one per date, on the top half of each calendar card.

Place the top card on the stack and fasten with a loose piece of yarn.

The Lord Comes to Us...
1 2 3 4 5 6 7 8 9
10 11 12 13 14 15 16 17 18
19 20 21 22 23 24

For Family Celebrations

Materials Needed: 25 slip-cover match boxes; foil or colored paper; glue, paste or tape; construction paper; scissors; markings pens, crayons; paper bag or hat; masking tape.

On the day of this celebration, decorate the slip-covers of 25 match boxes with foil or brightly colored paper. Cut small pieces of construction paper to fit firmly inside each box. Number the paper pieces on one side from 1 to 25 for the days of December. Place each dated paper in a paper bag or hat and let each participant draw random numbers until each has several and all numbers are drawn.

Then let each member of the family complete the phrase, "The Lord Comes To Us..." with different sayings on the back of each date drawn. Place each date inside the 25 match boxes. With masking tape backings, attach the closed match boxes (in consecutive order) to the kitchen refrigerator, thus making a three-dimensional Advent calendar.

SHARING CENTER

When the participants gather, briefly talk about Advent as a time when we prepare for the Lord's coming — not just at Christmas, but in the many episodes and moments of our lives. Instruct the participants in the use of their Advent calendars by giving the Witness Center activity assignment.

It would be fitting to suggest to everyone that by the Advent calendar activities we will make ready the coming of the savior by freeing our hearts of wrongdoing and filling our lives with helpful and caring concern for others and all of creation — through which the Lord comes and makes His dwelling as Immanuel. We must not be taken by sur-

prise as we were when playing "Hide-And-Go-Seek." Rather, we must look for the Lord who comes to us at every moment of our lives.

Sing "Do You Know?" and conclude with a blessing, such as is written here. (Invite the participants to open their arms receptively as this blessing is prayed upon them.)

May God our Father
bless you through the coming of our Lord
Jesus.
May He fill you with the Holy Spirit
to prepare a place for the peace and love
of the savior.
Amen.

WITNESS CENTER

For Classroom Celebrations

On each morning of December, begin the school day allowing a child to lead the class in prayer by turning over his/her card on his/her date. Let the day's leader choose a favorite Advent song at the conclusion of the morning prayer for all to sing.

On Fridays, turn over two additional dates in the afternoon before dismissal for Saturday and Sunday. Before Christmas vacation, duplicate a handout of the remaining dates for use at home.

Each day, help the participants look for "the Lord's coming to us" as suggested by the leader's card. No doubt there will be some repetition of phrases, but this will all be a part of the fun and suspense of a classroom Advent Calendar.

For Parish Celebrations

The participants should be instructed to use their Advent Calendars at home, flipping to the next date as each day of Advent dawns. Everyone should seek "the Lord's coming to us" in the way suggested on each date.

For Family Celebrations

The Advent calendar can provide an opportunity for the family to pray together at the beginning of each day before Christmas. Perhaps at breakfast each morning, members of the family could take turns leading a prayer and opening the new Advent calendar date-box. The completed phrase is read aloud and every member of the family looks for "the Lord's coming to us" according to the day's idea. Morning prayer could be concluded with a refrain from "Wake Up, Wake Up" or another favorite Advent song chosen by the day's leader.

It might be an enjoyable and valuable family experience to share with one another the day's encounters with "the Lord's coming" at the evening's close or, perhaps, at the dinner table.

THE FAMILY OF JESUS

Isaiah 11:1-10
Psalm 62
Romans 15:4-9
Matthew 3:1-12

Isaiah 11:1-10

Romans 15:5-13

Today's celebration will focus upon the biblical personalities and the events of salvation history. It will help us to understand the historical context of Jesus' birth by recalling his royal ancestral line, as is suggested in today's first reading. Thus, by looking at Jesus' family who prepared and waited for his birth, we come to realize that we are now his family who must keep his message alive for others to hear.

*For Parish Programs
and in the Religious Education Classroom*

The product of the Praise Center activity might later be placed in the church sanctuary as part of the parish Advent decorations.

In the Family Home

The Greeting Center discussion will probably lead to a valuable sharing of family memories and relationships. Take advantage of this opportunity to explore the love which binds the members of a family. The Creation and Praise Center activities might be extended to a week-long celebration. The first four verses of "Wait for the Savior" could be prepared for and sung today, then an additional verse could be sung after dinner each night during the week. Families might want to add their Jesse Tree ornaments to the family Christmas tree instead of putting them on a separate bare branch. Either would be a beautiful Advent custom for the family to initiate.

GREETING CENTER

When the participants have arrived, begin with the song "Howdy Friends." After everyone's name has been sung, lead a short discussion inviting answers to some of these questions:

1. What is a name? — a title, description
2. Who gives us names? — parents (friends sometimes give us nicknames!)
3. What is a family name? — a last name
4. Why do we have family names? — to identify relatives (or to distinguish between "Toms" or "Susans")
5. What is a family tree? — it is a listing of all the people who prepared and waited for us to be born!

Conclude by telling the participants that today's celebration will help us recall the many people who prepared and waited for the birth of our savior, Jesus.

WORD CENTER

Proclaim the following reading with great expression.

Isaiah 11:1-10

The royal line of David is like a tree that has been cut down; but just as new branches sprout from a stump, so a new king will arise from among David's descendants.

*The spirit of the Lord will give him wisdom
  and the knowledge and skill to rule his people.
He will know the Lord's will
  and will have reverence for him,
  and find pleasure in obeying him.
He will not judge by appearance or hearsay:
  he will judge the poor fairly
  and defend the rights of the helpless.
At his command the people will be punished,
  and evil persons will die.
He will rule his people with justice and integrity.
Wolves and sheep will live together in peace,
  and leopards will lie down with young goats.
Calves and lion cubs will feed together
  and little children will take care of them.
Cows and bears will eat together,
  and their calves and cubs will lie down in peace.
Lions will eat straw as cattle do.
Even a baby will not be harmed
  if it plays near a poisonous snake.
On Zion, God's holy hill,
  there will be nothing harmful or evil.
The land will be as full of knowledge of the Lord
  as the seas are full of water.*

A day is coming when the new king from the royal line of David will be a symbol to the nations. They will gather in his royal city and give him honor.

After the reading is completed, divide the participants into two evenly numbered groups. Ask one group what a wolf sounds like — they should growl. Ask the other what a sheep sounds like — they'll give a helpless "baah." Help the children to understand that wolves and sheep don't live in peace. Then explain that this story in Isaiah helps us understand that when the savior is in our midst we don't live like wolves and sheep. No, Jesus brings peace and love to our lives!

Then briefly talk about the symbolism of a family tree and how a family tree of salvation in Jesus is described in this reading from Isaiah.

CREATION CENTER

Jesse Tree Ornaments

Materials needed: white construction paper; scissors; crayons or felt tip markers; paper punch; and multicolored yarn pieces.

As a preparation activity for the Praise Center activity, divide the children into small groups. Each participant should cut a circle (about 6'' in diameter) or a square (each side about 6'') from white construction paper. An adult helper should supervise each group and begin by telling or reading one of these stories of biblical personalities. The participants in each group should then draw a picture of the story they have heard or, perhaps, of just one character in the story. Punch a hole in each circle or square and thread it with a piece of yarn, tying a bow with enough slack for use as an ornament hanger.

Genesis 3:20-23 — Adam and Eve

Adam named his wife Eve, because she was the mother of all human beings. And the Lord God made clothes out of animal skins for Adam and his wife, and he clothed them.

Then the Lord God said, "Now the man has become like one of us and has knowledge of what is good and what is bad. He must not be allowed to eat fruit from the tree of life, and live forever." So the Lord God sent him out of the Garden of Eden and made him cultivate the soil from which he had been formed.

Genesis 9:8-13 — Noah

God said to Noah and his sons, "I am now making my covenant with you and with your descendants, and with all living beings — all birds and all animals — everything that came out of the boat with you. With these words I make my covenant with you: I promise that never again will all living beings be destroyed by a flood; never again will a flood destroy the earth. As a sign of this everlasting covenant which I am making with you and with all living beings, I am putting my bow in the clouds. It will be the sign of my covenant with the world.

Genesis 12:1-3 — Abraham

The Lord said to Abram, "Leave your native land, your relatives, and your father's home, and go to a country that I am going to show you. I will give you many descendants, and they will become a great nation. I will bless you and make your name famous, so that you will be a blessing.

I will bless those who bless you,
But I will curse those who curse you.
And through you I will bless all the nations.

Exodus 3:1-6 — Moses

One day while Moses was taking care of the sheep and goats of his father-in-law Jethro, the priest of Midian, he led the flock across the desert and came to Sinai, the holy mountain. There the angel of the Lord appeared to him as a flame coming from the middle of a bush. "This is strange," he thought. "Why isn't the bush burning up? I will go closer and see."

When the Lord saw that Moses was coming closer, he called to him from the middle of the bush and said, "Moses! Moses!" He answered, "Yes, here I am."

God said, "Do not come any closer. Take off your sandals, because you are standing on holy ground. I am the God of your ancestors, the God of Abraham, Isaac, and Jacob." So Moses covered his face, because he was afraid to look at God.

Exodus 33:7-11a — Moses and the Israelites

Whenever the people of Israel set up camp, Moses would take the sacred Tent and put it up some distance outside the camp. It was called the Tent of the Lord's presence, and anyone who wanted to consult the Lord would go out to it. Whenever Moses went out there, the people would stand at the door of their tents and watch Moses until he entered it. After Moses had gone in, the pillar of cloud would come down and stay at the door of the Tent, and the Lord would speak to Moses from the cloud. As soon as the people saw the pillar of cloud at the door of the Tent, they would bow down. The Lord would speak with Moses face-to-face, just as a man speaks with a friend. Then Moses would return to the camp.

1 Samuel 16:17-23 — David

Saul ordered them, "Find me a man who plays well and bring him to me." One of the attendants said, "Jesse of the town of Bethlehem has a son who is a good musician. He is also a brave and handsome man, a good soldier, and an able speaker. The Lord is with him."

So Saul sent messengers to Jesse to say, "Send me your son David, the one who takes care of the sheep." Jesse sent David to Saul with a young goat, a donkey loaded with bread, and a leather bag full of wine. David came to Saul and entered his service. Saul liked him very much and chose him as the man to carry his weapons. Then Saul sent a message to Jesse: "I like David. Let him stay here in my service." From then on, whenever the evil spirit sent by God came on Saul, David would get his harp and play it. The evil spirit would leave, and Saul would feel better and be all right again.

Isaiah 7:10-14 — Isaiah

The Lord sent another message to Ahaz: "Ask the Lord your God to give you a sign. It can be from deep in the world of the dead or from high up in heaven."

Ahaz answered, "I will not ask for a sign. I refuse to put the Lord to the test."

To that Isaiah replied, "Listen, now, descendants of King David. It's bad enough for you to wear out the patience of men — do you have to wear out God's patience too? Well, then, the Lord himself will give you a sign: a young woman who is pregnant will have a son and will name him "Immanuel."

Jonah 1:12-17 — Jonah

Jonah answered, "Throw me into the sea, and it will calm down. I know it is my fault that you are caught in this violent storm."

Instead, the sailors tried to get the ship to shore, rowing with all their might. But the storm was becoming worse and worse, and they got nowhere. So they cried out to the Lord, "O Lord, we pray, don't punish us with death for taking this man's life! You, O Lord, are responsible for all this, it is your doing." Then they picked Jonah up and threw him into the sea, and it calmed down at once. This made the sailors so afraid of the Lord that they offered a sacrifice and promised to serve him.

At the Lord's command a large fish swallowed Jonah, and he was inside the fish for three days and three nights.

Matthew 1:18-21 — Joseph and Mary

This is how the birth of Jesus Christ took place. His mother Mary was engaged to Joseph, but before they were married, she found out that she was going to have a baby by the Holy Spirit. Joseph was a man who always did what was right, but he did not want to disgrace Mary publicly; so he made plans to break the engagement privately. While he was thinking about this, an angel of the Lord appeared to him in a dream and said, "Joseph, descendant of David, do not be afraid to take Mary to be your wife. For it is by the Holy Spirit that she has conceived. She will have a son, and you will name him Jesus — because he will save his people from their sins."

Mark 1:4-8 — John the Baptist

So John appeared in the desert, baptizing and preaching. "Turn away from your sins and be baptized," he told the people, "and God will forgive your sins." Many people from the province of Judea and the city of Jerusalem went out to hear John. They confessed their sins, and he baptized them in the Jordan River.

John wore clothes made of camel's hair, with a leather belt around his waist, and his food was locusts and wild honey. He announced to the people, "The Man who will come after me is much greater than I am. I am not good enough even to bend down and untie his sandals. I baptize you with water, but he will baptize you with the Holy Spirit."

PRAISE CENTER

The Jesse Tree

Materials Needed: a bare tree branch, spray paint and a pot of sand or rocks.

Gather the participants together, each holding his/her "ornament." A large bare branch of a tree should have been potted and spray-painted black or gold and placed in the middle of this Center. Again ask the participants "what is a family tree?" When they respond, "It is a listing of all the people who prepared and waited for us to be born," explain that everyone will help decorate the "family tree" of Jesus. On it will be placed their pictures of some of those persons who prepared and waited for Jesus' birth.

Sing "Wait for the Savior" and let each group place its ornaments upon the Jesse tree as its biblical story is retold in the verses of the song. Why is it called a "Jesse tree?" Because Jesse was the father of kings from whom Jesus is a descendant.

If time allows, briefly summarize for the entire group the biblical events which the participants have illustrated for the Jesse tree.

After the song is sung and the tree is decorated, conclude by initiating a Secret Message Prayer, such as "God, our Father, we are waiting for the savior."

SHARING CENTER

Those who believe in Jesus have a special name of their own — "Christians." It's the name of the family of believers in Jesus!

Talk with the children about being a Christian. How do we Christians differ from the personalities in the song "Wait for the Savior" and the other great personalities of the Old Testament? — We have known Jesus!

The Witness Center activity should be given before praying this blessing upon the participants:

Romans 15:5-13 (paraphrased)

May God, the source of patience and encouragement, enable you to have the same point of view among yourselves by following the example of Christ Jesus, so that all of you together may praise with one voice the God and Father of our Lord Jesus Christ. Accept one another, then, for the glory of God, as Christ has accepted you.

May God, the source of hope, fill you with all joy and peace by means of your faith in him, so that your hope will continue to grow by the power of the Holy Spirit. AMEN.

Conclude with a favorite Advent song such as "Rejoice! Be Glad!" or sing the refrain of "Wait for the Savior" once again.

WITNESS CENTER

Encourage the participants to ask a different friend everyday during the week, "Do you know my family name?" When their friends answer, "Smith" or "Jones," tell the participants to respond, "Yes, but I have another family too — the Christian family." Suggest that everyone keep a record of his/her friends' responses to bring with them to their next celebration.

OR, you might suggest that during this week, instead of giving negative feedback to our friends by calling them names such as "meany" or "stupid" or "bully" when they misbehave, give them positive feedback when they are peaceful and loving by calling them "Christian." This usually leads to some interesting conversations about being a Christian and could be the basis for an enlightening discussion at next week's celebration. (This would be an excellent addition to the daily Advent Calendar project initiated last week.)

BE PATIENT

Isaiah 35:1-6, 10
Psalm 146
James 5:7-10
Matthew 11:2-11

Isaiah 35:1-6, 10

James 5:7-10
Matthew 11:2-11

The season of Advent celebrates the prophetic telling of the coming of the long-awaited savior to the people of Judah. Today's Center Celebration focuses upon two of the great prophets who spoke of the coming of the savior, Isaiah and John the Baptist. Because their prophetic message is captured in the words of the epistle reading, today's theme comes from the letter of James: "Be Patient!"

GREETING CENTER

When the participants are ready for the celebration, begin with a favorite song, such as "Sing A Song of Praise."

Then lead a discussion including answers to these questions:

1. Have you ever waited for a long time for an important event? Maybe a fun event? (school's end, vacation trip, visit from a far-away relative, field trip, etc.)
2. Were you excited about the coming event?
3. Did you wait patiently?
4. Was the event worth your waiting?

A reader could be selected from among the participants to proclaim this short selection of the Epistle from James.

James 5:7-10

Be patient, then, my brothers, until the Lord comes. See how patient a farmer is as he waits for his land to produce precious crops. He waits patiently for the autumn and spring rains. You also must be patient. Keep your hopes high, for the day of the Lord's coming is near.

Do not complain against one another, my brothers, so that God will not judge you. The Judge is near, ready to appear. My brothers, remember the prophets who spoke in the name of the Lord. Take them as examples of patient endurance under suffering.

After the reading, briefly discuss the meaning of being patient. You might compare our eagerness for the coming of Christmas and all of its gifts with the awaiting of the Israelites for the coming of the savior.

Then ask the participants if they know what a prophet does, as James suggests in his letter. A prophet tries to tell the people of his/her place and time that there are special needs and problems of which everyone must be aware. He tries to get the people to act upon the needs and problems of the day.

CREATION CENTER

Briefly describe for the participants the prophets Isaiah and John the Baptist. (A simple map of the Holy Land might be an effective visual aid.)

Isaiah was a citizen of Jerusalem. He lived about 750 years before Jesus was born. He was marrried and had at least two children. He was a prophet among four kings of Judah and frequently visited the royal palace. He told the people of Judah that they must have faith and trust in God's ways. They must not be impatient and lose hope because God will indeed send a savior.

John the Baptist was the son of a priest, Zechariah, and his wife, Elizabeth, the cousin of Mary. John was about six months older than Jesus, and he lived in Judea. He went into the desert of Judea wearing clothes made of camel's hair with a leather belt around his waist. He ate locusts and wild honey. He preached about Jesus when the people came to him from Jerusalem. They confessed their sins, and he baptized them in the Jordan river, but he told them they should look for Jesus, for he was greater than John himself.

Paper Bag Prophets

Materials Needed: paper lunch bags for hand puppets or large grocery bags for sack masks, glue, crayons or marking pens, buttons and old fabric, newspapers and scissors.

After your description, divide the participants into two groups.

For Hand Puppets

Distribute to each a brown paper lunch bag (unopened). Have one group draw a face of Isaiah on the bottom of the bag with crayons. The other group should draw John the Baptist. Hair can be added with pieces of yarn and glue. Old scraps of fabric could be used for clothing below the face, if desired. You might use old buttons for eyes, etc. Old newspapers can be folded and added as hats, if time permits.

For Sack Masks

Distribute to each a large paper grocery bag large enough to fit over their heads. Cut out holes for the nose and eyes. For ears, cut out two shapes and paste them to each side of the head. One group becomes many "John the Baptists" while the other becomes a group of "Isaiahs!"

WORD CENTER

When the participants assemble, have them sit in their two groups, each set of prophets facing the other.

Allow the "Isaiahs" to stand and pretend to be preaching this message of the prophet as it is read aloud by an adult leader, pausing, as indicated, to sing the refrain of "Wait for the Savior." Conclude with verse 7 of the song.

Introduction: One day Isaiah the prophet gathered the people together and with an outburst of joy he spoke with confidence about the coming of the savior. He described what would happen with beautiful imagery. He said:

Isaiah 35:1-6, 10

The desert will rejoice,
  and flowers will bloom in the wastelands.
The desert will sing and shout for joy:
  it will be as beautiful as the Lebanon Mountains
  and as fertile as the fields of Carmel and Sharon.
Everyone will see the Lord's splendor,
  see his greatness and power.

refrain

Give strength to hands that are tired
  and to knees that tremble with weakness.
Tell everyone who is discouraged,
  "Be strong and don't be afraid!
God is coming to your rescue,
  coming to punish your enemies."

refrain

The blind will be able to see,
  and the deaf will hear.
The lame will leap and dance,
  and those who cannot speak will shout for joy.
Streams of water will flow through the desert;
They will reach Jerusalem with gladness,
  singing and shouting for joy.
They will be happy forever,
  forever free from sorrow and grief.

refrain and verse 7

When the reading is finished, talk with the children about the people who waited for the coming of the savior. They were growing impatient. Isaiah told them these things so that they would know that when the savior comes, all of creation will rejoice. The coming of the savior would be worth their waiting.

Then, let the "Baptists" stand and pretend that this story is about them.

Matthew 11:2-11

When John the Baptist heard in prison about the thing that Christ was doing, he sent some of his disciples to him. "Tell us," they asked Jesus, "are you the one John said was going to come, or should we expect someone else?"

Jesus answered, "Go back and tell John what you are hearing and seeing: the blind can see, the lame can walk, those who suffer from dreaded skin diseases are made clean, the deaf hear, the dead are brought back to life, and the Good News is preached to the poor. How happy are those who have doubts about me!"

While John's disciples were leaving, Jesus spoke about him to the crowds: "When you went out to John in the desert, what did you expect to see? A blade of grass bending in the wind? What did you go out to see? A man dressed up in fancy clothes? People who dress like that live in palaces! Tell me, what did you go out to see? A prophet? Yes indeed, but you saw much more than a prophet. For John is the one of whom the scripture says: 'God said, I will send my messenger ahead of you to open the way for you.' I assure you that John the Baptist is greater than any man who has ever lived. But he who is least in the kingdom of heaven is greater than John."

Sing verse 10 and the refrain of "Wait for the Savior."

Talk with the participants about John the Baptist. He told the people that they must be sorry for their sins. He told them that Jesus was in the country preaching the Good News. He asked them to go to Jesus. He told them they had no need to be impatient because Jesus, their savior, was in their midst. They need only go and find him in the land. (It might be appropriate to pause and sing "John the Baptist".)

In this reading we hear Jesus responding to the disciples of John. When they asked if he was the savior, Jesus said they must judge for themselves. What evidence did Jesus give? Was his evidence anything like the preaching of Isaiah?

PRAISE CENTER

Sing "Do You Know?" in its entirety, allowing different children or groups to take each verse in response to the leader's questions. Talk about the words of the song helping the participants to understand that when we free ourselves of selfishness and wrongdoing, the Lord comes to us with love and peace.

Then lead the participants in this, or any other Repetition Prayer of praise:

> God our Father
> we give you thanks today
> for your endless love.
> Help us to prepare
> for the coming of our savior.
> May we live lovingly
> and patiently
> with hearts open free
> to welcome our savior
> when we are in need.
> We make this prayer
> through Jesus, our savior.
> Amen.

SHARING CENTER

The participants could be reminded at this time about the purpose of the prophets. Prophets come to people and speak about special needs and problems. We are called to be prophets today. We should tell people that there is a need to love more caringly. We should announce to everyone that Jesus comes to make our hearts free and open to love. Don't let people become impatient with the failings of other people. Let them know that Jesus helps us to love and care for others and to be more patient with the failings of others.

Give the Witness Center assignment and conclude with a favorite Advent song, such as the refrain to "Wait for the Savior" or "Prepare Ye The Way."

WITNESS CENTER

As a reminder to each of us that we must be prophets of Jesus, let everyone bring his/her paper bag prophet home and display it where it will be seen daily. Encourage everyone to cut out a heart from red paper at home and paste it upon the chest of the paper prophets. This will be a reminder to us that we must be prophets of love, inviting other people to be free of hatred and sadness and impatience and to be open to receive the Savior at Christmas and everyday of their lives.

GRACE AND PEACE BE

Isaiah 7:10-14
Psalm 24
Romans 1:1-7
Matthew 1:18-24

Romans 1:1-7
Matthew 1:18-24

Jesus' birth is described in today's passage from Matthew's gospel. It is because of Jesus' birth and life with us (indeed, God-with-us) that St. Paul can wish his friends the grace and peace of God, our Father. His wish becomes our wish for our friends at Christmas and the theme of our celebration today.

In the Religious Education Classroom

If the first option of the Creation Center activities is chosen, it can be combined with the Sharing Center activity.

In the Family Home

Families will probably want to choose the second option of the Creation Center activities. Be sure to combine this activity with the suggestion at the Praise Center.

GREETING CENTER

Materials Needed: prepare a hand-printed copy of this reading and place it in a sealed envelope before the celebration.

When the participants have gathered, this celebration could begin with a song of praise or thanksgiving such as "Sing a Song of Praise." After singing, an envelope should be presented to the group in which the following letter is printed on personal stationery:

Romans 1:1-7

From Paul, a servant of Christ Jesus and an apostle chosen and called by God to preach his Good News.

The Good News was promised long ago by God through his prophets, as written in the Holy Scriptures. It is about his Son, our Lord Jesus Christ: as to his humanity, he was born a descendant of David; as to his divine holiness, he was shown with great power to be the Son of God by being raised from death. Through him God gave me the privilege of being an apostle for the sake of Christ, in order to lead people of all nations to believe and obey. This also includes you who are in Rome, whom God has called to belong to Jesus Christ.

And so I write to all of you in Rome whom God loves and has called to be his own people:

May God our Father and the Lord Jesus Christ give you grace and peace.

One of the participants could be asked to read the letter aloud. When the reading is concluded, a discussion including these questions and answers could begin.

1. Who was Paul? — a disciple of Jesus.
2. Who were the Romans? — Christians living in Rome after Jesus died and rose from the dead.
3. Why did Paul write this letter? — he was about to journey through Rome to Spain. He was announcing his impending visit. He wrote particularly about his understanding of the gospel.
4. What was Paul's greeting and wish for the Romans? — "May God, our Father and the Lord Jesus Christ give you grace and peace."

Invite the participants to sing "A Blessing Song," the lyrics of which are somewhat reminiscent of Paul's prayer in his letters.

When the song is completed, ask the children if they've ever received a greeting or a wish for peace in the mail. Hopefully they will think of birthday or Christmas cards. Ask the children if they know why we send Christmas cards. After a few responses, send everyone to the Word Center.

YOURS

WORD CENTER

Ask one of the participants to read aloud this short telling of the Christmas story. The other participants should listen carefully for a reason for our sending Christmas cards.

Matthew 1:18-24

This is how the birth of Jesus Christ took place. His mother Mary was engaged to Joseph, but before they were married, she found out that she was going to have a baby by the Holy Spirit. Joseph was a man who always did what was right, but he did not want to disgrace Mary publicly; so he made plans to break the engagement privately. While he was thinking about this, an angel of the Lord appeared to him in a dream and said, "Joseph, descendant of David, do not be afraid to take Mary to be your wife. For it is by the Holy Spirit that she has conceived. She will have a son, and you will name him Jesus — because he will save his people from their sins."

Now all this happened in order to make come true what the Lord had said through the prophet, "A virgin will become pregnant and have a son, and he will be called 'Immanuel' (which means, "God is with us").

So, when Joseph woke up, he married Mary, as the angel of the Lord had told him to.

After the reading you might want to sing "Wait For the Savior" with verses 9 and 11.

Continue the discussion about our sending Christmas cards — are there any helpful hints from the reading or the song? Help the children come to an understanding of our sending Christmas cards as our wish that Jesus will be with our friends. He is Immanuel, God-with-us. When we allow God to be with us, we have grace and peace. So, we wish one another "Peace" at Christmas when we celebrate Jesus' coming to birth among us.

CREATION CENTER

You might want to talk about the origin of our custom of sending Christmas cards as an introduction to this activity.

The sending of printed Christmas cards began in England when school children away from home would write Christmas letters to their parents on paper decorated with bible scenes or with pictures of nature's many beauties. Hoping for generous Christmas gifts, they reported on their progress at school. Grownups sometimes wrote Christmas verses to friends on similar paper or on small cards.

Through the ages, different nations have adopted this custom, usually by purchasing ready-made cards with Christmas decorations and joyous messages. However the card is made, it is a way of telling people that we remember them, care what happens to them, feel grateful toward them, think they are fun, like them or love them.

An exchange of Christmas cards often helps keep alive a friendship between people too far apart to see each other. Wherever we send the cards, they bring with them the spirit of Christmas, Christ's peace, by our reaching out to others and sharing our love and happiness.

Christmas Greeting Cards

Materials Needed: construction paper, drawing pens, pencils, or crayons. Or: a coat hanger, paper punch, and ribbon pieces.

One of these activities, whichever might be most appropriate, could be adopted:

1. On construction paper, have each child prepare a Christmas greeting card for another "anonymous" participant. Collect these cards for a random exchange at the Sharing Center.

2. Families might take the time to review the cards they have received from friends and relatives during the previous weeks. Be sure to take time talking about each greeting. Then, fasten the cards (punch a hole on the folded side) with inexpensive ribbon bows to a rounded-out coat hanger, forming a greeting wreath of Christmas wishes for the entry-way of the house.

PRAISE CENTER

When everyone gathers, the leader should ask each participant to mention a friend for whom he/she is grateful. Some might want to add a reason for their gratefulness. Then, in a form of litany, sing this short prayer ("Father, Care") after each one mentions a friend's name.

FATHER, CARE

Dick Hilliard

Fa-ther, care for (this friend / these friends) of ours. give (him/her / them) grace and peace this hour.

Families might continue their Christmas card activity at this time. Before fastening the cards to the wreath, each participant could take a stack of cards and read the names of the senders. After each stack is read, this prayer song could be sung. Then return to the Creation Center for making the entryway wreath.

An example of this litany might be:

Participant: For the McConnells and the Kellys and the Rossi Family, too.

All: Father, care for these friends of ours. Give them grace and peace this hour.

Participant: For Juan Mendoza who is never selfish.

All: Father, care...

Participant: For Sr. Joan Anselm because she makes school so much fun.

All: Father, care...

Participant: For our Moms and Dads who never forget to love us.

All: Father, care...

SHARING CENTER

Christmas time is an occasion for us to be thankful for our many friendships. Like St. Paul in his wish for the Romans, we should wish our friends and relatives the grace and peace of God our Father and the Lord Jesus Christ, Immanuel, God-with-us.

Ask the participants for their ideas for ways to show peace to our friends and relatives. Incorporate their ideas into the Witness Center activity assignment.

Then, exchange a sign of peace among the participants. If you have chosen to make cards for one another, now is an appropriate time to exchange cards by random distribution. Supervise this exchange by instructing the participants to give a card only to those who have not yet received a card. This will help ensure that no one is forgotten or duplicated.

Conclude by singing "A Blessing Song."

WITNESS CENTER

No doubt friends or relatives will be visiting our homes at Christmas. We, too, will probably visit other homes. When we meet these friends or relatives, let us make a special point to wish each one "The grace and peace of God our Father and the Lord Jesus Christ" as did St. Paul.

You might suggest this Italian custom: children prepare and compose letters of thankfulness and well-wishing for their parents and place them under their parents' dinner plates on Christmas eve.

AS CLAY IN GOD'S

Isaiah 63:16-17, 19; 64:2-7   Isaiah 63:16-17; 64:2-9
Psalm 80
1 Corinthians 1:3-9
Mark 13:33-37

Our celebration of the season of Advent would be lacking an essential aspect if we did not celebrate the loving concern of God for his people.

Today's celebration takes its theme from the image of humankind as clay and God as potter in the concluding verse of the reading from Isaiah. This celebration will help us all to begin our Advent preparation by acknowledging the Lord of creation who enables us to celebrate Christmas by sending us his Son, Jesus.

GREETING CENTER

When everyone has assembled a song such as "Sing a Song of Praise" should begin this celebration.

At the conclusion of this song, briefly discuss with the participants the many gifts they have received in life for which they are grateful to God, our Father. Perhaps the words of "Sing A Song of Praise" will help the younger participants contribute to this discussion.

When this short discussion is nearing its climax, ask the participants to close their eyes and follow these instructions as they are given aloud and slowly:

Imagine that the world is completely empty. It is very dark. There are no creatures in this world. It is silent. There is nothing to be seen or heard.

Now pretend that you are God. You are the creator of this empty, dark, and quiet world. You can see nothing and you can hear nothing. You are alone.

But you have the power to fill this world with anything you desire! Where it is empty, you can put anything you want. Where it is silent, you can fill it with sound. Where it is dark, you can bring light.

So you create a world of your very own with beautiful mountains, hills and valleys. You give it the light of the sun, the moon and the stars. And you fill it with the sounds of running rivers and splashing oceans and large and small animals.

But you are still alone. So you decide to share this world which you have created with a creature you love very much.

I wonder what kind of creature you created? You created this creature so that you could share your world. You love this creature very much. I wonder what kind of creature you created?

Now, without saying a word or making a single noise, open your eyes.

(When all eyes are opened, repeat your wondering:)

I wonder what kind of creature you created?

The participants should then assemble at the Creation Center — but they'd better not make a sound on their way!

HANDS

CREATION CENTER

Clay Creatures

Materials Needed: modelling clay for each participant.

Each participant should be given a stick of inexpensive modelling clay.

Recalling the activity of the Greeting Center, let each participant mold the creature he/she created in his/her imagination.

When all molding is completed, let each participant stand and describe his/her creature. At the conclusion of this sharing, lead the participants to the Word Center.

WORD CENTER

Hopefully many of the participants will have created models of human beings out of their clay. Briefly recall the story line of the Greeting Center activity, emphasizing the special choosing of humankind by God our Father in the plan of creation. Discuss with the participants our responsibility in caring for creation, for one another, and for God.

Then introduce this reading from Isaiah by explaining that sometimes we human beings forget to care for creation, for one another and for God. This is a prayer of the prophet asking God for forgiveness for the times when he and his people were selfish and turned away from God's loving ways.

(When celebrating with younger children, this reading could be shortened as necessary.)

Isaiah 63:16-17; 64:2-9

You are our father. Our ancestors Abraham and Jacob do not acknowledge us, but you, Lord, are our father, the one who has always rescued us. Why do you let us stray from your ways? Why do you make us so stubborn that we turn away from you? Come back, for the sake of those who serve you, for the sake of the people who have always been yours.

They would tremble like water boiling over a hot fire.

There was a time when you came and did terrifying things that we did not expect; the mountains saw you and shook with fear. No one has ever seen or heard of a God like you, who does such deeds for those who put their hope in him.

You welcome those who find joy in doing what is right, those who remember how you want them to live.

You were angry with us, but we went on sinning; in spite of your great anger we have continued to do wrong since ancient times. All of us have been sinful; even our best actions are filthy through and through. Because of our sins we are like leaves that wither and are blown away by the wind.

No one turns to you in prayer; no one goes to you for help. You have hidden yourself from us and have abandoned us because of our sins.

But you are our father, Lord. We are like clay, and you are like the potter. You created us, so do not be too angry with us or hold our sins against us forever. We are your people; be merciful to us.

At the conclusion of the reading, ask the participants which part(s) of the prayer they like best. Lead a discussion allowing each to share his/her reason(s) for liking a particular part of the reading.

If none of the participants selects the image of the clay in the hands of the potter, select this as your favorite part. Discuss the image of the molding of clay, comparing it with the Father's creation of humankind.

PRAISE CENTER

Continue your discussion of the image of the clay and the potter in a manner such as this:

When we create things out of clay, we have complete control over them. If we don't like the way things turn out, we can change them or destroy them and start again. (Illustrate by making your own clay creation.)

If they don't stand just the way we want them, or if they don't move just the way we'd like, we can say "Oh, forget it" and demolish our creature in an instant! (Illustrate with your own clay creation.)

Isaiah says to God, our Father: "We are like clay, and you are like the potter, You created us."

I bet there are many times when our loving Father looks at us and sees that we are not acting the way he would like us to act. But he doesn't destroy us in an instant. He doesn't just say, "Oh, forget it" and turn his back on us.

God has given us so many beautiful things in creation. He has blessed us with a world which makes us happy. When we decide not to care for creation or for one another, we are saying, "We don't care for you, God." We seem to be turning our backs on God!

But God our Father doesn't destroy us in an instant. He doesn't turn his back on us. But he could! He's the potter ...we're like the clay.

Instead, God continues to love us and care for us. He waits for us to come back to him and ask for forgiveness and promise to show our love for Him always.

Let us think for a moment about the times when we have not acted as God wants us to act. Let us ask God our Father for forgiveness.

"Bring Us Back" would be an appropriate song of reconciliation to sing with the participants.

After a brief pause, all pray this conclusion to the reading of Isaiah as a Repetition Prayer:

You, Lord, are our father.
We are like clay,
and you are like the potter.
You created us,
so do not be too angry with us.
Do not hold our sins against us forever.
We are your people.
Show us your forgiveness.
Amen.

SHARING CENTER

Lead a discussion among the participants by asking, "Why did God our Father send us Jesus?"

Help all to understand that Jesus is the gift of God our Father to us. Jesus shows us how to act in a way which is pleasing to our Father.

With your clay creation, demonstrate that clay quickly hardens — in a day or so — if it is not kneaded occasionally. It dries up very quickly if it is not moistened. It will lose its color if it is not protected from the harm of wind and hot sun.

Then continue by saying something such as this, demonstrating with a randomly-selected participant:

Materials Needed: handkerchiefs; cup of water and a band-aid.

We are very much like clay creatures. If we aren't cared for by one another (kiss, hug, hold hands) we become hard and mean. If we aren't comforted and refreshed by one another (pretend to wipe a tear with a handkerchief or put arm around the other, offer drink of water) then we dry up and become lonely. If we aren't protected by each other (put band-aid on participant's arm) we could be hurt by other people.

Give the Witness Center activity assignment.

Then continue with a conclusion such as:

Advent is a season when we thank God for all His gifts to us, especially his gift of Jesus, who teaches us how to act in a way which is pleasing in God's eyes. It is a time when we prepare to celebrate Jesus' birthday, his coming to us, on Christmas Day by being sorry for our sins.

This Advent let us remember to thank God our Father in our prayer and to prepare for Christmas Day by acting as Jesus taught us.

Sing "My Thankful Prayer," or any favorite song of gratitude.

WITNESS CENTER

The participants should take their clay creations home and put them on their dressers. During this week, whenever they go into their rooms and see their clay creations, they should be encouraged to pray to God and thank him for creating us!

The clay models should also be a reminder to us that we must care for other people as Jesus taught us. We mustn't let others harden or dry up or become hurt.

49

WE'VE GOT THINGS TO

Isaiah 40:1-5, 9-11
Psalm 85
2 Peter 3:8-14
Mark 1:1-8

Isaiah 40:1-5. 9-11

Mark 1:1-8

John the Baptist is the central figure of today's celebration, which includes readings from Isaiah and the gospel of Mark. As one who announced the time of preparation for the coming of the savior, John stands as a herald for us, too. We must heed his proclamation and make ready the way of the Lord. We've got things to do!

GREETING CENTER

Begin today's celebration with the refrain and verse 7 of "Wait for the Savior."

Then ask the participants if they know who Isaiah was. Give them enough clues and instruction so that they come to realize that he was a great prophet through whom God spoke to the Israelites in Jerusalem and Judah long before the time of Jesus. (A map of the Holy Land might be an effective visual aid.)

Some of the participants could be selected to read this selection of Isaiah written for the exiled people of Judah when they were suffering in Babylon and losing their hope of going home to Jerusalem.

Isaiah 40:1-5, 9-11

Reader 1:
Comfort, give comfort to my people, says our God. Encourage the people of Jerusalem.
Tell them they have suffered long enough and their sins are now forgiven.

Reader 2:
A voice cries out,
"Prepare in the wilderness a road for the Lord! Clear the way in the desert for our God!"

Reader 3:
Fill every valley;
level every mountain.
The hills will become a plain,
and the rough country will be made smooth.

Reader 4:
Then the glory of the Lord will be revealed, and all people will see it.
The Lord himself has promised this.

Reader 5:
Proclaim the good news!
Call out with a loud voice,
Tell the towns of Judah that their God is coming!

Reader 6:
The Lord is coming to rule with power, bringing with him the people he has rescued.

He will take care of his flock like a shepherd;
he will gather the lambs together and carry them in his arms.

At the conclusion of the reading, tell the participants that the voice Isaiah was talking about (reader 2) would probably be the voice of John the Baptist. Let them know that our celebration will focus upon the person of John the Baptist today.

WORD CENTER

Before this gospel reading is announced, lead a discussion among the participants by asking such questions as:

1. Have you ever prepared for meeting someone for the very first time? Perhaps a friend of your parents or the cousin of your best friend?

2. How did you prepare? Did you ask questions about the person you would meet?

3. Were you nervous? Did you want to make a good impression?

Then introduce this reading by telling the participants that it is about John the Baptist and how he prepared the people of Israel to meet the savior. Tell them to be sure and listen to how John described the savior.

Another participant could be selected to proclaim this gospel passage from Mark.

Mark 1:1-8

This is the Good News about Jesus Christ, the Son of God. It began as the prophet Isaiah had written:

"God said, 'I will send my messenger ahead of you to open the way for you.' Someone is shouting in the desert, 'Get the road ready for the Lord; make a straight path for him to travel!'"

So John appeared in the desert, baptizing and preaching. "Turn away from your sins and be baptized," he told the people, "and God will forgive your sins." Many people from the province of Judea and the city of Jerusalem went out to hear John. They confessed their sins, and he baptized them in the Jordan River.

John wore clothes made of camel's hair, with a leather belt around his waist, and his food was locusts and wild honey. He announced to the people, "The man who will come after me is much greater than I am. I am not good enough even to bend down and untie his sandals. I baptize you with water, but he will baptize you with the Holy Spirit."

Sing verse 10 of "Wait for the Savior" and the chorus as a response to this reading, or sing "John the Baptist."

Then summarize the lesson of this reading by leading a discussion about John's instructions to the people. Ask the participants for suggestions about how, in John's words, to "turn away from your sins."

DO!

PRAISE CENTER

Continue or summarize the discussion which followed the Word Center reading. Help the participants to understand that the best way we can turn away from our sins and prepare for the Lord's coming is to be thankful for the many gifts and talents God has given us.

Ask each participant to offer a short prayer of thanks to God for whatever particular gift he/she chooses, such as

"Thank you, God, for all of creation;" or,

"I give thanks to God for my friends;" or,

"I praise you, Father, for giving me a beautiful voice to sing for others."

When everyone has taken part in this litany of thanksgiving, all could sing "Sing a Song of Praise."

CREATION CENTER

"Things To Do" Lists

Materials Needed: lined paper for each participant, and pencils.

Ask the participants to pretend that they have never heard about Jesus, the savior, just like the people to whom Isaiah and John had spoken. When they have gotten into this mood, announce that the savior is soon to arrive in their midst. Tell the participants that they must quickly prepare to meet the savior.

Distribute lined paper to each participant. At the top of the sheet, each should write, "Things To Do." Then ask everyone to make a personal list of things he/she must do to prepare for the savior's coming.

Give the Witness Center assignment and conclude by singing "Rejoice, Be Glad," or "Wake Up! Wake Up!"

SHARING CENTER

Lead a free discussion inviting the participants to share all or part of their "Things To Do" lists. Be sure to highlight some points shared by each participant as important ways for all of us to prepare for the savior's coming.

Give the Witness Center assignment and conclude by signing "Rejoice, Be Glad," or "Wake Up! Wake Up!"

WITNESS CENTER

The participants should take their "Things To Do" lists home. Instruct them to read this list each morning during the coming week as a reminder of things they should be doing in preparation for our celebration of the Savior's birth. Just as John the Baptist announced the way for the people of Israel to prepare for the coming of the savior, so we will announce each morning the ways in which we are preparing to celebrate the savior's coming into our lives.

At the end of each day a check mark could be place beside each item which was observed during that day.

THE LORD CHOOSES ME

Isaiah 61:1-2, 10-11
Luke 1: 46ff
1Thessalonians 5:16-24
John 1:6-8, 19-28

Isaiah 61:1-2, 10-11

1 Thessalonians 5:16-23

Today's celebration takes its theme from the first two readings for the third Sunday of Advent. We find in Isaiah an example of one who responds well to the calling of the Father by spreading the good news of the coming of the savior. As we prepare to celebrate the coming of our savior, Jesus Christ, at Christmas, we must remember that we, too, must spread his good news, because we are indeed called in a special way by the Father.

In the Religious Education Classroom

The teacher will probably need some help with the puppet show at the Word Center. Call upon a school aide for assistance.

In the Family Home

The Greeting Center activity could lead to a valuable discussion of family events. You might want to take time recalling the feelings and memories of those events. Mom and Dad could present the puppet show at the Word Center. Perhaps the children could paint the backdrop earlier in the day.

GREETING CENTER

When the participants have gathered, begin with the song, "The Lord Blesses Me."

Then, briefly ask the children such things as:

1. Have you ever received good news? — such as going on a vacation or that Mom was going to have another baby?
2. How did you react to the good news? — happy, sad, disappointed, jumped for joy?
3. Did you keep it a secret or spread it around?

Before moving from this center, conclude with a Repetition Prayer, such as:

God, our Father,
you give us many blessings.
Please bless us again today
with the good news of Jesus.
Send your Holy Spirit
to help us spread
his good news.
Amen.

GOOD NEWS!

WORD CENTER

Materials Needed: puppets of Isaiah, puppets of some poverty-stricken people, puppets of some prisoners, and a puppet stage.

This familiar passage of Isaiah should serve as a reminder to all of us that we are called by the Father to proclaim the good news that we have been saved by Jesus. The passage is proclaimed as a puppet show dramatizing the task given to Isaiah and his joy at being chosen and sent by God. Since we, too, are chosen and sent by God, the participants should come to realize the joy of their Christian calling.

THE SONG OF ISAIAH

(A puppet show telling of Isaiah 61:1-2, 10-11)

The prophet Isaiah appears on stage against the background of a decaying city: buildings are in need of repair, poor people are begging for food, prisoners are locked in a jail, visitors to the jail are crying, etc. Isaiah walks about the street scene looking over the situation. A quiet musical arrangement is played in the background.

Finally, Isaiah, somewhat bewildered (scratching his head), turns to his audience and, sitting on a rock or bench says:

"The Lord has filled me with his spirit. He has chosen me and sent me!"

Isaiah throws his arms up in confusion, then hangs his head in sorrow. He then sits up and sings, somewhat hesitatingly,

He repeats this melody and looks over his clothes (he is well-dressed). He picks a flower and repeats the melody. Looking to the sun shining, he sings the melody again with great happiness and confidence. He ignores the scene behind him and jumps for joy.

After a few moments he turns to the poor people begging for food. He turns back to his audience and says:

"The Lord has filled me with his spirit. He has chosen me and sent me!"

He pauses, looks back at the beggars, then turns to his audience and says:

"He has chosen me and sent me to bring good news to the poor."

He thinks quietly for a brief moment, then takes the flower in his hand and gives it to the poor people. Pleased with their receptive response, he sings the melody again. He is so pleased, he begins dancing, repeating the melody over and over with great merriment. Motioning with his hand, he invites his audience to sing with him.

He then dances by the jail and sees the crying visitors outside. He looks over the situation, then says to his audience, "The Lord has filled me with his spirit. He has chosen me and sent me to heal the broken-hearted."

He goes to the visitors and puts his arms around them in comfort. They stop crying, and he sings his song again. The visitors join him and the audience and sing also. But the visitors stop suddenly and walk back to the jail. Isaiah stops and watches. Then he turns to his audience and says: "The Lord has filled me with his spirit. He has chosen me and sent me to announce release to captives and freedom to those in prison."

He runs to the jail and swings open the barred doors. He begins singing his simple melody with the visitors and audience. The beggars join too. Then he quiets his friends and mounts the rock or bench and delivers this speech: "The Lord has filled me with his spirit. He has chosen me and sent me to proclaim that the time has come when the Lord will save his people and defeat their enemies."

The other puppets begin a quiet mumble of questioning. Isaiah quiets them and continues: "The Lord has filled me with his spirit. He has chosen me and sent me to comfort all who mourn!"

Isaiah dances to the music through the assembly while singing and then takes a place at the other side of the stage. He then delivers this final speech: "Jerusalem rejoices because of what the Lord has done. She is like a bride dressed for her wedding. As surely as seeds sprout and grow, the Lord will save his people, and all the nations will praise him."

The people cheer for Isaiah as he and all the others sing his simple song. The curtain closes on the merry-making of this spirit-filled city.

After the dramatization, it would be helpful to talk with the participants about the meaning of this passage. It is "good news" for the poor, comfort for the broken-hearted, a message of hope for all prisoners of wrongdoing. As we prepare for the celebration of Christmas, we should be reminded that we must bring Christ's good news of peace and hope to people in everything we do.

PRAISE CENTER

Because we have received so many blessings from God, we should, as St. Paul reminds us, always be joyful and pray with thanksgiving at all times. Talk with the participants about the good news with which Jesus blessed us after he was born. You might ask, "What was Jesus' good news?" Hopefully the children will think of some of the episodes in Jesus' life which were occasions for him to bring good news to the poor, broken-hearted and prisoners of wrongdoing.

The short passage from 1 Thessalonians could be read with verse 23 becoming a Movement Prayer, as indicated. The participants could imitate the movement of the prayer leader and his/her partner.

1 Thessalonians 5:16-23

Be joyful always, pray at all times, be thankful in all circumstances. This is what God wants from you in your life in union with Christ Jesus. Do not restrain the Holy Spirit; do not despise inspired messages. Put all things to the test: keep what is good and avoid every kind of evil.

(In what follows, the **bold** is verse 23, while the *italic* suggests corresponding movements.)

May the God who gives us peace *(all raise hands in praise to God; bring arms down, crisscrossed upon the heart;)*

make you holy *(participants pair off, bestowing hands upon heads or shoulders of partners;)*

in every way *(lift hands, and make a circular sweep around partner from head to feet;)*

and keep your whole being — spirit, soul, and body *(bring hands together at feet and bend up to standing position, bringing extended hands to holding hands of partner;)*

free from every fault *(with hands held, pull partner close to self in exchange of positions;)*

at the coming of our Lord Jesus Christ. Amen. *(All make sign of the cross.)*

"My Thankful Prayer," or any song of thankfulness, could be sung as a conclusion to this center activity.

CREATION CENTER

Good News Buttons

Materials needed: colored construction paper, scissors, crayons, and safety pins.

As a reminder for the participants to spread the "good news" to everyone they meet during the week, each one can cut out a circle, 3" in diameter, from colored construction paper. Each could draw a smile on the circle, then write the words "I have good news!" above the smile. With a safety pin, it could be fastened to the participants' clothing. Now everyone has a "Good News Button." (Older children might want to pin their circles on school notebooks, bicycle seats or the like. Boys, especially, prefer not to have things pinned to their clothing!)

SHARING CENTER

Discuss what it means to realize that we are blessed by the Lord. It means we are specially chosen to bring the good news of Jesus to others. Invite suggestions of ways in which we could all prepare for our celebration of Jesus' good news at Christmas. A variety of acts of kindness and comfort and continued prayer of thanksgiving and praise to God are just a few examples.

Give the Witness Center assignment, and conclude with a song, such as "The Lord Blesses Me" or "The Lord is Comin'."

WITNESS CENTER

Ask the participants to wear or display their "Good News Buttons" every day during the coming week. Hopefully those we meet will ask us, "What's your good news?" when they see us wearing our buttons. If someone asks us, our answer might be, "Jesus is coming" or "the Lord blesses me"! Solicit other possible answers from the children.

I'M GONNA BE AN

2 Samuel 7:1-5, 8-11, 16
Psalm 89
Romans 16:25-27
Luke 1:26-38

Luke 1:26-35, 38

The activities of today's celebration focus upon the Annunciation to Mary, retold in this Sunday's gospel reading. The participants will be asked to become like the angel Gabriel, announcing the good news that the savior is among us.

The Word Center activity suggests a simple dramatization of the angel's appearance to Mary. Suggestions for adaptation by different groups are presented in the instructions.

The Creation Center activity requires a special preparatory errand, so be sure to look it over in advance.

In the Family Home

Families might adapt the Creation Center activity by allowing each family member to draw from a hat the name of another family member. Each could then prepare a special message for the person whose name was drawn. The messages could be opened and shared by all when the family celebrates Christmas by the exchange of gifts as suggested in the Witness Center.

GREETING CENTER

Today's celebration of God's Word should begin with an Advent song of joy, such as "Rejoice, Be Glad!"

Secret Message Game

Gather the participants close together and initiate a secret message by whispering in someone's ear: "The Lord is with you." Allow the participants time to whisper this secret message to all others sharing in the celebration. Ask the last receiver to announce the message to the group! (Usually by the time the message reaches the last receiver it is jumbled! This adds to the fun of the activity.)

Then lead the participants in a discussion including answers to these, or similar questions:

1. Have you ever been asked to deliver a message to someone? At home? At school?
2. Was it an important message?
3. How did you feel as the messenger? Willing? Important?
4. How did the receiver react to the message? Surprised? Pleased? Disappointed?

Then explain that today's celebration will be about an important message delivered by a very important messenger to a most important person!

WORD CENTER

The Annunciation story in the Gospel of Luke allows for a simple, yet interesting, dramatization for the participants. The script is provided, but it should be interpreted in whatever way is best for your setting. Larger groups might choose to separate into smaller groupings, each preparing this passage as a skit to be viewed, in turn, by the other groupings. Families and smaller numbers of participants might read through the script together, then discuss how best to perform this little gospel drama. Sometimes it is effective just to provide the storyline and allow the participants to make up their own dialogue and narration as their dramatization gets underway.

Luke 1:26-35, 38

Narrator: In the sixth month of Elizabeth's pregnancy God sent the angel Gabriel to a town in Galilee named Nazareth. He had a message for a girl promised in marriage to a man named Joseph, who was a descendant of King David. The girl's name was Mary. The angel came to her and said,

Gabriel: Peace be with you! The Lord is with you and has greatly blessed you!

Narrator: Mary was deeply troubled by the angel's message, and she wondered what his words meant. The angel said to her,

Gabriel: Don't be afraid, Mary; God has been gracious to you. You will become pregnant and give birth to a son, and you will name him Jesus. He will be great and will be called the Son of the Most High God. The Lord God will make him a king, as his ancestor David was, and he will be the king of the descendants of Jacob forever; His kingdom will never end!

Narrator: Mary said to the angel,

Mary: I am a virgin. How, then, can this be?

Narrator: The angel answered,

Gabriel: The Holy Spirit will come on you, and God's power will rest upon you. For this reason the holy child will be called the Son of God.

Narrator: Mary said,

Mary: I am the Lord's servant; may it happen to me as you have said.

Narrator: And the angel left her.

After the dramatization, the participants can discuss any possible reactions which might have been Mary's upon hearing the words of the angel. (If time permits, you might want to sing "See How The Virgin Waits.") Emphasize not only Mary's willingness to be the mother of the Son of God, but especially the role of the angel Gabriel as the messenger of God's Word. Ask the participants to describe how the angel might have felt as the one sent with such an important message for the woman who would give birth to the savior.

ANGEL

PRAISE CENTER

Talk with the participants about the joy which filled Mary when she received the message that the Lord was truly with her and had greatly blessed her by choosing her to be the Mother of Jesus.

After Mary was visited by the angel Gabriel, she went to visit her relative, Elizabeth. After telling Elizabeth the good news she had received from the angel, she sang a song of praise to God.

Pause and sing "The Lord Blesses Me!", a version of Mary's song for children (and adults).

Conclude with a Repetition Movement Prayer in words such as these:

Dear Father, *(hands outstretched heavenward;)*

bless us this day *(arms crossed upon chest;)*

with a heart *(hands place upon heart;)*

filled with your joy. *(spread arms in circular motion coming to rest at smiling mouth;)*

Help us spread your message *(extend arms outward;)*

that our savior is with us. *(raise arms heavenward coming to rest crossed upon chest;)*

Amen. *(bow heads.)*

CREATION CENTER

Peace-grams

If possible, ask your local Western Union office for enough "Mailgram" envelopes for distribution to each participant. Most offices will be happy to furnish these envelopes if you explain the purpose as described here. Regular white mailing envelopes would be a suitable substitute.

Each participant should be given a blank piece of paper upon which they could write an important message to their families about the meaning of Christmas. An example, taken from today's gospel reading, might be:

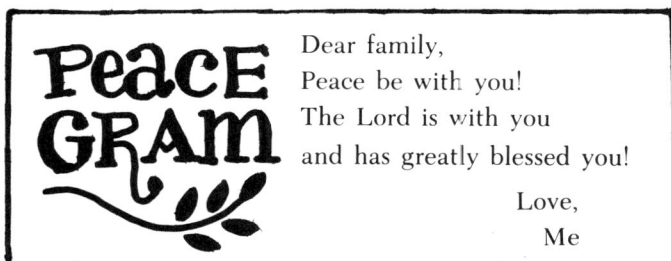

PEACE GRAM

Dear family,
Peace be with you!
The Lord is with you
and has greatly blessed you!

Love,
Me

Smaller children, unable to print, could draw a picture about Christmas instead of writing a message.

Each message should then be folded and placed inside the Mailgram envelope. The envelope should be addressed to each participant's family. Further instructions are given as the Witness Center activity assignment.

SHARING CENTER

When the participants gather together, a summary of today's lesson could be given in words such as these:

Very few people have ever had the opportunity to see an angel. Most of us have probably seen artists' paintings of what they think angels look like. You know, those floating-in-the-air people with wings and halos. No doubt many of us have been angels in school Christmas plays. We've been dressed up in pretty gowns with glitter and with a tinsel halo above our heads! But very few people have ever had the opportunity to see an angel.

The story of the Annunciation of Mary from the bible tells us that there are angels. In fact, Mary is one of those people who has seen an angel.

Do you know what the word angel means? It comes from an ancient Greek word that means "messenger."

Now, even if we've never seen an angel before, we would all probably agree that an angel is at least a messenger sent by God. God has sent special messages through angels in the past and God, our Father, continues to send important messages to us even today. In fact, he asks us to spread the good news that the savior is born for us. God asks us to be his messengers...and since angels are messengers sent by God, I guess that makes us God's angels today!

In a way we're like the angel Gabriel. We must announce the good news that Jesus is born and is with us today.

Then ask the participants for some suggestions for a special message we might spread in God's name. Some might share the message they have written for their families at the Creation Center.

Give the Witness Center activity assignment and conclude with a secret message such as "Spread the Good News!" or pray this version of the "Hail Mary":

Hail Mary, full of grace
the Lord is with you.
He has greatly blessed you
and your Son, Jesus.
Holy Mary, Mother of God,
pray for us now
and when we die.
Amen.

WITNESS CENTER

Encourage each participant to be an "angel" this Christmas by taking home the mailgram message prepared for their families. When the family gathers at Christmas to open their gifts, the participant should deliver his/her message for the family to read aloud. The message written by the participant will remind each family of the true Christmas gift: Jesus, our savior, is among us!

GOD KEEPS HIS PROMISES

Jeremiah 33:14-15
Psalm 25
1 Thessalonians 3:12-4:2
Luke 21:25-28, 34-36

Jeremiah 33:14-16
Psalm 25:4-21
1 Thessalonians 3:12-13

The theme of today's celebration is found in the selection of the prophet Jermiah where it is written that the Lord will fulfil the promise he made with Israel and Judah. It is a fitting beginning for our observance of the Advent season and an appropriate theme for this week's celebration of the lighting of the Advent wreath.

The origin of the Advent Wreath custom is explained in the Creation Center activity.

In the Parish Program

Display the Advent Wreath in the room's center during the season. It might be appropriate to duplicate the Creation, Praise and Witness Center activities as handouts for the participants to bring home for family celebration, perhaps as a ''kidsletter'' supplement.

In the Religious Education Classroom

Display the Advent Wreath in the center of the classroom for all of the season. Begin each school day with the lighting of the wreath if the participants are together.

In the Family Home

Families will appreciate displaying their Advent Wreaths in the front window, perhaps suspended from the ceiling, as was an early custom. The Witness Center activity could be a family prayer each day at breakfast or dinner time.

GREETING CENTER

A song of glory, thanksgiving or praise, such as ''Sing A Song of Praise'' or ''Come Out of Egypt,'' would be appropriate for the start of today's celebration.

Then talk with the participants about the season of Advent, the time the Church sets aside for us to celebrate the promise God made to his people long ago — his promise to send the Messiah, His Son, the ''Light of the World.''

Ask the participants if they have ever made a promise. Let them share their many varied experiences. Then ask about God's promise to send his Son to save his people. Why did God promise to send a savior?

Sing ''Do You Know?''

A discussion of the song's text might be appropriate before assembling at the Word Center.

WORD CENTER

Before reading Psalm 25, instruct the participants in words such as these:

God made a promise to his people, the Israelites, that he would send a savior to them and restore their happiness. But the people grew impatient with God because they did not know how or when God would send the savior. Some began to lose trust in God. Some even turned aside and ignored God's way.

Listen to this prayer which one of God's people wrote. It was a song. It asks God to make known his ways.

Psalm 25:4-5, 8-12

Teach me your ways, O Lord;
 make them known to me.
Teach me to live according to your truth,
 for you are my God, who saves me.
I always trust in you.
Because the Lord is righteous and good,
 he teaches sinners the path they should follow.
He leads the humble in the right way
 and teaches them his will.
With faithfulness and love he leads all
 who keep his covenant and obey his commands.
Keep your promise, Lord, and forgive my sins,
 for they are many.
Those who obey the Lord
 will learn from him the path they should follow.

CREATION CENTER

The Advent Wreath

Materials Needed: evergreen branches, green pipe cleaners, 4 red (1 pink, 3 red) candles, a purple ribbon strip and a small, portable table.

Several participants should be selected as Readers of the explanations for the different materials which make the Advent Wreath. As each is read aloud, the other participants should be designated, in turn, to assist in the formation of the wreath.

A. Evergreens

Reader 1: Long before there was a Christmas, ancient peoples placed evergreen branches above their doors during the winter months because they believed that there were spirits of the woods who were forced to wander around in the cold, but we know better! By offering them shelter in the branches of evergreens, the ancient people hoped for good health during the year!

Early Romans exchanged green branches at their winter festival, the Saturnalia, as a wish for good luck and hope that the sun would return. To the Druids, an ancient tribe, evergreens were sacred, a symbol of life.

Reader 2: Evergreens were soon made a symbol of Christmas by Christians. Because evergreens never change color, they remind us of God, whose loving care for us never changes. It is God who protects us all year 'round and sends us Jesus to guide our lives. God is indeed sacred: He is our only life and hope!

In the middle ages the evergreen branches were bent so that the ends touched. This represents life without beginning or end. When we make a circle out of our greens to form a wreath we are symbolizing our belief in God, who has no beginning and will have no end. God is everlasting and his love for us will last forever.

Activity: Attach the evergreens with green-colored pipe cleaners forming a wreath for placement on a table.

B. Candles

Reader 3: Candles have been used by many religious groups since long before the time of Jesus. As a matter of fact, many forms of light are used at religious festivals as a sign of joy. In times before Jesus, people lighted large torches welcoming the winter months. At the Saturnalia, the Romans put lighted candles on trees in honor of Saturn, the god they believed would come and protect their crops during the cold winter months.

Reader 4: The ancient Hebrews lighted candles, one each night, for eight nights at their first Feast of Lights in 165 B.C. For three years a foreign conqueror had placed false idols in their Temple in Jerusalem. When the Hebrews regained their Temple from the intruders, their candles were lighted to purify this holy place from the presence of the false idols. Jewish people commemorate this ancient event even today. It is called Hannukah.

The Irish people have a legend that says the Christ child visits homes every Christmas. Sometimes, however, he sends a stranger in His place. The Irish people place a candle in their windows for the stranger which means: We are waiting for you. You are welcome here!

Reader 5: Christians have made the burning candle a symbol of Christ, the "Light of the World." We place four candles on our evergreen wreath, one for each week of Advent, as a sign that we are waiting for Christ, the light of the world, telling everyone that Christ is welcome in our lives and as a reminder to us that we should purify our hearts of wrongdoing and prepare a holy place within us for Christ to dwell in.

Reader 6: The candles should be red, an exciting color which stands for love. When the candles are lighted each night during Advent, we should call to mind the kind actions we performed during the day as our "Advent purification." Some people's custom is to place a pink candle for the third week of Advent. Pink is a joyful color, reminding us that Christmas is not far away.

On Christmas Day a pure white candle should be lighted and placed in the center of the wreath. White stands for light and glory. On Christmas Day we give glory to God because Jesus, the light of the world, is our reason for celebration.

Activity: Arrange the four Advent candles on the wreath placed upon table.

C. Ribbon

Reader 7: Our Advent Wreath is complete when a large purple ribbon is attached. Ribbons are decorations which people have placed on gifts for years. Our purple ribbon reminds us that we must give other people the love of Christ through our good deeds and kind words during Advent. The Church chooses purple because it is a color which represents hard work — our giving to others will be hard work, too.

On Christmas morning, the purple ribbon is exchanged with a bright golden ribbon bow. Gold represents sunlight and radiance. Our gold bow represents God our Father's gift to us at Christmas: Jesus, the Light of the World.

Activity: Place gold ribbon, interwoven through the greens, on the Advent wreath.

PRAISE CENTER

If possible, darken the room.

Begin with an introduction, such as this:

Today (tonight) we light the first candle on our Advent wreath, recalling the great promise God made to his people. Our light will remind us this week that God kept his promise. He sent Jesus, the savior, to be a light for the world.

Ask one of the participants to light the first candle as another reads this short passage from Jeremiah.

Jeremiah 33:14-16
The Lord said, "The time is coming when I will fulfill the promise that I made to the people of Israel and Judah. At that time I will choose as king a righteous descendant of David. That king will do what is right and just throughout the land. The people of Judah and of Jerusalem will be rescued and will live in safety. The city will be called "The Lord Our Salvation."

Sing "The Advent Wreath Song" or the refrain of "Wait for the Savior."

Pause for a silent moment of personal prayer, then conclude with this Repetition Prayer, Psalm 25:4-5:

> Teach me your ways, O Lord;
> make them known to me.
> Teach me to live according to your truth;
> for you are my God.
> I always trust in you.
> Amen.

SHARING CENTER

Ask the participants to repeat some of the promises they mentioned at the Greeting Center. Then ask if anyone has ever broken a promise — or if perhaps friends have ever broken promises they made to us. Help the participants to speak openly. Keeping promises is a difficult task: it requires patience and honesty.

Discuss with everyone the importance and meaning of making and keeping promises. We should be grateful to God our Father for making and keeping His promise to send us Jesus, our savior.

Give the Witness Center assignment and conclude with this blessing from the first letter of Paul to the Thessalonians.

1 Thessalonians 3:12-13
May the Lord make your love for one another and for all people grow more and more and become as great as our love for you. In this way he will strengthen you, and you will be perfect and holy in the presence of our God and Father when our Lord Jesus comes with all who belong to him.

All sing a favorite verse of "Sing A Song of Praise."

WITNESS CENTER

During the first week of Advent, the Advent wreath should be lit each day with these divisions of Psalm 25 prayed during the lighting ceremony, as indicated.

Monday
Remember, O Lord, your kindness and constant love which you have shown from long ago.
Forgive the sins and errors we have made.
In your constant love and goodness, remember us, Lord!

Tuesday
Because the Lord is righteous and good, he teaches sinners the path they should follow.
He leads the humble in the right way and teaches them his will.
With faithfulness and love he leads all who keep his covenant and obey his commands.

Wednesday
Keep your promise, Lord, and forgive our sins.
Those who obey the Lord will learn from him the path they should follow.
The Lord is the friend of those who obey him and he affirms his covenant with them.

Thursday
We look to the Lord for help at all times, and he restores us from danger.
Turn to us, Lord, and be merciful.

Friday
Protect us and save us, Lord; keep us from defeat.
May our goodness and honesty preserve us, because we trust in you.

Saturday
Teach us your ways, O Lord, make them known to us.
Teach us to live according to your truth, for you are our God, who saves us.
We trust in you.

Each lighting service could be concluded by singing "An Advent Wreath Song" or the refrain of "Wait for the Savior."

AN ADVENT WREATH SONG

The ritual of the Advent Wreath lighting captures the spirit of joyful expectation which should accompany the season of Advent. This short song is about the light of the Advent Wreath candles, a sign of Christmas waiting. It should be sung during the service of lighting the Advent Wreath.

Dick Hilliard
arr. Rev. John H. Olivier, S.S.

Can-dle, can-dle, burn-ing bright, be our sign of wait-ing light. Light for our Sav - ior who comes to set us free. We make read - y to re - ceive the Lord. To Him all glo - ry be!

THIS WAY TO THE

Baruch 5:1-9
Psalm 126
Philippians 1:4-6, 8-11
Luke 3:1-6

Psalm 126:1-3
Philippians 1:4-7, 9, 11
Luke 3:1-6, 15-16, 18

Today's celebration is intended to help us realize that we can point the way to the presence of the Lord in our lives. Advent is a season during which we consider the ways we prepare to make the Lord's message of salvation known to all who seek to find Him. Our theme is taken from the gospel lesson of this Sunday's liturgy, Luke's retelling of the mission of John the Baptist. We continue our lighting of the Advent Wreath during this time together and all throughout these four Sundays of Advent.

GREETING CENTER

Today's celebration might begin with a favorite Advent song such as "Come Out of Egypt" or an introductory song of friendship, such as "Howdy Friends." After everyone is settled, lead a short discussion allowing the participants to respond to these or similar questions:

1. Have you ever been lost?
2. Did you ask someone for directions?
3. Has anyone ever asked you for directions?
4. Could you give accurate directions when someone was lost?

WORD CENTER

Select three participants to prepare and proclaim this reading from the gospel of Luke:

Luke 3:1-6

Narrator: *It was the fifteenth year of the rule of Emperor Tiberius; Pontius Pilate was governor of Judea, Herod was ruler of Galilee, and his brother Philip was ruler of the territory nearby; and Annas and Caiaphas were high priests.*

At that time the word of God came to John, son of Zachariah, in the desert. So John went throughout the whole territory of the Jordan River, preaching,

John: *"Turn away from your sins and be baptized, and God will forgive your sins."*

Narrator: *As it is written in the book of the prophet Isaiah:*

Isaiah:
Someone is shouting in the desert:
"Get the road ready for the Lord;
make a straight path for him to travel!
Every valley must be filled up,
every hill and mountain leveled off.
The winding roads must be made straight.
and the rough paths made smooth.
All mankind will see God's salvation!"

Narrator: *This is the gospel of the Lord!*

Then lead the participants in singing verses 10 and 11 of "Wait for the Savior."

A free discussion about the reading should follow, helping the participants recognize these important aspects of the reading's lesson:

1. John the Baptist was a prophet.
2. He proclaimed in the desert a message about the savior as predicted by Isaiah.
3. John's message was, in effect, simple "directions" for finding the savior, because people didn't seem to know the way.

You might encourage the participants to express John's directions freely in words of their own. (John's words, as found in the gospel, are "Turn away from your sins and be baptized.") You might want to sing "John the Baptist."

John's directions are as appropriate for our time as they were two thousand years ago. Help the participants to suggest ways for us to "turn away from our sins" and find our savior, the Lord Jesus.

CREATION CENTER

Paper Road Signs

Materials Needed: white construction paper, crayons, chalk, water base paints (or marking pens), and scissors.

Ask the participants to describe familiar road signs (stop, go back, one way, etc.). Road signs give directions. They help us to obey the rules of driving so that we don't hurt others and also so that we don't get lost.

Distribute white paper to each participant. On the paper each participant should draw and cut his/her favorite road sign.

SHARING CENTER

The participants should share with one another the meaning of the road sign they have chosen to illustrate. As each different type of sign is described, the leader might ask: "If someone asked you, 'Where can I find Jesus?', how would your sign help?"

Some clues might be:

Stop Sign — Don't go any further. Jesus is in you! or Stop! Don't hurt each other.

One Way — There is only one way to Jesus: through the loving and peaceful hearts of people.

Wrong Way — You are looking the wrong way for Jesus. You won't find him if you're bad.

Slow/Yield — Slow down and join the rest of the gang. Jesus is found wherever two or three are gathered in his name.

Speed Limit — Don't be impatient. Jesus is with us!

SAVIOR

Then sing "Do You Know?" Encourage the participants to hold up their signs if they think it is about one of the verses being sung.

Suggestions:
verse 1: speed limit sign
verse 2: wrong way
verse 3: stop sign
verse 4: slow/yield
verse 5: one way

PRAISE CENTER

The Advent wreath, with one lighted candle from the previous week's celebration, should be displayed appropriately, and around it all the participants should gather. A lighted candle is itself an old symbol used to "show the way" to expected visitors. It is a simple sign giving "directions" at the place of destination.

One of the participants can light the second Advent candle while another participant reads this passage from Psalm 125, a prayer which was sung when the exiled Israelite people were brought back to their homeland.

Psalm 126:1-3

When the Lord brought us back to Jerusalem, it was like a dream! How we laughed, how we sang for joy! Then the other nations said about us, "The Lord did great things for them." Indeed he did great things for us; how happy we were!

All sing "An Advent Wreath Song."

SHARING CENTER

Before concluding today's celebration, give the Witness Center assignment and pray this blessing from Paul's letter to the Philippians:

Philippians 1:4-7, 9, 11

I thank my God for you every time I think of you; and every time I pray for you all, I pray with joy because of the way in which you have helped me in the work of the good news.

May God, who began this good work in you, carry it on until it is finished on the Day of Christ Jesus.

I pray that your love will keep on growing more and more, so that you will be able to choose what is best in Christ Jesus, the Lord.

Sing verse 11 and the chorus of "Wait for the Savior."

WITNESS CENTER

The participants should take their "road signs" home as a reminder to follow the way to the Lord, our savior, as they discussed at the first Sharing Center activity.

Teachers will want to distribute a duplication of these readings for this coming week of lighting the Advent wreath during family prayer times (below), perhaps as part of the "kidsletter." Each day's lighting service could include a favorite Advent song, such as "An Advent Wreath Song" or the chorus of "Wait for the Savior."

Suggested readings to accompany the lighting of the Advent Wreath during the second week of Advent (taken from the third chapter of Luke's gospel):

Monday

John the Baptist went throughout the whole territory of the Jordan River preaching, "Turn away from your sins and be baptized, and God will forgive your sins."

Tuesday

As it is written in the book of the prophet Isaiah: "Someone is shouting in the desert; Get the road ready for the Lord; make a straight path for him to travel!"

Wednesday

The prophet Isaiah has written:
"Every valley must be filled up,
every hill and mountain leveled off.
The winding roads must be made straight,
and the rough paths made smooth.
All mankind will see God's salvation!"

Thursday

People's hopes began to rise, and they began to wonder whether John perhaps might be the Messiah. So John said to all of them, "I baptize you with water, but someone is coming who is much greater than I am. I am not good enough even to untie his sandals. He will baptize you with the Holy Spirit and fire.

Friday

In many different ways John preached the Good News to the people and urged them to change their ways.

Saturday

All of the above.

REJOICE!

THE LORD

Zephaniah 3:14-18
Isaiah 12:2-6
Philippians 4:4-7
Luke 3:10-18

Zephaniah 3:14-18, 20
Isaiah 12:2-4
Philippians 4:4-6

WILBUR IN THE WILDERNESS
by Dick Hilliard

Today's theme is taken from the responsorial and the first two readings of this Sunday's liturgy. Supplemented with a short tale, "Wilbur in the Wilderness," this celebration should help us to recognize that at this midpoint in the Advent Season we should rejoice with anticipation at the coming feast of our savior's birth. The center activities should flow together smoothly as they are unified not only by theme, but by prayerful bodily expression.

GREETING CENTER

After the participants are ready for this prayer-filled celebration, begin with an Advent song of joyfulness, such as "Rejoice, Be Glad."

Begin discussion of the celebration's theme by asking the children questions such as these listed. (Be sure to allow them time to tell their tales in their own creative detail.)

1. Did you ever expect a visitor from far away? Perhaps it was a relative?
2. How did you feel as you prepared for this visit? Anxious? Nervous? Excited? Joyful?
3. Were you happy when the visitor arrived? Did your visitor bring you anything?

or

1. Did you ever expect a very important phone call? Perhaps it was long distance from your grandparents on your birthday?
2. How did you prepare for this phone call? Did you make a list of things to say?
3. Were you excited when the phone rang? Did the caller have special news for you?

When the participants have finished telling their tales, prepare them for this short adventuresome story by practicing some of the prayer gestures which they will make as the story is told.

It wasn't too long before the sun set behind the distant mountaintop that ten-year-old Wilbur realized he was lost in the forest near his family's campground. As it grew dark among the very tall trees in the wilderness, Wilbur bundled up in his heavy coat and found a place in the brush to sleep through the night. He knew he shouldn't wander through the woods in the dark, and his chances of being saved would be greatest if he stayed right where he was until morning.

As he closed his eyes to sleep he remembered what his father had told the family before their camping trip: "If anyone should get lost, don't wander far away. Stay in one area and listen for dad's rescue horn. It will be a joyful sound that help is coming near!"

Wilbur paused and prayed before he fell asleep. He said (*invite the children to repeat these words and gestures*):

Dear Father (*raise open arms heavenward*)
protect me with your love (*cross arms upon chest*)
Let me hear the sound of joy (*cup hand behind ear*)
that help is coming near. (*move arm in welcoming motion*)

About midnight Wilbur was startled from his sleep by a distant sound going "hoot-hoot-hoot." He opened his eyes very wide and smiled with joy. Again he heard "hoot-hoot-hoot." He jumped up with happiness for he was certain the sound was the "hoot-hoot-hoot" of his father's rescue horn. The sound stopped for a while but then there was another "hoot-hoot-hoot."

COMES!

Poor Wilbur frowned with disappointment because he realized the "hoot-hoot-hoot" was the voice of an owl above him in the trees. He lay down again in the brush after he paused to pray:

Dear Father *(arms open heavenward)*
thank you for this sound of joy. *(cup hand behind ear)*
Let me rest with all these birds *(flap arms at sides)*
and awake when help is near. *(move arms in welcoming motion coming to rest crisscrossed upon chest)*

The night became very cold in the snow-tipped forest, but Wilbur slept quite soundly inside his big warm jacket until about six o'clock in the morning when he was awakened by another distant sound, "ow-ooh, ow-ooh." He quickly stood to listen more carefully. The sound grew louder and louder, "ow-ooh, ow-ooh." He listened again, "ow-ooh, ow-ooh."

"That must be my dad's rescue horn," he thought to himself. But the "ow-ooh" faded away over the mountain ridge as Wilbur realized it was the morning sound of a wild coyote. He walked around the area because he knew the sun would soon be shining. He paused and prayed:

Thank you, dear Father *(arms open heavenward)*
for this and every day. *(bring arms in circular motion to sides)*
May I hear dad's horn of joy *(cup hand at ear)*
and know that help is on the way. *(move arms in welcoming motion to rest crisscrossed upon chest)*

The birds began to chirp and sing. The squirrels rustled through the leaves. The snow melted drops from the treetops. The sun shone brightly through the woods. And little Wilbur was lost in the wilderness.

He almost started to cry because he was feeling disappointed that he was not yet rescued, but then he heard a loud and funny sound, "beep-beep, beep-beep!" He giggled as he looked around — he thought for sure it was the sound of a happy chipmunk. "Beep-beep! beep-beep!" That sound was heard again.

"Where is the little chipmunk," Wilbur thought as he looked all around. "Over here, little chipmunk," he said quietly.

But the "beep-beep, beep-beep" grew louder and closer and Wilbur still couldn't see any chipmunk. "Beep-beep. Beep-beep!" Wilbur was puzzled as he wondered, "Where could this joyous sound be coming from?"

Then he heard a rustle among the fallen leaves across the valley. "Beep-beep. Beep-beep!" Then Wilbur realized it was much too funny a sound to be coming from a little chipmunk. Wilbur turned all around trying to find the source of this joyful noise. "Beep-beep." And Wilbur jumped with gladness. Through the trees he saw his dad blowing a horn! "Beep-beep. Beep-beep."

Wilbur started running among the brush and trees and he landed right in the arms of his father. "I've been saved!" Wilbur yelled as he hugged his dad. He was so happy that he blew the horn himself. "Beep-beep. Beep-beep!"

They paused to pray before their long hike back to their campground.

(Invite one of the participants to lead the group in Wilbur's prayer of thanksgiving.)

When the story is finished, briefly talk about Wilbur and his eagerness to hear the joyful sound of his father's rescue horn. Is his experience anything like our expectation of a visitor's coming or of the long-awaited ring of the telephone?

WORD CENTER

This reading from Zephaniah could be introduced in words similar to these:

God's chosen people were once disappointed that the savior had not yet come. Some were so disappointed they began to lose hope. Although they wanted desperately to be saved, they stopped listening to the prophets and they did as they pleased.

One time, however, the prophet Zephaniah was in their midst. He gathered the people together and said:

(One of the participants should be selected to read this passage.)

Zephaniah 3:14-18

Sing and shout for joy, people of Israel!
Rejoice with all your heart, Jerusalem!
The Lord has stopped your punishment;
he has removed all your enemies.
The Lord is with you; there is no reason now to be afraid.
The time is coming when they will say,
"Do not be afraid!"
The Lord your God is with you;
his power gives you victory.
The Lord will take delight in you,
and in his love he will give you new life.
He will sing and be joyful over you,
as joyful as people at a festival."

At the conclusion of this reading, ask the participants if they have ever been sent to their rooms for misbehaving. Did you want to be freed from your punishment? Explain that this freedom is like the freedom desired by the people of Israel. They thought they were being punished because God would not send the savior to them. But Zephaniah announced good news to them saying: "Rejoice! You will be saved!" (Perhaps it was the kind of sound that our friend Wilbur was waiting for?)

Sing the refrain of "Rejoice, Be Glad!"

PRAISE CENTER

A short preparation for the service of lighting the Advent wreath candle should be given in words similar to these below. (The first two candles should already be burning.)

Our friend Wilbur rejoiced when he heard the sound of his father's horn announcing help was on the way.

We rejoice when we hear the doorbell ring announcing the arrival of an expected visitor.

The people of Israel rejoiced when they heard that the savior was soon to be in their midst.

Today we light the third candle of the Advent wreath as a sign of rejoicing...we know that we will soon celebrate the feast of our savior's birth. Let us pray together in the words of the prophet Isaiah (12:2-4 paraphrased).

I praise you, God! (arms raised heavenward)
You are my savior; (bring arms crossed upon chest)
I trust you (arms openly extended)
and am not afraid. (palms down, move arms in opposite direction in front of self)
I give thanks to you, Lord. (hands upon heart, then extend heavenward)
You are my savior! (bring arms crossed upon chest)
Amen. (bow head)

At the conclusion of the prayer, light the third candles as all sing "An Advent Wreath Song."

CREATION CENTER

Megaphones

Materials Needed: colored construction paper sheets, scissors for each participant, and tape.

Each participant should be given a large piece of colored construction paper. Allow each to cut the corners of the paper sheet as illustrated. Demonstrate the rolling of the paper into a megaphone. Let each tape his/her megaphone into place.

SHARING CENTER

When the participants are gathered, each with his/her own megaphone, they should sit in a circle while this brief instruction from St. Paul is read.

Philippians 4:4-6

May you always be joyful in your union with the Lord. I say it again: rejoice!

Show a gentle attitude toward everyone. The Lord is coming soon. Don't worry about anything, but in all your prayers ask God for what you need, always, asking him with a thankful heart.

Highlight Paul's emphasis upon rejoicing with thankfulness at the coming of the Lord. It is very much the mood of Wilbur in the Wilderness and the message of Zephaniah and Isaiah.

Then invite each participant to stand and, speaking through a megaphone, announce with joy his/her own reason for praying to God, as Paul instructs, with a thankful heart. Examples might be:

"Because God is my savior!,"

"because God makes me happy!,"

"because Jesus' day is near," etc...

Together join in singing "Sing a Song of Praise."

Give the Witness Center activity assignment and conclude, if time allows, with the chorus of "Rejoice, Be Glad!"

WITNESS CENTER

This week's assignment might be given in words similar to these:

Megaphones are used to make important announcements. Cheerleaders sing and shout for joy through megaphones. Officials give urgent instructions when speaking through a megaphone.

Take your megaphone home and let it be a reminder to you that you should announce the day of the Lord's coming. Like the horn of Wilbur's father, let your megaphone resound with a joyful noise!

Teachers should distribute a copy of these readings for lighting the Advent wreath at family prayer during the coming week, as printed below. It could be attached to the "kidsletter."

Readings from *Zephaniah 3:14-20* for lighting the Advent Wreath candles during Week 3:

Monday

Sing and shout for joy, people of Israel!
Rejoice with all your heart!
The Lord has stopped your punishment;
He has removed all your enemies.

Tuesday

The Lord, the king of Israel, is with you;
There is no reason now to be afraid.
The time is coming when they will say
"Do not be afraid!"

Wednesday

The Lord your God is with you;
his power gives you victory.
The Lord will take delight in you,
and in his love he will give you new life,
He will sing and be joyful over you,
as joyful as people at a festival.

Thursday

The Lord says,
"I have ended the threat of doom
and taken away your disgrace."

Friday

"The time is coming!
I will bring your scattered people home;
I will make you famous throughout the world
and make you prosperous once again,"
says the Lord, our God.

Saturday

(all of the above)

Each day's lighting service could conclude with "An Advent Wreath Song" or the chorus to "Rejoice, Be Glad" or another favorite Advent song.

WHAT A SURPRISE!

Micah 5:1-4   Micah 5:2-4
Psalm 80
Hebrews 10:5-10
Luke 1:39-45   Luke 1:38-45, 56
                                         Luke 1:68-74, 78-79

"The least expected" is a theme which is characteristic of the readings today and gives reason for our choosing "What A Surprise!" as today's celebration theme. The town of Bethlehem and the person of Mary are the central figures of today's lesson and the readings are supplemented with a short tale, "Disaster at the Damascus Zoo," to be told at the Greeting Center.

This week concludes our celebrating the lighting of the Advent wreath as we recall the prayer of Zechariah in the Witness Center activities. It is a fitting ending to our Advent season ceremonies.

GREETING CENTER

When the participants are ready, the celebration can start with an Advent song of waiting, such as "Wait for the Savior" (chorus only), or "The Lord Is Comin'."

Then everyone can gather close together for a telling of this little tale, "Disaster At the Damascus Zoo."

DISASTER AT THE DAMASCUS ZOO!
by Dick Hilliard

At nine o'clock in the morning on December 20, Mr. Kilpepper Klinger began a memorable day as keeper at the Damascus Zoo. He opened the gates promptly as the clock struck nine, and in went Mrs. Henrietta Harper and her 29 second grade students from the Damascus Day School.

Mr. Klinger was proud to have his zoo be the destination of Mrs. Harper's class field trip. It was a brisk and breezy day in December as the children made their entry among the zoo's population of preposterous pets.

At about 9:30 that morning, Mr. Kilpepper Klinger gathered Mrs. Henrietta Harper's class of second graders together to begin their official Christmastime tour of the Damascus Zoo.

"Over here to our left you see our elated, elegant family of elephants," announced Mr. Klinger. "We call them the Ellisons," he said. "Why, that's Elisha Ellison right in front of us," he announced as he pointed to the mama elephant.

"Go ahead and swing from her trunk," whined a wicked voice from behind the youngsters. Everyone turned around to find this voice coming from the mouth of Quincy, the crooked crocodile.

"Don't listen to Quincy," cautioned Mr. Klinger. "He'll just get us into trouble."

Just then the breeze grew so strong at the Damascus Zoo that it blew the bonnet from the head of one little girl. It soared high into the air and landed at the top of a nearby oak tree.

"O, dear!" said Mrs. Harper. "I'm afraid you're going to have to say good-bye to that bonnet."

"Not in the least," commented Quincy, that crooked crocodile. "Mr. Klinger will choose one of us smart animals to rescue that hat!"

"How about Priscilla, Mr. Klinger," laughed Quincy as he made his way toward the zoo-keeper.

"O, don't listen to Quincy, children," Mr. Klinger said. "Poor Priscilla is our prickly porcupine. She'd just get stuck in the tree. That's Quincy for you. He'd suggest anything just to get us in trouble."

"Hey, Gifford!," shouted Mr. Klinger. "Get that bonnet for this sweet little girl."

So Gifford the giant giraffe reached to the top of that tall oak tree and retrieved the bonnet blown by the breeze.

As Gifford backed away he accidentally hit the brick wall of the big bird bath. Down splashed the water through the crumbling bricks, and the wall fell into a pile of rubble.

"O, dear!," said Mrs. Harper. "I'm afraid your bath's destroyed."

"Not in the least," commented Quincy, that crooked crocodile. "Mr. Klinger will choose one of us smart animals to repair that wall."

"How about Priscilla, Mr. Klinger," joked Quincy.

"Don't Listen to Quincy, children," Mr. Klinger said. "Poor Priscilla, our prickly porcupine, would get stuck in cement trying to repair those bricks! That's Quincy for you. He'll suggest anything just to get us in trouble."

"Bertrand!" yelled Mr. Klinger. "Come fix this brick wall for us."

So, Bertrand the bashful beaver hobbled over to repair the brick wall for the big bird bath. To Bertrand it was just like building another dam!

As Bertrand was finishing his work, the second graders from Damascus Day School heard an awful noise from near the zoo's entrance. Old Clarence the clown took a terrible spill off the ladder from which he sold brightly colored balloons.

"O, dear!," said Mrs. Harper. "I'm afraid your balloons are going to pop!"

"Not in the least," commented Quincy, that crooked crocodile. "Mr. Klinger will choose one of us smart animals to replace that clown."

"How about Priscilla, Mr. Klinger," roared Quincy with great laughter.

By then the second graders from the Damascus Day School had caught on to Quincy's crooked ways, so they said to Mr. Klinger, "Don't listen to Quincy! He'll suggest anything just to get us in trouble. Priscilla would pop those balloons with the prickly needles of her porcupine skin!"

But Mr. Klinger paused for a moment and thought about this present disaster at the Damascus Zoo. After a few moments he shouted with dignified certainty, "Hey, Priscilla! Kindly replace Clarence the clown and gather those balloons for sale."

As Priscilla the prickly porcupine raced her way to the zoo's entrance, the children from the Damascus Day School were puzzled. Why would Mr. Klinger pick a prickly porcupine to gather up the balloons?

Quincy, too, was stunned. Never before had Mr. Klinger ever paid attention to Quincy's advice. Quincy might be crooked, but he was smart! He knew also that Priscilla's prickly porcupine quills would pop those balloons. Quincy couldn't figure out Mr. Klinger's decision.

"You see, Quincy," Mr. Klinger announced. "The joke is on you! Those balloons over there are filled with helium. With this breeze today they'll stay way up in the air. They'll never fall to Priscilla's prickly porcupine skin!"

When the second graders from the Damascus Day School heard Mr. Klinger's explanation they laughed with all their might at Quincy, the crooked crocodile. For once the joke was on Quincy!

At the conclusion of the story, discuss with the participants the main characters of the tale. Emphasize particularly the fact that Priscilla was the one most of us would least expect to be chosen for the task of selling balloons!

PRAISE CENTER

Bring the participants around the Advent wreath with three candles already burning. Before lighting the fourth and final candle, this passage from the prophet Micah should be read aloud. It is Micah's telling of the Lord's promise to the people of Bethlehem, the smallest town of Judah.

Micah 5:2-4

The Lord says, "Bethlehem, you are one of the smallest towns in Judah, but out of you I will bring a ruler for Israel, whose family line goes back to ancient times."

So the Lord will abandon his people to their enemies until the one who is to give birth has her son. Then his fellow countrymen who are in exile will be reunited with their own people. When he comes, he will rule his people with the strength that comes from the Lord and with the majesty of the Lord God himself. His people will live in safety because people all over the earth will acknowledge his greatness, and he will bring peace.

A short discussion about the passage may be necessary. Highlight the fact that although Bethlehem was one of the smallest and least important of the cities of Judah, it was to become the most famous because it would be the city in which the savior would be born. Like Priscilla in "Disaster at the Damascus Zoo," Bethlehem was the city least expected for the birth of the savior.

Light the fourth candle and then lead the participants in a Repetition Movement Prayer such as this:

God, our Father (*open arms heavenward*) **help us open our hearts** (*cover heart with hands, then open hands outward*) **to receive our savior.** (*welcoming motion, then placing hands upon heart again*) **When he is born in our lives** (*extend arms above heads, then bring arms to sides*) **we will be very important** (*grip thumbs on shirt/blouse under shoulders*) **We will be filled** (*gathering motion with arms*) **with his love and peace.** (*bring arms crossed upon heart*)

"An Advent Wreath Song" or "Rejoice, Be Glad!" could be sung as a conclusion to the lighting ceremony.

WORD CENTER

Before the reading of the delightful telling of the Visitation, invite the participants to retell the story of the angel Gabriel's Annunciation to Mary (cf. Luke 1:26-38). Then select three participants for this dramatization. If it is appropriate, simply tell the storyline to the three dramatists and allow them to enact the tale using their own words.

Luke 1:38-45, 56

Narrator: *Before the angel Gabriel left Mary's house, Mary said,*

Mary: *"I am the Lord's servant. May it happen to me as you have said."*

Narrator: *After the angel left her, Mary got ready and hurried off to a town in the hill country of Judea. She went into Zechariah's house and greeted Elizabeth. When Elizabeth heard Mary's greeting, the baby moved within her. Elizabeth was filled with the Holy Spirit and said in a loud voice,*

Elizabeth: *"You are the most blessed of all women, and blessed is the child you will bear! Why should this great thing happen to me, that my Lord's mother comes to visit me? For as soon as I heard your greeting, the baby within me jumped with gladness. How happy you are to believe that the Lord's message to you will come true!"*

Narrator: *Mary stayed about three months with Elizabeth and then went back home. During her stay she sang a song of praise to the Lord, our God.*

Then sing "The Lord Blesses Me!"

Briefly discuss with the participants Mary's willingness to accept the Lord's desire that she give birth to the savior. Highlight especially her attitude of joyfulness as expressed in her song, the Magnificat. Just as Bethlehem was the town least expected to be chosen for the birth of the savior, so too was Mary the woman least expected to be chosen to give birth to the Christ child. Perhaps the predicament of Priscilla in "Disaster at the Damascus Zoo." is much like Bethlehem and Mary!

CREATION CENTER

Balloons

Materials Needed: balloons (one for each participant), and string (cut into 15-inch strips, one for each participant).

Distribute one balloon to each participant. Allow each to inflate his/her balloon.

Distribute one 15-inch piece of string to each participant. Assist each in tying one end of the string to the balloon. Tie the other end to the participant's wrist.

SHARING CENTER

When the participants are assembled, the lesson of today's theme could be summarized in words such as these:

In the story of "Disaster at the Damascus Zoo" we saw Priscilla, the prickly porcupine, chosen for a very special task. No one ever expected her to be selected to care for the balloons.

Like Priscilla, the town of Bethlehem was a place no one ever expected would be selected for the birth of the savior. It was chosen for a very important event.

And Mary, too, was not expected to be blessed by the Lord as the mother of the savior. But she, like Priscilla and the town of Bethlehem, willingly accepted the responsibility.

We probably didn't expect it, but Jesus chooses us to be his special people. We must accept the responsibility as his people and spread the good news that Jesus is born, the savior is in our lives.

Give the Witness Center activity assignment and conclude with a song, such as "Wake Up! Wake Up!" or the traditional "O Little Town of Bethlehem."

WITNESS CENTER

Each balloon should be taken home as a reminder to us that although we didn't expect it, we are Jesus' chosen people. Watch out, though. You might not be expecting that balloon to pop, but it just might! Let it be a reminder to us to be ready to respond to the Lord with good actions and faithful prayer.

Teachers will want to distribute copies of these readings for the final week of lighting the Advent wreath, perhaps as an attachment to the "kidsletter." They should be used until December 23.

Readings for lighting the Advent wreath during the last week before Christmas: (These readings are selected verses of the Canticle of Zechariah in Luke 1:67-69).

Monday

Let us praise the Lord, the God of Israel!
He has come to the help of his people and has set them free.
He has provided for us a mighty Savior, as descendant of his servant David.

Tuesday

He promised through his holy prophets long ago that he would save us from our enemies, from the power of all those who hate us.

Wednesday

The Lord said he would show mercy to our ancestors and remember his sacred covenant.
With a solemn oath to our ancestor Abraham he promised to rescue us from our enemies and allow us to serve him without fear.

Thursday

Our God is merciful and tender.
He will cause the bright dawn of salvation to rise on us and to shine from heaven on all those who live in the shadow of death, and to guide our steps into the path of peace.

Friday

All of the above.

Each lighting service could be concluded with a favorite Advent chorus, such as "An Advent Wreath Song," "Wait for the Savior," or "Rejoice, Be Glad."

Songs For Celebrating The Christmas Season

Title/Composer	Modern Liturgy Vol:No	Gather 'Round Page	Gather 'Round, Too! Page	The Lord Blesses Me Page	My Heart is Happy
A BLESSING SONG Dick Hilliard					X
ADVENT SONG (vs 2) JoAnn Brown	4:6		84		
AS A FAMILY Paul F. Page	1:5	38			
BRING US BACK Dick Hilliard	5:4				X
DO YOU KNOW? Dick Hilliard					X
FOLLOW THE STAR Beverly Hilliard				88	
GLORY TO GOD Dick Hilliard					X
IF YOU BELIEVE Dick Hilliard					X
KEEP US CLOSE Dick Hilliard				75	
THE LORD BLESSES ME! Dick Hilliard	4:6		89	28	X
MY THANKFUL PRAYER Dick Hilliard	4:7				X
QUIETLY HE CAME Paulette Davis	1:8	51			
SING A SONG OF PRAISE Dick Hilliard					X
TO THE LIVING GOD Paul F. Page	1:8	53			
TODAY IS BORN OUR SAVIOR Dick Hilliard	X	X	74		

INTRODUCTION TO THE CHRISTMAS SEASON

The event marked by weeks of personal and communal preparation during the Advent Season comes with joyful anticipation on Christmas day. It is a day which heralds a brief, but deeply spiritual, season in the Christian liturgical calendar.

Filled with scenarios and tales from the gospel narratives, the birth and first manifestations of Jesus blossom forth into the few, but rich, stories of his childhood during our liturgical celebrations. The Church considers this Christmas Season, which celebrates the Lord's coming as man and the early events of his life, second only to the annual celebration of the Easter mystery.[1]

It would be hard for us to deny that the valued customs of a family Christmas celebration make our observance of the Lord's Nativity all the more religious. Christmas is our favorite family holyday because it allows the child within us all to recognize the deep symbolic treasure of the day's meaning. For this reason a classroom or parish-wide Center Celebration is not encouraged on Christmas day itself. Rather, a simple family celebration on the eve of Christmas is suggested as a prayerful climax to our Advent celebrations and as a spiritual preparation for the holiday traditions and community Eucharist which will be so much a part of Christmas morning.

The Sunday following Christmas day is the feast of the Holy Family. Our reverence for Mary, Joseph and Jesus deepens our reflection upon our own family living. Thus, the celebration for Holy Family Sunday are simple liturgies for dedication of the family members to Christian love and peace.

On January 1 we commemorate Mary, the Mother of God. The suggested liturgy focuses upon the motherhood of Mary, a devotion which has long been a part of our Christian heritage. Although January 6 is the traditional feast of the Epiphany of our Lord, this holyday is celebrated in the United States on the Sunday after January 1.[2] It is a time when the Church recalls the first showing of Jesus, the savior, to other men. The Christmas Season concludes as the Church remembers the Baptism of the Lord on the Sunday following January 6.[3]

1. *The Roman Calendar, Text and Commentary*, #32, (Washington: United States Catholic Conference, 1976), p. 9.
2. Ibid., #7b, p. 6.
3. The "Second Sunday of Christmas" with the readings suggested in the Lectionary is not celebrated in the United States because of the transfer of the Epiphany from January 6. Therefore, no Center Celebration is included for the "Second Sunday."

JESUS CHRIST IS BORN!

(Mass At Midnight)
Isaiah 9:1-6   Isaiah 9:2-7
Psalm 96
Titus 2:11-14
Luke 2:1-14   Luke 2:2-7

This simple and quiet evening prayer takes its theme from the readings selected for the Christmas Vigil Midnight Mass. It is suggested for families as a conclusion to their Advent celebrations before bedtime on Christmas Eve. (There is no Creation Center activity planned for this celebration.)

GREETING CENTER

When the family comes together at the Greeting Center, the celebration begins with an Advent song such as, "Rejoice! Be Glad!" or "Advent Song," or a song of Christmas glory, such as, "Glory to God."

Then, one member of the family should read this telling of the Christmas story:

Luke 2:1-14

At that time Emperor Augustus ordered a census to be taken throughout the Roman Empire. When this first census took place, Quirinius was the governor of Syria. Everyone, then, went to register himself, each to his own home town.

Joseph went from the town of Nazareth in Galilee to the town of Bethlehem in Judea, the birthplace of King David. Joseph went there because he was a descendant of David. He went to register with Mary, who was promised in marriage to him. She was pregnant, and while they were in Bethlehem, the time came for her to have her baby. She gave birth to her first son, wrapped him in cloths and laid him in a manger — there was no room for them to stay in the inn.

There were some shepherds in that part of the country who were spending the night in the fields, taking care of their flocks. An angel of the Lord appeared to them, and the glory of the Lord shone over them. They were terribly afraid, but the angel said to them, "Don't be afraid! I am here with good news for you, which will bring great joy to all the people. This very day in David's town your Savior was born — Christ the Lord! And this is what will prove it to you: you will find a baby wrapped in cloths and lying in a manger."

Suddenly a great army of heaven's angels appeared with the angel, singing praises to God:

> *"Glory to God in the highest heaven,*
> *and peace on earth to those with*
> *whom he is pleased!"*

Suggestions:

1. Sing "Quietly He Came," the traditional "Silent Night," or pause together briefly for quiet prayer.
2. Discuss with the family the importance of this holy night for all Christian people. Perhaps some of the Advent activities could be recaptured as a way of having prepared for this evening of joy.

WORD CENTER

Materials Needed: 1 free-standing candle and some matches.

Darken the room except for a burning candle placed at the center of the family gathering. When everyone is quiet, remind the family of the historical Christmas and the long preparation for that event by the people of Judah. This prophecy of Isaiah captures the mood of this sacred evening and recounts the marvelous joy which overtook God's chosen people at the announcement of the birth of Jesus.

Every member of the family should focus upon the candle's flame as this reading is proclaimed. If possible, an instrumental version of "Today Is Born Our Savior" could be played as a background setting for this reading.

Isaiah 9:2-7

The people who walked in darkness
   have seen a great light.
They lived in a land of shadows,
   but now light is shining on them.
You have given them great joy, Lord;
   you have made them happy.
They rejoice in what you have done,
   as people rejoice when they harvest grain
   or when they divide captured wealth.
For you have broken the yoke that burdened them
   and the rod that beat their shoulders.
You have defeated the nation that oppressed
   and exploited your people, just as you defeated
   the army of Midian long ago.
The boots of the invading army and all their
   bloodstained clothing will be destroyed by fire.
A child is born to us!
A son is given to us!
And he will be our ruler.
He will be called, "Wonderful Counselor,"
   "Mighty God," "Eternal Father," "Prince of Peace."
His royal power will continue to grow,
   and his kngdom will always be at peace.
He will rule as King David's successor,
   basing his power on right and justice,
   from now until the end of time.
The Lord Almighty is determined to do all this."

At the conclusion of this reading, the family could stand, holding hands, in a circle around the burning candle and sing "Today Is Born Our Savior."

PRAISE CENTER

Every Christmas burning candles appear in the windows of family homes all through the world according to local customs. Lighted candles are symbols for occasions of joy. For Christian people, the lighted candle has a special meaning at Christmas because it represents Christ, the Light of the World.

This activity of prayerful praise could be conducted while still standing around the burning candle at the Word Center.

Because the light of candles helps guide our way in darkness, the peoples of many countries (Italy, Denmark, Phillipines, Russia, Greece, Mexico, Labrador and Spain) place a burning candle in their windows on the night before Christmas to guide the Christ child.

The oldest child can carry the burning candle from the Word Center location as the family follows to a front window. When it is in place, the family prays together in words such as these:

> Come, Lord Jesus
> into our hearts this Christmas.
> Fill our home with your peace and love
> and be a light
> to guide us in dark times.
> Amen.

SHARING CENTER

The family might exchange a kiss of peace while gathered at the burning candle placed in the front window.

Then the children can be sent off to bed. (Be sure to extinguish the candle before the last adult member of the family retires!)

WITNESS CENTER

It might be a touching reminder of this evening's prayer to place the candle on the Christmas dinner table the next day.

TODAY IS BORN OUR SAVIOR

This is a Christmas hymn of praise announcing the birth of the savior. It should be an entrance hymn or response to the proclamation of God's Word on Christmas Day.
Based on Luke 2:11 and Psa. 96
Christmas Midnight Mass

Dick Hilliard
arr. Rev. John H. Olivier, S.S.

1. To-day is born our Sav-ior, Christ the Lord. Sing a new song
2. To-day is born our Sav-ior, Christ the Lord. Let the earth be
3. To-day is born our Sav-ior, Christ the Lord. Come be-fore the

1. to the Lord! To-day is born our Sav-ior, Christ the
2. glad and sing! To-day is born our Sav-ior, Christ the
3. Lord, our King! To-day is born our Sav-ior, Christ the

1. Lord. Pro - claim the good news that we have been saved! *to refrain*
2. Lord. An - nounce the day of great-ness has be - gun!
3. Lord. He comes with peace and love to rule the world.

Praise the Lord, all people on earth, give glo-ry to our Lord!

peace is ours, re - joice and sing. Our Sav-ior has been born.

Keep Us Close

Families will enjoy singing this simple prayer of blessing. It is written for family celebrations of love, reconciliation and dedication to the way of the Lord.

Dick Hilliard
arr. Rev. John H. Olivier, S.S.

Bless our fam-'ly, Lord, we pray. Keep us close in your love. Fill us with peace and kind-ness, Lord. Keep us close in your love.

OUR LIFE TOGETHER

Sirach 3:2-6, 23:14
Psalm 128
Colossians 3:12-21 Colossians 3:12-14, 20-21
Matthew 2:13-15, 19-23 Matthew 2:13-15, 19-23

The Church's observance of the Feast of the Holy Family within the octave of Christmas allows us to look upon Mary, Joseph and the child Jesus as a model for family living.

This celebration begins with the account of the Holy Family's escape into Egypt from the threat of Herod's decree. It then focuses upon the epistle of St. Paul to the Colossians and becomes a prayerful opportunity for families to celebrate their vocation to live together in the peace and love of Christ.

*For Parish Programs
and in the Religious Education Classroom*

School and parish programs will have difficulty if they attempt to adapt this family celebration to other settings. During most calendar years, Holy Family Sunday falls during Christmas vacation and would thus not be a part of regular scheduling.

GREETING CENTER

Begin this family celebration by singing "My Thankful Prayer" or "As A Family."

Then ask for a volunteer to read this familiar story of the childhood of Jesus from Matthew's gospel:

Matthew 2:13-15, 19-23

After the wise men had left, an angel of the Lord appeared in a dream to Joseph and said, "Herod will be looking for the child in order to kill him. So get up, take the child and his mother and escape to Egypt, and stay there until I tell you to leave."

Joseph got up, took the child and his mother, and left during the night for Egypt, where he stayed until Herod died.

After Herod died, an angel of the Lord appeared in a dream to Joseph in Egypt and said, "Get up, take the child and his mother, and go back to the land of Israel, because those who tried to kill the child are dead." So Joseph got up, took the child and his mother, and went back to Israel.

But when Joseph heard that Archelaus had succeeded his father Herod as king of Judea, he was afraid to go there. He was given more instructions in a dream, so he went to the province of Galilee and made his home in a town named Nazareth.

At the conclusion of the reading, the gospel story can be discussed with the members of the family emphasizing the care Jesus' parents showed for him in seeking protection for his life. Mary and Joseph stand as models for all parents and thus, with Jesus, they are called the *Holy Family.*

WORD CENTER

Perhaps one of the parents could read this selection from St. Paul's letters:

Colossians 3:12-14, 20-21

You are the people of God; he loved you and chose you for his own. So then, you must clothe yourselves with compassion, kindness, humility, gentleness, and patience. Be tolerant with one another and forgive one another whenever any of you has a complaint against someone else. You must forgive one another just as the Lord has forgiven you. And to all these qualities add love, which binds all things together in perfect unity.

Children, it is your Christian duty to obey your parents always, for that is what pleases God.

Parents, do not irritate your children, or they will become discouraged.

After the reading, the leader can encourage family members to speak openly and honestly about how well each one observes the instructions given by St. Paul about family living. No doubt several deficiencies will be pointed out, but be sure to help everyone recognize the ways in which each one has carefully lived Paul's words. This could be a good opportunity for honest family dialogue.

PRAISE CENTER

True reconciliation begins at home. This celebration can be an opportunity for the family to offer and accept the reconciliation of each member for the failings and limitations that are a part of us all.

Suggestions:

1. Begin by repeating these words from St. Paul's letter: "You must forgive one another just as the Lord has forgiven you."

2. Initiate a litany of forgiveness among all the family members gathered by encouraging each to pray in words similar to these:

   I am sorry, Lord, for shouting at Carl.
   I am sorry, Lord, for not obeying Mom and Dad.
   I am sorry, Lord, for hitting Carol.
   Forgive me. Lord, for being impatient with our children.

3. All sing "Bring Us Back" with appropriately selected verses, or any song of reconciliation and peace.

SHARING CENTER

Materials Needed: paper and pencils or pens.

Once the family has been reconciled and has celebrated the Lord's presence in a prayer of forgiveness, all could discuss the events which have become fond memories of your family's life. Ask each member to jot down on a piece of paper their recollection of:

1. The family's funniest event.
2. The family's happiest event.
3. The family's saddest event.

Then share your answers with one another.

CREATION CENTER

Family Drawings

Materials Needed: drawing paper and crayons or marking pens.

With crayons or marking pens, each member of the family should draw a picture of some family event which they are certain the other members of the family have completely forgotten about.

SHARING CENTER

Discuss each other's drawings made at the Creation Center. Perhaps each could hold up his/her pictures for the other members of the family to guess the event which has been illustrated.

Give the Witness Center assignment and conclude with the song, "Keep Us Close," or any song of family blessing.

WITNESS CENTER

Mystery Persons Game

Materials Needed: small strips of paper, a pen, and a hat or bowl.

Write each family member's name on a piece of paper and drop all names in a hat or bowl. Each member draws a name. Everyone should perform some secret act every day during the week for the person whose name they have drawn. Each night at dinner some of the day's events which have happened to each person could be shared in a family discussion. Be sure that no one gives away who has performed the secret acts!

At the end of the week each member should guess who had drawn his/her name.

COME BEFORE THE

Sirach 3:2-6, 12-14
Psalm 128
Colossians 3:12-21
Luke 2:22-40

Luke 2:22-35, 39-40
Numbers 6:24-26

The Praise Center activity is a major event for this evening celebration. It is based upon the gospel story of the Presentation of the child Jesus in the Temple which is read at the Word Center. No Creation Center activity is suggested.

This is a family celebration of dedication to the Lord which is ritualized in the parish church in the prayerful presence of the parish priest. The Sharing and Witness Center activities attempt to continue the celebration of family life in the Lord.

*For Parish Programs
and in the Religious Education Classroom*

This family celebration can be adapted as a short Word Service for school and parish programs. The Praise, Sharing and Witness Center activities can be combined into the Witness Center activity assignment by preparing instructions for parents as part of a "kidsletter" or as a separate handout to be taken home by the participants.

GREETING CENTER

After singing a song of thanksgiving such as "My Thankful Prayer," family members should discuss the meaning of their family's surname. This might be an opportunity to talk about some important ancestors.

Then remind the family that we are also members of a larger, Christian family to which we were joined when we were presented to the priest, deacon and church for baptism.

WORD CENTER

According to Jewish law, the ritual of purification was celebrated for the oldest male child of the family. It marked his presentation to the Lord much as our Christian baptism signifies our presentation to the Lord for his care over us.

This account of the presentation of the child Jesus in the temple should be read by a family member. If little children are participating, the reading could be freely shortened as necessary.

Luke 2:22-35, 39-40

The time came for Joseph and Mary to perform the ceremony of purification, as the Law of Moses commanded. So they took the child to Jerusalem to present him to the Lord, as it is written in the law of the Lord: "Every first-born male is to be dedicated to the Lord." They also went to offer a sacrifice of a pair of doves or two young pigeons, as required by the law of the Lord.

At that time there was a man named Simeon living in Jerusalem. He was a good, God-fearing man and was waiting for Israel to be saved. The Holy Spirit was with him and had assured him that he would not die before he had seen the Lord's promised Messiah. Led by the Spirit, Simeon went into the Temple. When the parents brought the child Jesus into the Temple to do for him what the Law required, Simeon took the child in his arms and gave thanks to God: "Now, Lord, you have kept your promise, and you may let your servant go in peace. With my own eyes I have seen your salvation, which you have prepared in the presence of all peoples: A light to reveal your will to the Gentiles and bring glory to your people Israel.

The child's father and mother were amazed at the things Simeon said about him. Simeon blessed them and said to Mary, his mother, "This child is chosen by God for the destruction and the salvation of many in Israel. He will be a sign from God which many people will speak against, and so reveal their secret thoughts. And sorrow, like a sharp sword, will break your own heart."

When Joseph and Mary finished doing all that was required by the law of the Lord, they returned to their home of Nazareth in Galilee. The child grew and became strong; he was full of wisdom and God's blessings were upon him.

The event of the Presentation should be highlighted as the occasion of the Holy Family's dedication to the Father.

LORD

PRAISE CENTER

Arrange with your parish priest ahead of time for a convenient appointment to meet him this evening in your parish church. Bring the family to the sanctuary for this ritual of family presentation to the Lord as your prayer and Praise Center activity. An alternative might be for several families to share in this ceremony at the parish church.

Another way of implementing this activity would be to invite your parish priests, sisters and/or staff to your home for this ceremony. Other families could also be invited to participate.

If it is more convenient, families could adapt this service for private home use. Simply pray in dedication to the Lord. If a manger scene is in the home, it could be the site of this Praise Center activity.

As the family arrives at church:

Priest: Why are you gathered here this evening?

Father of the family: We are gathered to present ourselves to the Lord.

Mother of the family: We are gathered to dedicate our family life to His care.

Oldest child: We are gathered to ask His blessing upon our lives together.

Priest: Let us give thanks to the Lord, our God.

All: It is right to give Him thanks and praise.

All enter the sanctuary. The family kneels together as the priest prays over them.

Father, we look to your care and the lives of Mary, Joseph and Jesus as the pattern of all family life. Accept the (　　　　　　) family as your children. Watch over them, guide them, and be with them with your love and gentleness.

Then the family prays:
Father,
we want to live as Jesus, Mary and Joseph,
in peace with you and one another.
We present ourselves to you this day
and ask that you guide us
with your careful light and bless us
with the presence of the Holy Spirit.
Amen.

A candle should be lighted by the priest and presented to the father or mother of the family. (If the parish has prepared a crib scene in church, the priest should light the candle from one lighted in front of the crib scene.) If other members of the family have candles, they may be lighted from the father's or mother's candle. All stand.

All could sing "Keep Us Close" as a concluding song.

Blessing by Priest: (Blessing of Aaron in Numbers 6:24-26)

May the Lord bless you and take care of you;
May the Lord be kind and gracious to you;
May the Lord look on you with favor
and give you peace.
May almighty God bless you, the Father, and the Son, and the Holy Spirit.

Priest: Go in peace to love and serve the Lord.

All: Thanks be to God.

The family returns to the church entrance where they extinguish their candles.

SHARING CENTER

Materials Needed: family album or photos, or family slides and projector and screen, or family movies and projector and screen.

When the family arrives home, all could sit together and look through the family album or show slides or home movies of sacramental events which have captured the family's celebration of their presentation to the Lord's life. (Examples: family member's weddings, baptisms, first communions, confirmations, etc.)

Conclude this celebration by singing "Sing A Song of Praise," or "To The Living God."

WITNESS CENTER

Each night at dinner time during the week, relight the candle(s) received during the Praise Center activity and sing "Keep Us Close."

GROWING IN GOD'S

Sirach 3:2-6
Psalm 128
Colossians 3:12-21
Luke 2:41-52

Luke 2:41-52

This is a family celebration based on the gospel story of the finding of the child Jesus in the temple at Jerusalem. The Center activities are intended to bring the family closer together in their love for one another, and make them more aware of their dependence on God's favor for their growth in the Spirit.

GREETING CENTER

This family celebration could begin with a song, such as "Sing A Song of Praise," "As A Family," or "Glory to God!"

At the conclusion of the song, discuss some memorable events of the family together, perhaps on an outing when one or more of the family has been lost or separated from the others for a short time. Discuss how each person felt: secure? lonely? worried? helpless?

WORD CENTER

This is an opportunity to dramatize the story of the finding of the child Jesus in the Temple. Mom and Dad should play the parts of Mary and Joseph and one of the children should be selected to play the part of Jesus. The other children can be the teachers with Jesus in the temple. You may choose to have one of the older children read the gospel story aloud as the players perform their parts, or simply tell the story in your own words as the family performs.

Luke 2:41-52

Every year the parents of Jesus went to Jerusalem for the Passover Festival. When Jesus was twelve years old, they went to the festival as usual. When the festival was over, they started back home, but the boy Jesus stayed in Jerusalem. His parents did not know this; they thought that he was with the group, so they traveled a whole day and then started looking for him among their relatives and friends. They did not find him, so they went back to Jerusalem looking for him. On the third day they found him in the Temple, sitting with the Jewish teachers, listening to them and asking questions. All who heard him were amazed at his intelligent answers. His parents were astonished when they saw him, and his mother said to him, "Son, why have you done this to us? Your father and I have been terribly worried trying to find you."

He answered them, "Why did you have to look for me? Didn't you know that I had to be in my Father's house?" But they did not understand his answer.

So Jesus went back with them to Nazareth, where he was obedient to them. His mother treasured all these things in her heart. Jesus grew both in wisdom, and in body, gaining favor with God and men.

When the dramatization is completed, the participants could discuss the feelings which probably came to Mary, Joseph and Jesus. At the conclusion of this discussion, the final verses of this gospel story should be highlighted by emphasizing that the Holy Family grew in love with the grace of the Father protecting them.

FAVOR

PRAISE CENTER

Every family grows not only in love but in age as the children become adults and capable of making their own decisions. The Holy Family should be a model to our Christian families who seek to mature in the love of the Father as each child grows older.

Each member of the family should freely express to the others in a litany format the way in which he/she desires to be blessed by God. Each one might also pray a blessing upon the other members of the family.

Then, standing in a circle, lead the family in this Movement Prayer:

God, our Father *(arms raised heavenward)*

watch over our family *(arms extended outward in sign of blessing)*

protect us with your love. *(place arms around family members on either side)*

Guide our family *(holding hands)*

on the way of peace. *(move to circle's center, into a family hug)*

Conclude this prayer activity by singing "My Thankful Prayer" or "Keep Us Close."

CREATION CENTER

Petition Cards

Materials Needed: pens, crayons or pencils and cards or sheets of paper.

On a card or sheet of paper distributed to each family member should be written a completion statement to this phrase:

"I will ask God to bless our family..."

SHARING CENTER

Materials Needed: hat, jar, can, or any similarly-sized container.

Take the completed statements on the "Petition Cards" from the Creation Center activity, fold them, and place them in a jar, hat or can. Each family member should draw a folded paper from the container and read it aloud. The family could try to guess who wrote each statement as it is read.

Take time to discuss each person's statement when it is read aloud. This should make for a touching moment of family sharing.

Give the Witness Center assignment and conclude today's celebration of God's Word by singing "Keep Us Close."

WITNESS CENTER

Each day during the coming week (or however many days are needed) one family member should be chosen for whom the prayers and actions of the other family members are offered. In this way, every day the family seeks to grow in God's favor.

A HEART FILLED WITH

JANUARY 1 — OCTAVE OF CHRISTMAS

Numbers 6:22-27   Numbers 6:24-26
Psalm 67
Galatians 4:4-7
Luke 2:16-21   Luke 2:16-20

The Church has always held sacred the free response of Mary to the Father in accepting her role as the mother of our savior, Jesus. On this day we celebrate the motherhood of Mary and give thanks for her vocation and her example to us.

Our celebration's theme comes from the gospel for today's liturgy around which our activities are focused. Each center flows freely into another, culminating in the Sharing Center discussion which offers two alternative approaches, one for families and one for parish programs. Since January 1 is usually part of the Christmas recess from school, this celebration is not fully designed for the religious education classroom.

GREETING CENTER

"Today Is Born Our Savior" or any favorite Christmas carol would be a fitting opening to this celebration of our affection for Mary, the Mother of our savior.

When the song is finished, the participants could be led in a discussion which will probably allow their imaginations to run somewhat wild. A few will no doubt speak from the experience of watching their mothers care for a younger brother or sister, but invite everyone to suggest answers to these questions:

1. How does a mother care for her baby after the infant's birth?
2. Do you think mothers ever get tired of keeping watch over their babies?
3. How did you think your mother acted after you were born? Did she show you to her friends? Was she proud?

Spend some time talking about the responsibility which a mother and father assume with the birth of a child. Be sure to emphasize that a parent's care is rooted in love for a child.

WORD CENTER

This familiar tale from the gospel of Luke lends itself very well to simple dramatization. Gather the participants together and read the passage with great expression. Then, volunteers can play the parts of the shepherds, Mary and Joseph. Select a narrator to reread this selection aloud as the others interpret the story for the rest of the participants.

Luke 2:16-20
The shepherds went in haste to Bethlehem and found Mary and Joseph, and the baby lying in the manger; once they saw, they understood what had been told them concerning this child.
All who heard of it were astonished at the report given them by the shepherds.
Mary treasured all these things and reflected on them in her heart.
The shepherds returned, glorifying and praising God for all they had heard and seen, in accord with what had been told them.

Text from the New American Bible, © 1970 by the Confraternity of Christian Doctrine, Inc. Washington, D.C. Used by permission of the copyright owner.

After the dramatization, be sure to highlight any special interpretations which the performers might have included in the acting of their parts.

Then lead a discussion about the role of Mary in this story. Ask the participants what memories Mary might have had in mind (2:19, Mary treasured all these things and reflected on them in her heart). This verse refers to the many events which involved Mary and Joseph leading up to the birth of Jesus. You might conclude with a brief discussion of how a mother treasures all the preparatory events leading to the birth of her children. A mother rarely forgets these memories. Why?

TREASURES

PRAISE CENTER

Hopefully the Word Center discussion will have allowed the participants to recall the events of Mary's preparing for the the savior's birth from the time of the Annunciation and her visit to Elizabeth to the epiphany of the child to the magi.

As our thanksgiving for Mary's voluntary role in this saving act of the Father's gift of His son, all could pray this version of the ''Hail Mary,'' or pray the traditional words.

Hail Mary,
full of grace,
the Lord is with you.
He has greatly blessed you
and your son, Jesus.
Holy Mary, Mother of God,
pray for us now
and when we die.
Amen.

Sing Mary's song, ''The Lord Blesses Me!''

CREATION CENTER

Pocket Hearts

Materials Needed: red construction paper, staples, stapler, or paste; writing paper, pencils or crayons; and scissors.

Because the gospel passage of today's celebration reminds us that ''Mary treasured all these things in her heart,'' this activity is based on the image of the human heart.

Distribute one piece of red construction paper to each participant. Fold the paper in half width-wise. Draw a heart on one side of the folded paper. With scissors, carefully cut out the heart in double thickness. The two resulting hearts should be stapled or pasted at the bottom and side edges leaving a larger opening at the top.

Then distribute a sheet of writing paper to each participant. On it, each should write a list of the treasured moments celebrated at home during this Advent and Christmas season. When the list is completed, fold it and insert into the stapled heart.

SHARING CENTER

For families, an activity which involves sharing the written lists made at the Creation Center would be appropriate. Perhaps Mom could be chosen to read all the lists and the other family members could guess whose list is being read aloud. A touching discussion of the family's preparation and celebration of the Incarnation will no doubt be a part of this activity.

Give the Witness Center activity assignment and conclude with this blessing or sing ''Keep Us Close.''

Blessing: (Numbers 6:24-26)

May the Lord bless you and take care of you;
May the Lord be kind and gracious to you;
May the Lord look on you with favor
and give you peace.

Or

Parish programs could initiate a sharing activity among the participants by asking each to mention one treasured moment from his/her family celebration of the Christmas event. Give the Witness Center assignment and allow the participants to take their hearts home and present them to their Mom and Dad as a ''Thank You'' for making this Christmas season so special. (The words ''Thank You'' might be written on the outside of the heart pocket.)

Conclude with the blessing above and sing ''A Blessing Song.''

WITNESS CENTER

Each morning until the next celebration, the participants should lead their families in a prayer of thanksgiving to Mary. The ''Hail Mary'' would be appropriate.

FOLLOW THE STAR!

Isaiah 60:1-6
Psalm 72
Ephesians 3:2-3, 5-6
Matthew 2:1-12

Matthew 2:1-12

The gospel of the Epiphany is a favorite story of the Christmas season for young people. Today's celebration dramatizes that story from Matthew's gospel at the Word Center and follows the great star of the East through the other center activities. The star becomes a reminder to us that we, too, must show others the way to Jesus in all that we do.

GREETING CENTER

"Today is Born Our Savior" or "Quietly He Came" are appropriate songs to begin this celebration of the savior's coming among men and women.

Secret Message Game

After the opening song, initiate a "secret message" among the participants by whispering to someone, "Show me the way to Jesus." The message should be whispered from participant to participant. When the last person announces the message which has been passed along, lead a discussion including these questions:

1. Do you have a secret place to keep things of your own? — a dresser drawer? a clubhouse?
2. Do you think anyone else knows just where your place is?
3. Is there anything near it to remind you that it is close by? — a jewelry box? an oak tree?
4. Have you ever shown your secret place to a friend?

You might conclude this discussion by telling the participants that today's celebration is about Jesus' secret place of birth and how some very important visitors made their way to find him.

WORD CENTER

The participants will no doubt already be familiar with the story of the visitors from the East. Select some of the participants to dramatize this story. In some instances, a simple review of the Epiphany event would be sufficient before allowing the participants to enact this story in their own words.

Players Needed: Narrator, King Herod, priests, 3 astrologers, Mary and Joseph. The remaining participants can be the crowd in scene 1 and 2.

Materials Needed: paper crown for King Herod, cardboard star, and 3 boxes (as gold, frankincense, myrrh).

THE STORY OF THE THREE VISITORS FROM THE EAST

(Matthew 2:1-12)

Scene 1

Narrator: *Jesus was born in the town of Bethlehem in Judea, during the time when Herod was king. Soon afterward, some men who studied the stars came from the East to Jerusalem and asked,*

Astrologers: *"Where is the baby born to be the king of the Jews? We saw his star when it came up in the east, and we have come to worship him."*

Scene 2

Narrator: *When King Herod heard about this, he was very upset, and so was everyone else in Jerusalem. He called together all the chief priests and the teachers of the Law and asked them,*

King Herod: *"Where will the Messiah be born?"*

Priests: *"In the town of Bethlehem in Judea."*

Priest: *"This is what the prophet wrote: 'Bethlehem in the land of Judah, you are by no means the least of the leading cities of Judah; for from you will come a leader who will guide my people Israel.'"*

Narrator: *So Herod called the visitors from the East to a secret meeting and found out from them the exact time the star had appeared. Then he sent them to Bethlehem with these instructions:*

King Herod: *"Go and make a careful search for the child; and when you find him, let me know, so that I too may go and worship him."*

Scene 3

(The astrologers are with two others, Mary and Joseph, at the manger.)

Narrator: *And so they left, and on their way they saw the same star they had seen in the East. When they saw it, how happy they were, what joy was theirs! It went ahead of them until it stopped over the place where the child was. They went into the house, and when they saw the child with his mother Mary, they knelt down and worshipped him. They brought out their gifts of gold, frankincense, and myrrh, and presented them to him.*

Then they returned to their country by another road, since God had warned them in a dream not to go back to Herod.

When the dramatization is concluded, discuss with the participants the search made for Jesus by the three visitors. At first it appeared that Jesus' birthplace was a secret, but the star pointed the way. In fact, Jesus' presence is never a secret.

Invite the participants to suggest ways in which we can help others to find Jesus. They could be asked, "What are some of the things we can do to 'point the way' to Jesus as the star did?"

Then sing "Do You Know?" or "Follow the Star."

CREATION CENTER

Star Mobiles

Materials Needed: colored construction paper, a five-pointed star pattern, scissors, paper punch, and some strips of string.

Let each participant cut a five-pointed star from colored construction paper (a pattern may be provided). With a paper punch, put a hole near the tip of one of the star's points. Tie a two- or three-foot long piece of string through the hole.

These stars will be used again at the Praise and Sharing Centers and will become bedroom mobiles as part of the Witness Center activity assignment.

PRAISE CENTER

Remind the participants of the role the star played in the search of the Eastern magi for the child Jesus as they hold their own stars made at the Creation Center. The star pointed the way to Jesus.

Lead the participants in a spontaneous prayer of petition, allowing them to contribute their own prayers as they desire. The prayer should continue the theme of the Word Center discussion, asking our Father to help us point the way to Jesus. An example might be:

Help us, Father, to be like Jesus as we make friends at school.

Father, let us be kind and loving like Jesus with everyone we meet.

Lord, help me show others the way to Jesus by my actions of love.

and so on...

Then, with their stars dangling or held high, lead the participants in the fitting song, "Follow the Star."

SHARING CENTER

Materials Needed: crayons or marking pens.

With crayons or marking pens, let the participants write on their paper stars five things they will do to help show people the way to Jesus. Remind them of some of the suggestions already given at the Word Center and Praise Center. Each resolution might be written on one of the five points of their stars. An example might be:

pray every day
share my games
tell stories about Jesus
be loving
bring peace at home

Give the Witness Center assignment and conclude by singing "Follow the Star."

WITNESS CENTER

The participants should take their stars home and, with a tack or tape, attach the star's string to the ceiling of their bedroom. When it hangs it will be a colorful mobile!

Every day during the following week, the participants should choose one of their five activities listed on the star as their Christian Witness action for that day. Jesus is no secret...we will point the way to him!

PROCLAIM THIS FAITH

Isaiah 42:1-4, 6-7
Psalm 29
Acts 10:34-38
Matthew 3:13-17   Matthew 3:13-17

(Please Note: When the feast of the Epiphany is celebrated on January 7 or 8, the feast of the Baptism of the Lord in not celebrated on a Sunday. Instead, it becomes a weekday feast and the "Second Sunday in Ordinary Time" follows Epiphany Sunday.)

The Feast of the Baptism of the Lord is an opportune moment for us to reaffirm our faith in the Lord Jesus Christ whose birth and manifestation to men and women we have recently celebrated. The symbols of our Christian baptism become the signs of our center activities.

The lectionary suggests three separate gospel readings of the Baptism of Jesus for the three liturgical cycles. Because they are essentially the same telling of the event at the Jordan River, only one celebration has been developed for this feast. The gospel of Matthew for Year A is chosen for its simplicity and is proclaimed at the Word Center. Should the alternate readings be preferred, they are: Year B: Mark 1:7-11; Year C: Luke 3:15-16, 21-22.

GREETING CENTER

An appropriate opening for this celebration is "Howdy Friends." Be sure to let every participant announce his/her name as this song is sung. Following the song, ask the participants if they know when they received their names. Help them to realize that at our baptism the Christian community accepted us into their midst and called each of us by a name. At baptism, too, we all claim a common name in Jesus Christ. We become "Christian" for a lifetime.

As this brief discussion of baptismal names comes to an ending, direct the participants to the Sharing Center.

SHARING CENTER

Materials Needed: a container of water, a dried plant, and a paper airplane.

Continue the Greeting Center discussion of baptism by talking about the sacramental sign of water. Have a bowl or bucket of water handy so that the participants can experience the effects of water as the Christian symbolism is discussed.

Experience	Christian Symbolism
water a dried plant	water gives life, nourishment
splash water on participant's faces	water is refreshing
wash dirty hands	water cleanses
dip paper airplane into water	water can destroy

Encourage the participants to suggest similar experiences as each of the symbolisms is discussed.

Then conclude with a short instruction about our Christian celebration of baptism including such statements as:

1. At baptism we are given life in the Spirit of Jesus.
2. At baptism we celebrate our new faith in Christ.
3. At baptism we rid ourselves of sin.
4. At baptism we destroy the power of evil over us.

WORD CENTER

Remind the participants of the ministry of John the Baptist. He proclaimed the need of repentance to the people of Galilee and baptized them in the Jordan River. He prepared people to receive the savior by asking them to free themselves of evil ways.

Then proclaim this story of the Baptism of Jesus from Matthew's gospel:

Matthew 3:13-17

At that time Jesus arrived from Galilee and came to John at the Jordan to be baptized by him. But John tried to make him change his mind. "I ought to be baptized by you," John said, "and yet you have come to me!"

But Jesus answered him, "Let it be so for now. For in this way we shall do all that God requires." So John agreed.

As soon as Jesus was baptized, he came up out of the water. Then heaven was opened to him, and he saw the Spirit of God coming down like a dove and lighting on him. Then a voice said from heaven, "This is my own dear Son, with whom I am pleased."

At the conclusion of the reading, invite answers from the participants to the question, "Why did Jesus want to be baptized?"

When enough answers are shared, summarize the participants' responses by instructing them that Jesus was baptized by John in the Jordan River as a sign to the people that he cherished their desire to repent from the way of sin and to follow the savior. Jesus was now in their midst to lead them with the Spirit of God to the Father.

PRAISE CENTER

Occasionally it is important for us to ritualize the proclamation of faith which we made at our baptism. Lead the participants in a statement of faith using the Apostles Creed as indicated. All should stand, a significant human posture which we assume when we want to make an important statement about something we firmly believe.

Apostles' Creed

I believe in God
the Father almighty,
creator of heaven and earth.

I believe in Jesus Christ,
his only Son, our Lord.
He was conceived
by the power of the Holy Spirit
and born of the Virgin Mary.
He suffered under Pontius Pilate,
was crucified,
died,
and was buried.
He descended to the dead.
On the third day he rose again.
He ascended into heaven,
and is seated
at the right hand of the Father.
He will come again
to judge the living and the dead.

I believe in the Holy Spirit,
the holy catholic Church,
the communion of saints,
the forgiveness of sins,
the resurrection of the body,
and the life everlasting,
Amen.

(English translation of the Apostle's Creed by the International Consultation on English Texts. Used with permission.)
Then sing "If You Believe."

CREATION CENTER

Paper Baptismal Stoles
Materials Needed: white shelf paper, scissors, and crayons.
Using strips of white shelf paper, each participant should decorate a stole, the baptismal garment, with the symbol of water. Paper should be cut into pieces about six inches wide and two yards long. Crayon drawings of water drops at the end of the stole would be effective.

The baptismal stole is a symbol for a clothing in new life, the life of Christ which one receives at baptism. The stole is also a reminder of the priesthood of Christ to which we are joined at baptism. We are all called to be ministers of Christian faith, hope and love.

SHARING CENTER

Invite the participants to name one part of their Christian faith for which they are most proud to profess. Some examples might be:
life everlasting
Jesus' birth
forgiveness of sins
redemption through the cross
the Spirit's presence
Younger children will give less sophisticated responses but, nonetheless, just as significant.

As each makes his/her proclamation, the leader of this celebration could clothe the participant in his/her paper stole.

Give the Witness Center assignment and conclude with "A Blessing Song." Families might sing "Keep Us Close."

WITNESS CENTER

Allow the participants to wear their stoles as they leave this celebration and encourage them to hang the stole in a convenient space at home, perhaps above their beds. Tell the participants to be reminded during the week of their Christian faith whenever they see their stole. Encourage them to recite the Apostles' Creed each evening. It might be printed and attached to the "kidsletter."

FOLLOW THE STAR

The star of Bethlehem shone brightly in the sky heralding the birth of Jesus. This song for children is appropriate for Christmas and Epiphany celebrations.

Beverly Hilliard
arr. Rev. John H. Olivier, S.S.

(Capo 1)

Leader: Fol-low the star   All: Follow the star   Leader:
1. O - ver the hill   2. The wind blows cold   3. Soon we'll be there   4. Its light is bright
All:
O - ver the hill   The wind blows cold   Soon we'll be there   Its light is bright

Leader: Fol-low the star   All: Fol-low the star   Leader: Yon-der   All: Yon-der.

Refrain   I want to shine like you do, leading all to Je - sus.

If I could shine like you do, then Je - sus would be near to

1. me.   2. me.

Songs For Celebrating The Lenten Season

Title/Composer	Modern Liturgy Vol:No	Gather 'Round Page	Gather 'Round, Too! Page	The Lord Blesses Me Page	My Heart is Happy
BALLAD OF GOD'S LOVE — Dick Hilliard					X
BE HAPPY! — Dick Hilliard					X
BELIEVE/COME LORD — Dick Hilliard			97		
BRING US BACK — Dick Hilliard	5:4				X
CALL MY NAME — Dick Hilliard					X
CARRY THE CROSS — Dick Hilliard			135		
DO YOU KNOW? — Dick Hilliard					X
FATHER, I ADORE YOU — Traditional	4:1	62			
FATHER, CARE — Dick Hilliard			44		
GLORY TO GOD — Dick Hilliard					X
GOD DID — Cathy Viger	2:5	83			
HOSANNA! — Dick Hilliard			126		
HOWDY, FRIENDS — Dick Hilliard					X
IF YOU BELIEVE — Dick Hilliard					X
KEEP US CLOSE — Dick Hilliard			75		
LET ME LORD — Paul F. Page	4:5	88			
MY THANKFUL PRAYER — Dick Hilliard	4:7				X
NOAH'S SONG — Dick Hilliard					X
THE OLD ARK — Nancy Marsters	3:8	54			
PRAISE THE LORD, REJOICE AND SING — Sr. Sheila Ann Dougherty	4:3	73			
PRAYER FOR MERCY — Dick Hilliard			109		
PROMENADE SONG — Dick Hilliard					X
PSALM 46 — Sr. Angela Murphy	4:5	83			
REJOICE! BE GLAD! — Dick Hilliard					X
SHEPHERD, LEAD ME — Dick Hilliard					X
SING A SONG OF PRAISE — Dick Hilliard					X
THANK YOU, GOD — Dick Hilliard					X
WHO AM I IN GOD'S EYE? — Beverly Hilliard					X
YOU ARE MY PEOPLE — Paul Lisicky	4:5	83			

INTRODUCTION TO THE LENTEN SEASON

Lent begins and ends with two rituals which have become favorite liturgical events among Catholics for centuries. From the imposition of ashes on the Wednesday following Mardi Gras to the procession of palms on Passion Sunday, the Lenten Season summons the Christian to prepare for the joyfully triumphant celebration of the Risen Lord on Easter Sunday.

Certain themes belong to Lent because of the way it has been observed through the tradition of the Church. Linked ultimately to the powerful proclamation of the Resurrection, Lent can be the Christian's time to rediscover the events of the Lord's revelation, which give fuller meaning to eternal life. Early in the Church's life, Lent became a time for preparing converts to Christianity, culminating in the sacrament of the waters of Baptism on Easter night. As time passed, Lenten observances became very complicated according to local custom. For many it is a time of penance, fasting and almsgiving. For others, Lent is a season of reconciliation and communal gathering. For still other Christians, the weeks before Easter are a time for disciplined prayer and study. However it is preserved throughout the Christian world, Lent offers us forty days of varied themes, practices and memories which have come to form a treasured season in our Church's liturgical heritage.

The Center Celebrations for the Lenten season which follow in the next pages have been prepared for children and families who seek to enrich themselves with the liturgical heritage of the Church. For children, the signs, symbols and customs which compose these celebrations will contribute to their appreciation of Christian ritual and worship. For the adults who celebrate these activities with young children, the practices which are suggested will ring a note of fond past observances and, hopefully, give renewed meaning and understanding to the old ways.

A theme of Christian vocation is interwoven among the five Lenten Sundays of Year A. The second set of celebrations for Year B develops the theme of God's covenant with his people. Reconciliation and God's mercy is the unifying theme for Year C. Together the celebrations of the Sundays of Lent compose a series of services which enable us to proclaim the salvation which is ours in Christ. Ancient Christian symbols, international customs of long standing, and the beckoning of Christian witness to the world of our day give color and texture to the composition. And the composition is framed between the touching events of Ash Wednesday and Palm Sunday.

May the Lenten Season be a time of religious renewal for you and help you once again to proclaim, "The Lord blesses me!"

LET US PRAY

Joel 2:12-18   Joel 2:13
Psalm 51
2 Corinthians 5:20-26
Matthew 6:1-6, 16-18   Matthew 6:1-6

The Church's celebration of the beginning of the Lenten season is one of the most treasured ritual practices among Catholics. This simple Center Celebration begins with a brief sharing of the meaning of the imposition of ashes and develops into a time for us to ponder the importance of prayer in our lives, especially during this season of the Church's liturgy.

*For Parish Programs
and in the Religious Education Classroom*

Leaders of religious education classes and parish programs which meet only once each week should carefully look over the Creation Center activity in light of the Witness Center assignment for which it is designed. A simple alteration from a large-scale model intended for school classes and family celebrations will make it more practical.

GREETING CENTER

Sing the "Promenade Song" as the participants gather for this simple celebration of God's Word.

When the song is finished, a discussion could follow about the meaning of the imposition of ashes on our foreheads earlier in the day (ashes not only remind us of our human condition and substance, but are used as a sign of our repentance). Be sure to share reactions and feelings which were felt this day because such an obvious mark of our religious tradition was worn on our foreheads.

1. Are we proud to proclaim our faith by displaying the ashes? Embarrassed?
2. Did we enounter many questions about the ashes on our foreheads?
3. Did we act differently because we were displaying a sign of our faith?
4. Did we understand what the ashes meant?

WORD CENTER

This reading from Matthew's gospel is one of Jesus' most direct teachings about the way of praying. One of the participants should be selected to proclaim this gospel passage.

Matthew 6:1-6

Make certain you do not perform your religious duties in public so that people will see what you do. If you do these things publicly, you will not have any reward from your Father in heaven.

So when you give something to a needy person, do not make a big show of it, as the hypocrites do in the houses of worship and on the streets. They do it so that people will praise them. I assure you, they have already been paid in full. But when you help a needy person, do it in such a way that even your closest friend will not know about it. Then it will be a private matter. And your Father, who sees what you do in private, will reward you.

At the conclusion of the reading, the participants should be asked to describe ways of praying either from the observations of others or from their own personal experience. Conclude by recalling Jesus' teaching just proclaimed: we must not brag about our ways of praying. Rather, we should pray often without boasting of our prayer times as though we were better than people who do not yet pray.

PRAISE CENTER

Ask the participants to suggest introductory phrases for beginning times of prayer, such as

"Dear Father"
"Jesus my Lord"
"God, our Father"
"Praise to you, Lord"
"Hi, God!"
"Brother Jesus"

However we choose to begin our personal prayer, we should feel comfortable using the words with which we address our God. We are assured by Jesus that our Father hears our prayer no matter what words we may choose. We must not overly concern ourselves with the words we use but, rather, enter into prayerful conversation with the words which are waiting upon our lips to be placed before the Lord

"Call My Name" would be an appropriate song to sing.

Volunteers could lead the group in a short prayer of praise, thanksgiving, forgiveness or petition. It might even be effective for the participants to compose a prayer together. This activity could be concluded by all praying together in the words Jesus gave us:

The Lord's Prayer

Our Father in heaven,
    holy is your name,
    may your kingdom come,
    your will be done on earth
    as in heaven.
Give us today
    our daily bread.
Forgive us our sins
    as we forgive those
    who sin against us.
Do not lead us to temptation
    but save us from evil.
For the kingdom and the power
    and the glory are yours
    now and forever.
Amen.

CREATION CENTER

Prayer Jar

Materials Needed: a large container (for families and classroom groups), or individual containers (for groups meeting once a week), paper strips, crayons, and paste or glue.

A large container such as a fish bowl, relish jar, cookie tin, coffee can or whatever is available, should be selected for use during the Lenten season by the group of participants. Individual containers such as juice cans, milk cartons or cigar boxes could be used by each participant in groups which do not come together daily.

The containers should be decorated with printed words of prayer selected by the participants. Examples might be: praise, bless, please, send, give, thanks, and so on. These words should be written down and cut out of paper strips and pasted onto the container's sides in a collage fashion. Individual containers might be wrapped in one solid piece of paper and written upon by the participants rather than burdening each participant with numerous pieces of paper strips.

Cut a hole into the container's top. Presto! A "Prayer Jar!"

SHARING CENTER

At the Sharing Center discuss ways of repenting during the season of Lent as we prepare to celebrate the Lord's victory over sin and evil on Easter Sunday. We must not be afraid to admit our sins and return to the Lord, because in Scripture it is written:

Joel 2:13b
Come back to the Lord your God.
He is kind and full of mercy;
he is patient and keeps his promises.
He is always ready to forgive and not punish.

Perhaps the best way for us to repent during Lent for our sinful failings is to be faithful in praying for our needs and the needs of others, and thankful for God's blessings upon us.

Give the Witness Center activity assignment and conclude in song with "My Thankful Prayer," or any song of gratitude.

WITNESS CENTER

Every day during Lent the participants should select an intention for which his/her prayer is offered that day. It might be for forgiveness of a sin, for the needs of a relative or friend, or in praise of God's presence in our lives. Whatever the daily intention may be, it is written in a few words on a slip of paper and deposited in the "Prayer Jar" assembled at the Creation Center. By this daily gesture, we all attempt to remain faithful to prayer during the days of Lent, and we also heed Jesus' command to pray privately because our intentions remain secret within our hearts.

Our jar of intentions, becoming more full as the days of Lent progress, should be a reminder to us that we live in a community marked with faith in prayer.

VERY SPECIAL PERSONS

Genesis 2:7-9, 3:1-7
Psalm 51
Romans 5:12-19
Matthew 4:1-11

Genesis 2:4-9, 3:1-7

THE GARDEN OF EDEN

The season of Lent affords us the opportunity to look closely at ourselves as God's favored people. Our looking often reveals our inadequacies and our failure to live up to being so specially regarded by the Creator.

Today's theme is found in the creation story of Genesis and allows us to begin our celebration of Lent by realizing that we are God's chosen people. Indeed, we are very special persons entrusted with the care of the Father over all of creation.

Suggestions For Celebration:

Two alternatives are suggested as the Witness Center activity for today's celebration. Families and classroom teachers will find either acceptable but weekly program leaders will probably find it necessary to disregard the first option.

GREETING CENTER

Materials Needed: a hand mirror.

Sing "Howdy Friends" as the participants assemble for this first celebration during the season of Lent.

Then pass around a hand mirror to the participants. As each person looks into the mirror, ask, "What do you see?" Don't pursue any deep explanation for their answers, which will probably be as simple as "Teddy" or "Marie" or "a girl" or "a face."

When everyone has shared in this activity, conclude by saying, in words such as these:

The bible tells us that we are made in God's image. That's right! We may not all look the same, but whenever we see ourselves or another person, we see the image of God! God is special, very special. So I guess if we're made in God's image, we must be very special persons!

WORD CENTER

Materials Needed: puppet stage, puppets of Adam, Eve, and a snake.

The adults responsible for this celebration may choose either to present this puppet show themselves for the other participants or to select some of the children to present the show as the script is read by adults.

A puppet show telling of Genesis 2:4-9, 3:1-7

(Action: the curtain opens to solid black background with small mounds of brown soil at the stage front.)

Narrator: When the Lord God made the universe, there were no plants on the earth and no seeds had sprouted, because he had not sent any rain, and there was no one to cultivate the land.

(Sprinkle soil from above landing on mounds.) Then the Lord God took some soil from the ground and formed a man out of it; he breathed lifegiving breath into his nostrils and the man began to live. *(Adam slowly stretches forth from below, then exercises freely.)*

Then the Lord God planted a garden in Eden, in the East, and there he put the man he had formed. *(Two trees — paper cutouts — rise onto the background to the astonishment of Adam.)*

He made all kinds of beautiful trees grow there and produce good fruit. *(Adam examines the trees on the backdrop.)*

In the middle of the garden stood the tree that gives life and the tree that gives knowledge of what is good and what is bad. *(Adam approaches and stands near this tree. Adam bows to the tree and leaves the stage.)*

(A snake appears on stage taunting the audience. Eve appears in the garden.) Now the snake was the most cunning animal that the Lord God had made.

Snake: Did God really tell you not to eat fruit from any tree in the garden?

Eve *(observes the tree)*: We may eat the fruit of any tree in the garden except the tree in the middle of it. God told us not to eat the fruit of that tree or even touch it; if we do, we will die.

Snake *(speaks with sneaky voice)*: That's not true; you will not die. God said that because he knows that when you eat it, you will be like God and know what is good and what is bad.

Narrator: The woman saw how beautiful the tree was and how good its fruit would be to eat, and she thought how wonderful it would be to become wise. So she took some of the fruit and ate it. *(Adam reappears in the garden.)* Then she gave some to her husband, and he also ate it. *(After tasting the fruit of the tree, both quickly leave the stage.)* As soon as they had eaten it, they were given understanding and realized that they were naked; so they sewed fig leaves together and covered themselves.

After the puppet show, discuss with the participants the meaning of this tale of creation. Include questions such as:

1. Who was your favorite character? Why?
2. Who was the villian? Why?
3. What would you have done if you were the man or the woman? Why?
4. Why do you think God acted the way he did?

The discussion could be concluded with a brief instruction emphasizing the many gifts which were given to God's first human creatures. God has specially chosen these people for his loving care. He made them in his image. They did not realize how special they were and so they lost their unique privileges.

The gifts of creation are also given to us. We must make careful use of God's blessing if we desire to remain in special relationship to the Father. We are made in God's image. We must be very special persons!

If time allows, "God Did" or any song about creation could be sung.

PRAISE CENTER

The story of creation in Genesis helps us to realize our unique role in the universe as God's special persons. It is fundamental to our Christian living that we are able to recognize this special relationship which the Father has chosen to have with all human beings...even you and me!

"Who Am I In God's Eye" would be a very appropriate song.

Briefly discuss in your own words the meaning of being "a very special person in God's eye." Conclude this activity with a Chain Prayer of thanksgiving with the participants: Sit in a circle and begin by praying, "Thank you, God, for (my life)." The next participant repeats your prayer and adds another gift from God, such as "Thank you, God, for (my life) and (my friends)." Continue around the circle, each participant repeating the previous prayer and adding his/her own intention, such as "Thank you, God, for (my life), (my friends), (food to eat), etc."

It will be more difficult as the prayer continues around the circle for each participant to repeat all the intentions, but this will add to the fun of the praying activity and also help us to realize how boundless the gifts of God are and how easily we forget his many blessings upon us. We have much to be grateful for!

CREATION CENTER

Creation Ornaments
Materials Needed: colored construction paper, scissors, paste, paper punch, and some nine-inch strips of yarn.

Colored construction paper should be available for all the participants to use. Let each participant think of one example of God's many gifts which we see in creation around us everyday (birds, people, the sun, clouds, etc.). Allow each to cut out of the construction paper an illustration of their example. Paste should also be available for multicolored examples. (Keep the examples simple by setting a time limit.)

When each example is completed, punch a hole at the top and thread a nine-inch strip of yarn through the hole.

SHARING CENTER

Tree of Creation
Materials Needed: a tree branch, a container of rocks of sand, and some spray paint, if desired.

Prepare a broken or bare branch for use with this activity. Put it in a container of sand or rocks so that it is sturdy. It may be painted a solid color, if desired. It will become a "Tree of Creation" for our celebration today.

When the participants gather with their examples of creation's gifts, summarize the celebration's theme by instructing that we, as God's special people, must take special care of the gifts he has given us. We should always give thanks and praise to God for his many blessings upon us.

Invite the participants to describe their examples before the group. "Sing A Song of Praise" could be sung as each participant takes a turn at hanging his/her illustration upon the "Tree of Creation."

Give the Witness Center assignment and conclude by singing,"Who Am I In God's Eye?" or "God Did."

WITNESS CENTER

For Families and Classroom Groups:

The "Tree of Creation" should be displayed in a place where it can be seen by the participants during the week. Turns should be taken throughout the week allowing each participant to lead a prayer of thanksgiving and praise to God. Families might be able to make this a once-a-day event, whereas school classes may have to make this a three-times-a-day prayer so that all the participants have a turn as leader.

Or, you might choose the assignment suggested below.

For Parish or Weekly Groups:

As a Witness Center assignment, each participant can take his/her Creation Center project home and tape it to the bathroom mirror. Every day when they look into the mirror, they should be reminded to say a short prayer of thanks to God for making them the special person who will care for all of creation.

HOLY ONES, PRAY

Genesis 12:1-4
Psalm 33
2 Timothy 1:8-10
Matthew 17:1-9

Genesis 12:1-4

1 Corinthians 12:10

This celebration builds upon the theme celebrated last week. It is another opportunity for us to consider how blessed we are to be called and chosen by God as his own people.

By exploring different ways of praying and by observing the ancient Lenten custom of eating the baked pretzel, the participants should be helped to realize the importance of prayer in the Christian life.

GREETING CENTER

"Who Am I In God's Eye?" is an appropriate opening song for this celebration of our Christian vocation to holiness.

At the conclusion of this song, invite the participants to share ideas about what it means to be a "special person." Refer to last week's celebration and ask the participants about their performance of the Witness Center activity assigned at the last celebration.

Conclude by announcing that today's celebration theme is about being specially picked by God.

WORD CENTER

This reading from the book of Genesis tells the story of how the Lord chose Abram to be the father, or leader, of God's chosen people. Two participants should be selected to read the parts of the Lord and Abram. An adult could read the part of the narrator.

Genesis 12:1-4

Narrator: *The Lord said to Abram,*

Lord: *"Leave your native land, your relatives, and your father's home, and go to a country that I am going to show you. I will give you many descendants, and they will become a great nation. I will bless you and make your name famous, so that you will be a blessing.*

I will bless those who bless you, But I will curse those who curse you. And through you I will bless all the nations."

Narrator: *When Abram was seventy-five years old, he started out from Haran, as the Lord had told him to do; and Lot went with him.*

At the conclusion of the dramatized reading, ask the participants how they would feel if they were Abram being chosen by the Lord. (Surprised? Unworthy? Blessed?)

Discuss the meaning of the word "vocation," a calling. When we speak of a "vocation in life" we mean the way in which we respond to the Lord's choosing us to be his people. There are many ways we can respond to God's calling, but however we live our vocation we must strive to become holier and closer to the life of the Lord. This is our Christian vocation: to follow the way of the sinless Christ to holy union with the Lord in the Spirit. Indeed, we Christians are very special persons!

PRAISE CENTER

There are many ways for us to respond to the Lord's calling in the Church. These ministries are elaborated by St. Paul in his first letter to the Corinthians.

1 Corinthians 12:10

The Spirit gives faith to one person, while to another person he gives the power to heal. The Spirit gives one person the power to work miracles; to another, the gift of speaking God's message; and to yet another, the ability to tell the difference between gifts that come from the Spirit and those that do not. To one person he gives the ability to speak in strange tongues and to another he gives the ability to explain what is said.

Today we share more fully in the ministries of the Church as priests, religious teachers and proclaimers, and through many liturgical services. Invite the participants to pray for all the ministers of the Church. They could mention the names of the ministers in the local parish and sing "Father, Care" (p. 44) after every few are mentioned

Then allow some silent moments in quiet prayer for our own understanding of God's will for us. After several moments, pray these, or similar words:

> Father,
> You are the Holy One.
> Let your will be known to us.
> Make us holy.
> May we always follow your way.

Conclude by singing "Shepherd, Lead Me."

CREATION CENTER

There is a Lenten custom which began during the early years of the Church, and which could have special meaning for our Lenten observance. The pretzel was baked by the Germanic peoples as a symbol of prayer, its shape resembling crossed arms upon the breast, a common posture for prayer among many Christian people. The eating of these little breads was a reminder of the prayerful attitude which should be a part of the Christian striving for holiness.

If time allows, let the participants mix the ingredients for the baking of soft pretzels. If your situation does not permit for this activity, explain the meaning of the pretzel and distribute packaged pretzels to the participants.

Soft Pretzels

1 cake yeast dissolved into 1 ½ cups warm water.
add 1 teaspoon salt, and 1 tablespoon sugar.
Blend in 4 cups of flour.

Knead dough until smooth. Cut into small pieces. Roll into ropes, and twist into desired shape. Place on lightly greased cookie sheets. Brush pretzel with 1 beaten egg. Sprinkle with coarse salt. Bake immediately in 425° oven for 12 to 15 minutes.

Pretzels

1 cup butter
1 ½ cups sifted flour
6 eggs, beaten
¼ cup cream
1 teaspoon vanilla
1 cup sugar
½ teaspoon salt
1 egg white for icing
1 tablespoon milk

Cut shortening into the flour as for pie crust. Combine beaten eggs, cream, vanilla, sugar and salt. Add to flour and shortening mixture and chill. Form into rolls about 8 inches long as thick as a lead pencil. Shape like a pretzel, brush with egg white which has been beaten slightly and to which has been added 1 tablespoon milk. Bake in moderate oven 350° oven about 12-15 minutes. Makes about 5 dozen pretzels.

SHARING CENTER

Materials Needed: pretzels (from Creation Center activity), napkins, refreshment drink, and cups.

The pretzel is a reminder of our praying vocation. Perhaps the participants can suggest different postures for praying, or simply lead them in these gestures:

kneeling, hands folded;
standing, arms crossed upon breast;
sitting, head bowed, hands on lap

Indeed, there are many ways for us to pray.

The participants could now eat the pretzels and drink a simple liquid refreshment.

Give the Witness Center assignment and conclude with verse 1 of "Shepherd, Lead Me" or "The Lord Blesses Me!"

WITNESS CENTER

Encourage the participants to pray each day asking God to make known his will. Suggest that they experiment with different postures of prayer, such as arms crossed as symbolized in the pretzel's shape.

Suggest that they tell their friends about the religious significance of the crossed pretzel.

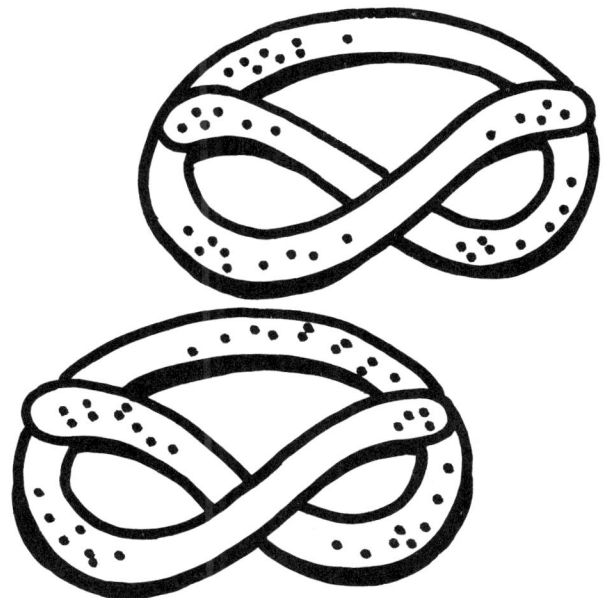

THE GIFT OF FAITH

Exodus 17:3-7
Psalm 95
Romans 5:1-2, 5-8
John 4:5-42   John 4:5-15, 19-26, 28-30, 39-42

We recognize our Christian vocation to become more holy because of the gift of faith given us by the Holy Spirit. It is fitting, then, as we continue our Lenten focus upon our religious calling, that we celebrate our profession of faith as a community. The story of Jesus meeting the Samaritan woman at Jacob's well provides an appropriate gospel text for us to listen to and pray over as we reconsider our own response in faith.

GREETING CENTER

A song of thanksgiving such as "Thank You, God" or "Father, I Adore You" should be the opening prayer for this celebration.

An experience of believing and doubting should be provided to younger children to help them understand the meaning of God's Word spoken in today's Word Center activity. This game of "We Doubt It" is suggested as a possible experience.

We Doubt It!

Each participant thinks of some spectacular occurrence which has happened or might happen to him/her. It can be fact or simply imaginative. In turn, each participant announces the spectacular event or seemingly incredible fact to the other participants who must play the role of the judges. After the announcement, the judges either say "We believe it" or "We doubt it," depending on how they judge the participant to be telling factual truth. The idea is to stump the judges. The participant must tell the real truth after the judges' decision is voiced.

An example might be:

Participant 1: I've been to the moon.

Judges: We doubt it.

Participant 1: Right!

Participant 2: I have eight brothers and five sisters.

Judges: We doubt it.

Participant 2: Wrong! I do have eight brothers and five sisters.

Participant 3: The pope is my uncle.

Judges: We doubt it.

Participant 3: Right!

Participant 4: I've been to Disney World four times this year.

Judges: We believe it.

Participant 4: Wrong! I've only been once.

WORD CENTER

Materials Needed: puppet stage, and puppet of Jesus and a woman.

Involve the participants in this puppet showing of Jesus and the Woman of Samaria by leading them in the short refrain, ''Believe!'' as indicated in the script.

BELIEVE

A puppet show telling of John 4:5-15, 19-26, 28-30, 37-42

Narrator: *In Samaria Jesus came to a town named Sychar, which was not far from the field that Jacob had given to his son, Joseph. Jacob's well was there, and Jesus, tired out by the trip, sat down by the well. It was about noon.*

A Samaritan woman came to draw some water, and Jesus said to her,

Jesus: *Give me a drink of water.*

Woman: *You are a Jew, and I am a Samaritan — so how can you ask me for a drink?*

Narrator: *(Jews will not use the same cups and bowls that Samaritans use.) But Jesus answered:*

Jesus: *If you only knew what God gives and who it is that is asking you for a drink, you would ask him, and he would give you life-giving water.*

All sing refrain.

BELIEVE

Dick Hilliard

Be-lieve the Lord lives and he cares for you.

Be-lieve the Lord lives and he cares for you.

© 1978 by Resource Publications. All Rights Reserved.

Narrator: *Soon the woman said to Jesus:*

Woman: *Sir, you don't have a bucket, and the well is deep. Where would you get that life-giving water? It was our ancestor Jacob who gave us this well; he and his sons and his flocks all drank from it. You don't claim to be greater than Jacob, do you?*

All sing refrain

Narrator: *Then Jesus answered the woman:*

Jesus: *Whoever drinks this water will get thirsty again, but whoever drinks the water that I will give him will never be thirsty again. The water that I will give him will become in him a spring which will provide him with life-giving water and give him eternal life.*

All sing refrain.

Narrator: *The woman then said to Jesus:*

Woman: *Sir, give me that water! Then I will never be thirsty again, nor will I have to come here to draw water.*

All sing refrain.

Woman: *I see you are prophet, sir. My Samaritan ancestors worshiped God on the mountain, but you Jews say that Jerusalem is the place we should worship God.*

Jesus: *Believe me, woman, the time will come when people will not worship the Father either on this mountain or in Jerusalem. You Samaritans do not really know whom you worship; but we Jews know whom we worship, because it is from the Jews that salvation comes. But the time is coming and is already here, when by the power of God's Spirit people will worship the Father as he really is, offering him the true worship that he wants. God is Spirit, and only by the power of his Spirit can people worship him as he really is.*

All sing refrain.

Woman: *I know that the Messiah will come, and when he comes, he will tell us everything.*

Jesus: *I am he, I who am talking with you.*

All sing refrain.

Narrator: *Then the women left her water jar, went back to the town, and said to the people there:*

Woman: *Come and see the man who told me everything I have ever done. Could he be the Messiah?*

Narrator: *So they left the town and followed her.*

Many of the Samaritans in that town believed in Jesus because the woman had said ''He told me everything I have ever done.'' So when the Samaritans came to him, they begged him to stay with them, and Jesus stayed there two days.

All sing refrain.

Narrator: *Many more believed because of his message, and they told the woman, ''We believe now, not because of what you said, but because we ourselves have heard him, and we know that he really is the Savior of the world.''*

All sing refrain.

At the conclusion of the show, ask the participants about the woman at the well. How quickly did she place her trust in Jesus? How quickly did she tell others of her faith in the Lord? Was she hesitant to believe? Or to spread the good news of faith? If she had been playing ''We Doubt It,'' what would her response to Jesus have been?

PRAISE CENTER

What is our response to the Lord? Are we quick to say "We believe" or do we sometimes say "We doubt it?"

Believing in Jesus comes from our hearing his message of love and hope proclaimed and our placing trust in his ways. When we believe, we are convinced of the truth. Believing is a gift from God to his chosen people. How blessed are we to be called his people for we are gifted with faith!

This Repetition Prayer could be introduced in words such as these: "Let us give thanks to God for the gift of faith and pray that we will always remain close to the truth which Jesus teaches."

Act Of Faith

My God and Father
I really believe
that you are Lord of all.
I really believe
that Jesus is your son
and he is my savior and brother.
I really believe
that Your Holy Spirit
lives today in the Church.
I really believe
that the Church teaches your truth
which you make known to us.
Keep me close to you
and to your truth
until I die
and share your life eternally.
Amen.

CREATION CENTER

Holy Water Cans

Materials Needed: tuna or cat food cans, vinyl or masking tape, construction paper, scissors, marking pens or crayons, clear tape, and holy water.

Directions: Clean tuna or cat food cans thoroughly. Strip them of advertising labels and place masking tape around the top edge to cover any sharp edges.

Distribute the cans to the participants. On construction paper sized and cut to wrap around the outer side of the cans, let each participant write the words, "I Believe." With tape, help them attach this "I Believe" label as an outer wrapping for the cans.

Ask at the parish office for holy water to fill each of the cans about one-third full.

SHARING CENTER

The participants should assemble with their holy water containers in hand from the Creation Center activity.

Everyone should be reminded of the symbolic meaning of water (refreshing sign of rebirths, cleansing sign of new life). Water is used at baptism as a sign of our new belief professed in Christ. When we bless ourselves with water, we should be reminded of the faith we professed at our baptism.

Sing "If You Believe," a fitting statement of faith.

Give the Witness Center assignment and conclude with the refrain, "Believe."

WITNESS CENTER

The participants should be encouraged to bless themselves with the water in their "I believe" containers each day as a reminder of the faith we profess as Christians. Invite them to use the water at the entrance to Church when they visit — another reminder of the faith of our baptism, the faith we share as a Christian community.

LIGHT THE WAY OF

1 Samuel 16:1, 6-7, 10-13
Psalm 23
Ephesians 5:8-14
John 9:1-41

Psalm 23:1, 3-4
Ephesians 5:8-14

Light and darkness are ancient religious symbols which have become precious to the liturgical celebration of Christians. Today's celebration allows us to listen to St. Paul's letter to the Ephesians about the meaning of living in the light of Christ's love. We will also pray the 23rd psalm, acknowledging the way of love led by the Shepherd Lord.

This celebration will prepare young children for the great night of the Easter celebration when the Church uses the symbol of darkness and light in its richest hour.

Suggestions for Celebration

Adequate adult supervision will be needed throughout these center activities because of the use of lighted candles. A small container of water should be kept handy should a lighted candle be dropped accidentally.

GREETING CENTER

Today's celebration may begin with a joyful song, such as the "Promenade Song" or "Praise the Lord, Rejoice and Sing."

Then ask the participants to suggest times and events when they have experienced complete darkness. Some might think of a local power blackout, being locked in a closed room, camping outside at night, walking into a cavern, and so on. Ask the participants to describe their reactions to the experience of darkness. Were they scared? excited? lonely? sad?

CREATION CENTER

The participants should assemble at the Creation Center to make candle holders for use during the rest of the center activities.

Candle Holders

Materials Needed: candle tapers for each participant, a cake-size paper plate for each participant, scissors, and a knife or screwdriver.

Distribute a paper plate and a small candle taper to each participant. With the end of a scissors or blunt-edged knife or screwdriver, punch a hole in the center of the plate's bottom. Allow the participants to slide their candles through the paper plates.

WORD CENTER

When the participants gather, the room or Word Center area should be darkened. Ask the participants to share reactions to the darkness.

Then light one candle. Again ask the participants to share reactions to the small light.

Then pass the light around by lighting each participant's candle. Once again invite reaction to the growing light. Hopefully, the reactions to the growing light will tell a story of movement from fear to security or from loneliness to a sense of community.

Then ask the participants to extinguish their candles as the passage from St. Paul's letter to the Ephesians is proclaimed. Follow the instructions interwoven into the text:

Ephesians 5:8-14

(in darkness)

You yourselves used to be in the darkness, but since you have become the Lord's people, you are in the light.

(light one candle)

So you must live like people who belong to the light, for it is the light that brings a rich harvest of every kind of goodness, righteousness, and truth. Try to learn what pleases the Lord.

(spread light to candles of the participants)

Have nothing to do with the worthless things that people do, things that belong to the darkness.

(extinguish your candle only)

Instead, bring them out to the light.

(invite one of the participants to relight your candle)

And when all things are brought out to the light, then their true nature is clearly revealed; for anything that is clearly revealed becomes light.

LOVE

We are called, as Christians, from a life of darkness, fear and loneliness to the way of light, security, and community by our faith in Jesus. This mystery should be discussed with the participants by using examples which illustrate these realities:

sin is tuning out the Lord's life just as darkness is a tuning out of light;

rejecting the Lord's love is like a dark place refusing to let light into its space;

the way of the Lord destroys evil just as light completely rids a place of darkness.

Refer to the experience of the light and darkness during the reading from St. Paul's letter to the Ephesians as you discuss the call of Christians to live in the light.

Christ is the light of the world. As Christians believing in Christ, we too, must be a light to others in darkness. This is the meaning of our Christian witness to those who have not heard of Jesus or have turned from his ways. This is another dimension of our vocation as Christians. We are called to be lights in a world of darkness just as Jesus is the light dispelling the darkness of sin and evil.

Extinguish the candles and gather at the Praise Center.

PRAISE CENTER

We become lights of Christ when we follow the way of the Lord. Let us pray to God and tell him that we place all our trust in his ways.

Psalm 23:1, 3-4
The Lord is my shepherd
I have everything I need.

He gives me new strength.

He guides me in the right paths,
as he has promised.

Even if I go through the deepest darkness,
I will not be afraid, Lord,
for you are with me.

All could sing "Shepherd, Lead Me," a musical version of Psalm 23.

SHARING CENTER

Invite the participants to suggest ways of living as lights of Christ, lighting the way of love. Examples might include:

helping older people to walk;
carrying groceries for mom or dad;
cutting the lawn at home;
playing with a new neighbor;
assisting your teacher with a special task.

Help the participants to realize the importance of living in love as Jesus taught. It is by our love for one another that people will know that we are Christians, lights of the Lord, Jesus Christ.

The "Ballad of God's Love" could be sung as a fitting reminder of the Christian's call to love.

Give the Witness Center assignment and conclude with a song about Christian vocation, such as "Who Am I In God's Eye?" or "Let Me Lord."

WITNESS CENTER

The participants should take their candles home and place them in a cup of sand or gravel upon their bedroom dressers. At the end of each day as they prepare for sleep, encourage them to light their candles and pray Psalm 23 with their parents. (Psalm 23 could be printed in the "kidsletter.") We are to be lights in the world showing the way of our Shepherd, the Lord Jesus.

HOPE IN GOD'S LIFE

Ezekiel 37:23-24
Psalm 130
Romans 8:8-11
John 11:1-45   John 11: 1, 3, 5-7, 11-14, 17-27, 32-36, 38-39, 43-45

Dick Hilliard

Come, Lord, be with us, we need you.

Come, Lord, be with us, we need you.

The story of Jesus' raising Lazarus back to life helps prepare us for the celebration of Easter as another, yet far more important story of God's triumph over darkness and sin. Today's center activities are focused upon the episode at Bethany, yet pave the way for the realization of the promise given to God's people: we will share in the life of the Lord eternally.

Hope in life everlasting is not only appropriate as a Lenten preparation for the great event of Easter, but a fitting conclusion to our celebrating the vocation of Christians on these past Sundays of Lent.

GREETING CENTER

At the start of this celebration, everyone should sing "Believe," while the leader asks each participant to mention some way in which the Lord has shown his care for them or for others during the past week. The "Believe" refrain should be repeated after every two or three participants offer examples of the Lord's care.

Then the leader should simply ask, "Did you need the Lord this week?" This might make for an opportune occasion to discuss our trust in the Lord and our need for his caring presence in all we do. Perhaps some of us think that we can get along well without the Lord's guidance. How would the participants respond to this kind of attitude? Can we ignore our need for the Lord?

"Wishing Game"

The "Wishing Game" is perfectly suited for this celebration. Invite the participants to offer a concluding phrase to the statement, "If I could have one wish come true, I'd wish..." Let each suggest his/her own wish without any further discussion. Then move to the Word Center.

WORD CENTER

Teach the participants the short refrain, "Come, Lord" (same melody as "Believe"). Then read the story of the summoning of Jesus by Mary and Martha, using the musical refrain as indicated.

John 11:1, 3, 5-7, 11-14, 17-27, 32-36, 38-39, 43-45.

A man named Lazarus, who lived in Bethany, became sick. Bethany was the town where Mary and her sister Martha lived. The sisters sent Jesus a message: "Lord, your dear friend is sick."

(Sing "Come, Lord.")

Jesus loved Martha and her sister and Lazarus. Yet when he received the news that Lazarus was sick, he stayed where he was for two more days. Then he said to the disciples, "Let us go back to Judea."

Jesus said to his disciples, "Our friend Lazarus has fallen asleep, but I will go and wake him up."

The disciples answered, "If he is asleep, Lord, he will get well."

Jesus meant that Lazarus had died, but they thought he meant natural sleep. So Jesus told them plainly, "Lazarus is dead."

When Jesus arrived, he found that Lazarus had been buried four days before. Bethany was less than two miles from Jerusalem, and many Judeans had come to see Martha and Mary to comfort them about their brother's death.

(Sing "Come, Lord.")

When Martha heard that Jesus was coming, she went out to meet him, but Mary stayed in the house. Martha said to Jesus, "If you had been here, Lord, my brother would not have died! But I know that even now God will give you whatever you ask him for."

"Your brother will rise to life," Jesus told her.

"I know," she replied, "that he will rise to life on the last day."

Jesus said to her, "I am the resurrection and the life. Whoever believes in me will live, even though he dies; and whoever lives and believes in me will never die. Do you believe this?"

"Yes, Lord!" she answered. "I do believe that you are the Messiah, the Son of God, who was to come into the world."

Mary arrived where Jesus was, and as soon as she saw him, she fell at his feet. "Lord," she said, "if you had been here, my brother would not have died!"

(Sing "Come, Lord.")

Jesus saw her weeping, and he saw how the people with her were weeping also; his heart was touched, and he was deeply moved. "Where have you buried him?" he asked them.

(Sing "Come, Lord.")

Jesus wept. "See how much he loved him!" the people said. Deeply moved once more, Jesus went to the tomb, which was a cave with a stone placed at the entrance. "Take the stone away!" Jesus ordered.

After he had said this, he called out in a loud voice, "Lazarus, come out." He came out, his hands and feet wrapped in grave cloths, and with a cloth around his face. "Untie him," Jesus told them, "and let him go."

Many of the people who had come to visit Mary saw what Jesus did, and they believed in him.

(Sing "Come, Lord.")

At the conclusion of this telling of the tale, invite some of the participants to re-enact this story by taking the roles of Jesus, Mary, Martha and Lazarus, and a messenger for delivering Mary and Martha's message to Jesus. The remaining participants can form the chorus and crowd at Bethany. One of the adults can give directions, if needed, by playing the role of a narrator.

(Once when this activity was performed by a group of second graders, the girls playing Mary and Martha openly wept in bitterness over Jesus' delay in coming to Bethany. Somewhat suspicious of Jesus' power, Mary and Martha shoved and pushed Jesus in anger, then watched with astonishment as Jesus miraculously raised Lazarus to new life. The young boy was so confident of his ability as Jesus that, after his raising of Lazarus, he walked over to the weeping Martha, poked his elbow in her side, and whispered nonchalantly, "See, I told you I could do it!")

Discuss with the participants the roles played by Lazarus, Mary and Martha. If Mary, Martha or Lazarus were to play the "Wishing Game," what might be their wishes? Why? Be sure to point out the hesitant faith which characterized these two women in this situation.

What is Jesus' response to each of the three persons? When we have faith and believe that the Lord has come for us, we have no need of making wishes because we are certain of the Lord's protection and care over us.

Hope is an attitude toward life. For the Christian it means trusting in the Lord's promises. The Lord brings hope to all. Yes, we need you, Lord!

PRAISE CENTER

Hope is the promise given to those who walk in the way of the Lord; to those who follow his command of love; and to those whose lives are modeled on the ministry of Jesus. Thus, for us who rely on the saving power of the Lord who calls us to live in holiness, faith and trust, our reward is knowing that the Father truly loves us, guides us, and will bring us to everlasting life. We need not be concerned about wishes for a better life because we are assured of the best life possible: life in the Lord who has saved us and has risen to demonstrate his care for us.

All pray an *Act of Hope*.

Dear Father
I trust in your loving power.
I trust in your promise of life eternal.
In hope I will live in your love.
In hope I will be pardoned for my sins.
In hope I will share your life forever
which you give us
through Jesus our Lord.

"My Thankful Prayer" or "Father, I Adore You" would be appropriate responses in song.

CREATION CENTER

Hope Chests

Materials Needed: a cigar, shoe or small gift box for each participant; colored construction paper or wrapping paper; glue, paste or tape; and some marking crayons.

The custom of the hope chest originated in England many centuries ago. In every house wooden chests were used to store away household linens and wearing apparel. In most homes a chest was set aside for every daughter into which were placed finery and handmade items which would eventually be used in "the home of her hopes" after she married. Let us remember this custom as we construct our own hope chests full of gifts which we would be happy to bring to our Lord with whom we hope to share our eternal home of life everlasting.

Each participant should decorate a cigar, shoe or small gift box. On its top write the words, "Hope Chest."

SHARING CENTER

Today's celebration should be concluded by reminding the participants of our Christian vocation which has been celebrated during these weeks of Lent. The leader could refer to the themes of the previous weeks as helpful clues to the development of our calling as God's chosen people.

Give the Witness Center assignment and conclude by singing "Who Am I In God's Eye?" or "Let Me Lord."

WITNESS CENTER

Each day during the coming week of Lent, the participants should be encouraged to deposit a list of gifts which they have made for the Lord into their "Hope Chests."

It might be a list of kind things performed for others or said to others. It might be a list of sacrifices which they made during the day. Or it might be a prayer written in thanksgiving or praise to God for his many blessings received during the day. Whatever the listing is, it is a gift to God which one would be proud to present to the Lord with whom we hope to share life everlasting.

A COLORFUL COVENANT

Genesis 9:8-15
Psalm 25
1 Peter 3:18-22
Mark 1:12-15

Genesis 7:1-5, 9:8-17

Mark 1:14-15

The tale of Noah and his Ark is a favorite bible story of children and adults alike. Its covenant theme makes it a fitting reading for the beginning of the Lenten season. As we focus upon the loving relationship which God, our Father, offers each of us, let us also be reminded of the consequences of our failure to keep the Lord's covenant.

We begin this Lenten season, then, by recalling God's blessing upon us and the sign of his love for us in those colors bowed in the sky.

GREETING CENTER

The participants should assemble at the Greeting Center location and begin this celebration by dancing and singing to the "Promenade Song."

At the conclusion of the song, the leader should ask the participants questions, such as these, about human agreements, promises and covenants:

1. Have you ever made a promise to do something?
2. Did you fulfill your promise?
3. Was your promise really a mutual agreement, an exchange of promises with another person?
4. Have you ever made a covenant, that is a promise with someone you love?

Today's celebration reminds us of a promise God made long ago!

WORD CENTER

When the participants have gathered at the Word Center, begin with this introductory section of the story of Noah in Genesis:

Genesis 7:1-5

The Lord said to Noah, "Go into the boat with your whole family; I have found that you are the only one in all the world who does what is right. Take with you seven pairs of each kind of ritually clean animal, but only one pair of each kind of unclean animal. Take also seven pairs of each kind of bird. Do this so that every kind of animal and bird will be kept alive to reproduce again on the earth. Seven days from now I am going to send rain that will fall for forty days and nights, in order to destroy all the living beings that I have made. And Noah did everything that the Lord commanded.

"Noah's Song" Game

Then interrupt the telling of the biblical narrative by inviting the participants to dramatize the loading of the Ark with the many animals. Line the participants in pairs and select one participant to be Noah.

Sing "Noah's Song" allowing each pair of participants to be the animals referred to in the verses of the song. Noah should attempt to load the animals onto his boat as they are called forth in the verses. As the song indicates, however, Noah encounters many incidents which contribute to his frustration!

After the song, dramatization and fun are concluded, continue the biblical telling of the Noah story.

Genesis 7:8-17

God said to Noah and his sons, "I am now making my covenant with you and with your descendants, and with all living beings — all birds and all animals — everything that came out of the boat with you. With these words I make my covenant with you: I promise that never again will all living beings be destroyed by a flood; never again will a flood destroy the earth. As a sign of this everlasting covenant which I am making with you and with all living beings, I am putting my bow in the clouds. It will be the sign of my covenant with the world. Whenever I cover the sky with clouds and the rainbow appears, I will remember my promise to you and to all the animals that a flood will never again destroy all living beings. When the rainbow appears in the clouds, I will see it and remember the everlasting covenant between me and all living beings on earth. That is the sign of the promise which I am making to all living beings."

The leader should discuss with the participants the meaning of this favorite Old Testament tale. Be sure to include such important factors as:

1. At a time when many people turned away from God to wicked ways, Noah remained faithful to God.
2. God chose Noah to be saved from the destruction of the flood because he was a good and just man.
3. Noah is given responsibility for caring for one pair of all clean animals.
4. The rainbow appeared as a sign of God's covenant: never again would the earth be destroyed by God.

You might conclude by asking the participants about the effect of the covenant throughout the ages. The rainbow continues to be a sign of the covenant of peace and God's merciful permission to continue life on earth even when men and women continue to be disloyal to God's ways. God is good! He continues to bless us!

CREATION CENTER

Rainbows

(Several adult leaders will be needed to supervise this activity if large numbers of participants are involved.)

Materials Needed: white paper, water color paints, brushes, water and some towels.

On white construction or painting paper, allow each participant to paint a rainbow. The simplest way might be to distribute a sheet of paper to each participant standing in a single line. Place six containers of watercolor paints (one for each color of the rainbow: purple, blue, green, yellow, orange, red) at different stations in the Creation Center area with a paint brush in each container. The line could move from one color to the next, stopping briefly at each container to make quick arched strokes of the rainbow on the sheet of paper.

The painted rainbows should be placed in an area for quick drying.

PRAISE CENTER

Continue the covenant theme of today's celebration as you lead a discussion asking the participants such questions as:

1. How do we keep God's covenant? — By following the Lord's commandments.
2. Does Jesus teach us ways to act in keeping with the covenant of our Father? — Love? Be patient? Be honest? Pray?
3. What happens when we don't keep God's covenant? — Are we punished? Forgiven?

Indeed, the ever-present loving forgiveness of our Father when we fail to keep the promise of the covenant leads us to give him thanks and praise. A favorite song of praise or thanksgiving such as "My Thankful Prayer" or "Praise the Lord, Rejoice and Sing" could be sung.

The participants should stop at the Creation Center to pick up the dried rainbow paintings on the way to the Sharing Center.

SHARING CENTER

Tell the participants that the rainbow is a reminder of God's covenant, of God's love for us, as we heard in the Word Center proclamation. Help the participants to realize that we must try continuously to keep the covenant God made with us through Noah. It is not easy to be just and faithful, but this is at the root of our relationship with God. That is why Jesus remarked when he appeared in Galilee proclaiming the good news:

Mark 1:14-15

"The right time has come and the Kingdom of God is near! Turn away from your sins and believe the Good News!"

Give the Witness Center assignment and conclude with the last verse and chorus of "Noah's Song" or, if time allows, sing "The Old Ark."

WITNESS CENTER

The participants should be instructed to take their rainbow paintings home as a reminder of our covenant with God during this Lenten season.

Suggest that the rainbow paintings be taped and hung on the bedroom door. At the end of every day during Lent when they close their door to go to sleep, each participant must decide whether or not he/she kept the covenant during that day. If not, the rainbow must be taped upside down as a reminder that we must make a change in our behavior during the next day. At the end of a day lived in agreement with God's covenant of love, the rainbow stands right side up shining its arch of blessing upon us just like the colors in the sky!

WHAT A SACRIFICE!

Genesis 22:1-2, 9, 10-13,
         15-18
               Genesis 22:1-2, 9-13, 15-18
Psalm 116
Romans 8:31-34
Mark 9:2-10

The many practices which have accompanied the Christian celebration of Lent throughout the ages are cherished even today. One of these practices, almsgiving, becomes the Witness Center activity at the conclusion of the celebration, which focuses on the sacrifice of Abraham and Isaac. It is a perfect opportunity to acquaint young children with the penitential spirit of sacrifice which is so much a part of our Christian tradition.

Our Lenten theme of covenantal relationship with the Lord continues as we ponder ways in which we can show our love for the Father through our charitable acts.

GREETING CENTER

As the participants arrive for this celebration, everyone should sing "My Thankful Prayer" or "Thank You, God."

Then lead a discussion about making sacrifices. The leader might want to include such questions as:

1. Do you have a favorite item at home that is all yours? — a special chair? a doll? a scooter or skateboard?
2. Did you ever have to give it up? How did you feel about not having it any longer? — upset? happy?
3. If not, how would you feel if you had to give it up? Would you be sorry? Willing? Stubborn?

WORD CENTER

A puppet stage should be set up for this dramatization of Abraham's offering of his son, Isaac. Be sincere as you speak the voices of the several characters. Follow the stage directions woven into the scriptural text.

ABRAHAM'S SACRIFICE

A puppet show telling of Genesis 22:1-2, 9-13, 15-18
(Abraham enters stage with mountain backdrop)

God's Voice: *Abraham!*

Abraham: (startled) *Yes, here I am!*

(Abraham summons Isaac and they journey together.)

God's Voice: *Take your son, your only son, Isaac, whom you love so much and go to the land of Moriah. There, on a mountain that I will show you, offer him as a sacrifice to me.*

Narrator: *When they came to the place which God had told him about, Abraham built an altar and arranged the wood on it. He tied up his son and placed him on the altar, on top of the wood.* (Abraham does as described here.)

But the angel of the Lord called to him from heaven.

Angel's Voice: *Abraham! Abraham!*

Abraham (stops): *Yes, here I am!*

Angel's Voice: *Don't hurt the boy or do anything to him. Now I know that you have obedient reverence for God, because you have not kept back your only son for him.*

Narrator: *Abraham looked around and saw a ram caught in a bush by its horns. He went and got it and offered it as a burnt offering instead of his son.* (Abraham does as described.)

The angel of the Lord called to Abraham from heaven a second time,

(Abraham hugs Isaac. The two leave the mountain.)

Angel's Voice: *I make a vow by my own name the Lord is speaking — that I will richly bless you. Because you did this and did not keep back your only son from me, I promise that I will give you as many descendants as there are stars in the sky or grains of sand along the seashore. Your descendants will conquer their enemies. All the nations will ask me to bless them as I have blessed your descendants — all because you obeyed my command.*

When the show is ended, ask for volunteers to retell the story in their own words. As they announce the tale, ask them these, or other, questions which highlight the role of Abraham:

1. Did Abraham hesitate to do as the Lord asked?
2. How did you think Abraham felt about God's request? (Remember, Isaac was Abraham's only son!)
3. Do you think it was a difficult sacrifice for Abraham? Was it easy for him, do you think, to give up his only son?
4. How did God reward Abraham for his willingness to make this sacrifice?

Younger children will probably identify more easily with Isaac. You might begin by asking them questions about how Isaac might have felt during this event, then continue by asking the questions about Abraham.

Indeed, Abraham realized how blessed he was by God. His readiness to respond to the request of the Father is an example to us of how eager we should be to live the Father's will.

PRAISE CENTER

Sometimes we have to make sacrifices in our lives even though we really don't want to. When we don't get to watch our favorite TV shows because something special is on or because the TV isn't working — that's a sacrifice for us! When we plan to do something that would be fun and for some reason we are prevented from doing it, that, too, is a sacrifice. At times when things don't go our way and we have to give in to others' demands, that is also a sacrifice for us. Like Abraham, we are often asked to make sacrifices.

Sacrifices very often make us sad. They make us feel sorry that we're not able to do what we want or have what we want. These sad times are occasions for us to think about the many gifts which God has given to us. God's covenant is full of many blessings upon us. This should make us happy, not sad!

Let us pray to God, asking him to bring us happiness and blessings when we are saddened by sacrifices as we sing "Be Happy." Or, let us be attentive to the words of the Lord as we sing "Psalm 46."

Conclude this activity by asking one of the participants to offer a prayer of his/her own for the whole group. Invite other participants to offer their prayer aloud also.

CREATION CENTER

Offering Cans

Materials Needed: a can, jar or other similar container; paste, tape or glue; wrapping paper; scissors; and a dull knife.

It has been a custom of Christian penance to give money to the poor, to offer alms, during the Lenten season. This custom is explained in the Witness Center, but let us make our "offering cans" here.

Take a large can, jar or plastic container. Strip it of its label and wrap it in colorful paper. With a dull-edged knife, make a slot in its lid large enough for the insertion of coins.

SHARING CENTER

The leader should discuss with the participants the meaning of making sacrifices. Refer to the story of Abraham as you talk about our hesitancy to make sacrifices. Abraham was willing to make his sacrifice and so stands as a model for us. The church has always taught that our sacrifices bring blessings and benefits either to us or to those for whom our sacrifices are made.

The participants should be invited to suggest things they might do in the spirit of Lenten sacrifice, such as:

> not watching my favorite TV show;
> not eating my favorite snack food;
> not riding my skateboard;
>
> eating the vegetables I don't really like;
> offering to cut the lawn;
> washing the dishes without complaining.

Give the Witness Center activity assignment and conclude with "Be Happy!", a song about people who make sacrifices.

WITNESS CENTER

Almsgiving is a penitential custom which existed long before the Christian Church and has become one of Christianity's most precious traditions. Originally public sinners were made to present gifts to the poor as a sign of their sorrow for sinning.

Throughout the ages, the Church has taught that the performance of charitable acts for the improvement of the poor is an honorable way of atoning for one's sins.

To give alms in the form of a gift is very often a special sacrifice which we are called upon to perform. The sacrifice of our money so that the poor may have the necessities of life is a difficult task for all of us.

The group of participants should place its "offering cans" in a prominent place for the remaining weeks of Lent. Everyone can contribute money sacrificed daily or weekly from his/her allowance to the can. At the end of Lent, the collection should be given to a charitable group in your parish such as Outreach or the St. Vincent de Paul.

LOVE GOD, LOVE ALL

Exodus 20:1-17
Psalm 19
1 Corinthians 1:22-25
John 2:13-25

Exodus 20:1-17

Repentance for sins is a common Lenten theme. Today's celebration allows us to consider this Christian spirit of human sorrow and God's mercy as we hear the Word of the Lord in the story of the Ten Commandments, another sign of God's covenant with his chosen people. The Praise Center activity helps us put ourselves into a spirit of Lenten penance.

GREETING CENTER

"Be Happy!" or "Shepherd, Lead Me" are appropriate opening songs for today's Center Celebration.

Ask the participants to announce the one regulation at home which is the most difficult for them to keep. Discuss the reasons they might give for the difficulty they find in complying with the rule.

Lead a discussion about the purposes of rules. Help the younger participants realize that rules are made to keep peace, to help all people to live in love, to enable people to understand the behavior which is expected of them.

Ask them if they can think of any regulations which God gives to us. If (or when) they suggest the Ten Commandments, move right on to the Word Center.

WORD CENTER

Materials Needed: poster board or drawing tablet and marking pen; or overhead projector and grease pencil; or blackboard and chalk.

Ask the participants to name the Ten Commandments (or as many as they can). List the commandments on a poster board, a large drawing tablet, an overhead projector or blackboard as they are announced.

Then read the story of the giving of the Ten Commandments.

Exodus 20:1-17
God spoke and these were his words: "I am the Lord your God who brought you out of Egypt, where you were slaves. Worship no god but me.

"Do not make for yourselves images of anything in heaven or on earth or in the water under the earth. Do not bow down to any idol or worship it, because I am the Lord your God and I tolerate no rivals. I bring punishment on those who hate me and on their descendants down to the third and fourth generation. But I show my love to thousands of generations of those who love me and obey my laws.

"Do not use my name for evil purposes, because I, the Lord your God, will punish anyone who misuses my name.

"Observe the Sabbath and keep it holy. You have six days in which to do your work, but the seventh day is a day of rest dedicated to me. On that day no one is to work — neither you, your children, your slaves, your animals, nor the foreigners who live in your country. In six days, I the Lord made the earth, the sky, the seas, and everything in them, but on the seventh day I rested. That is why I, the Lord, blessed the Sabbath and made it holy.

"Respect your father and your mother, so that you may live a long time in the land that I am giving you."

"Do not commit murder.

"Do not commit adultery.

"Do not steal.

"Do not accuse anyone falsely.

"Do not desire another man's house; do not desire his wife, his slaves, his cattle, his donkeys, or anything else that he owns."

Discuss with the participants the commandments which they find more difficult to observe than others.

Continue your discussion with these or similar questions:
1. Why are they difficult?
2. Why are the commandments given to us?
3. What happens when we don't correctly observe the commandments?
4. How do we feel when we don't keep God's covenant?
5. What can we do when we realize that we have broken the covenant with our Lord as it is described in the law of the Ten Commandments?

A discussion about the Ten Commandments might lead to a rich sharing about the meaning of sin. Sin should be thought of as our deliberate turning from the way of the Lord. Sin is our choosing not to be a part of the covenant with the Lord. The Ten Commandments are given to us to help us realize God's plan.

Parents and teachers might take advantage of this opportunity to point out the common failings of everyday living at home and at school and how these failings might lead us to turn deliberately from the Lord's way of love.

PRAISE CENTER

The Lenten season has always been a time for Christians to repent of their sins and prepare themselves for the great joy of the Easter celebration free of guilt. The reading of the Exodus account at the Word Center provides an opportunity for us to proclaim our sorrow for our sins and to ask God for his forgiveness.

Lead the participants in a litany of mercy, using the three acclamations of the "Prayer For Mercy" song as indicated.

PRAYER FOR MERCY

Freely — Dick Hilliard

Leader: Lord, have mer-cy. All: Lord, have mer-cy.
Leader: Christ, have mer-cy. All: Christ, have mer-cy.
Leader: Lord, have mer-cy. All: Lord, have mer-cy.

For the times we have not obeyed your commandments, we pray
   1 Lord, have mercy
For your forgiveness, and love, we pray
   2 Christ, have mercy
For your strength and care in all we do, we pray
   3 Lord, have mercy

Lord, make us attentive to your commands as we pray
   1 Lord, have mercy
Christ, make us aware of your pardon as we pray
   2 Christ, have mercy
Lord, show us your kindness and favor as we pray
   3 Lord, have mercy

Father, write your commandments in our hearts.
   1 Lord, have mercy
Jesus, remind us of your loving ways.
   2 Christ, have mercy
Holy Spirit, heal us of our sins with your power.
   3 Lord, have mercy

Conclude with a Repetition Prayer, such as:

> Father, Almighty God
> have mercy on us
> forgive us our sins
> and bring us to everlasting life.
> Amen.

The commandments which were given to the people of Israel have been handed down to us through Scripture, through the life of Jesus and through the teaching of our church. Jesus summarized the Ten Commandments in two simple statements. Ask the participants if they can recall Jesus' twofold command to "love God and love your neighbor as yourself."

Invite the participants to suggest ways of loving God and loving one's neighbor. Discuss the many suggestions which will no doubt be mentioned.

"Bring Us Back" or "Call My Name" could be sung at the conclusion of this prayer activity.

CREATION CENTER

Love Circles

Materials Needed: 4" circles from construction paper, marking pens or crayons, scissors, and safety pins, or stick-on labels and marking pens or crayons.

Cut out circles, each 4" in diameter. Make one for each participant. Distribute one circle with a crayon or marking pen to each participant.

Instruct them to write the words, "Love God, Love All," on the circles. When finished, attach the love circles onto the participant's shirts or blouses.

Then return with the participants to the Sharing Center.

SHARING CENTER

Give the Witness Center activity assignment when the participants have returned here with their "Love Circles" pinned to their clothing. Conclude by singing the "Ballad of God's Love."

WITNESS CENTER

The commandments of the Lord can easily be forgotten in detail, but the summary of these commandments, as Jesus taught it, can be remembered in the simple words: "Love God, Love All." This loving way of life is our way of keeping the Lord's covenant.

Instruct the participants to wear their love circles during the week as a reminder of the commandments the Lord gives us to help us live in peace and love. Ask everyone to be aware of people's reactions when they see the circles being worn! Does their behavior change? Do they look puzzled?

BELIEVE THE WAY OF

2 Chronicles 36:14-17, 19-23
Psalm 137
Ephesians 2:4-10
John 3:14-21

Ephesians 2:4-10
John 3:1, 16-17

All of the traditions and customs of Lent might be summarized as an attempt to say, "I believe," to our loving God. Today's gospel reading of Jesus teaching Nicodemus about the way to gain life everlasting serves as an appropriate occasion for us to consider our own statement, "I believe." Is this profession of faith really at the heart of our Lenten celebrations and at the core of our covenant with the Lord?

GREETING CENTER

"Thank You, God" or "My Thankful Prayer" would be fitting songs to begin this celebration.

Recall the spirit of penance which is appropriate to the season of Lent. Ask the participants to share in a discussion of the ways in which they are demonstrating their sorrow for their sins this Lent.

WORD CENTER

Salvation is a gift to those who believe and trust in the way of the Lord. It is a gift to those who keep the Lord's covenant. This passage from the gospel of John in one of Jesus' direct teachings about the way to obtain the saving gift of the Lord.

John 3:1, 16-17
There was a Jewish leader named Nicodemus, who belonged to the party of the Pharisees. One night Jesus said to Nicodemus: God loved the world so much that he gave his only Son, so that everyone who believes in him may not die but have eternal life. For God did not send his Son into the world to be its judge, but to be its savior.

Repeat this short selection and talk with the participants about the purpose of Jesus' coming into the world.

Sing "Do You Know?"

Then ask them, "What must we do to be saved?" the answer is simple: Believe! But is believing, really believing, as simple as it might sound?

SALVATION

PRAISE CENTER

For us who believe in the Lord Jesus and who place our trust in the Spirit of God, salvation is the Father's gift. As our Lenten season reaches its midpoint, it is right that we reaffirm our faith in the God who saves.

Then ask one of the participants to read from St. Paul's letter to the Ephesians.

Ephesians 2:4-10

God's mercy is so abundant, and his love for us is so great, that while we were spiritually dead in our disobedience he brought us to life with Christ. It is by God's grace that you have been saved. It is not the result of your own efforts, but God's gift, so that no one can boast about it. God has made us what we are, and in our union with Christ Jesus he has created us for a life of good deeds, which he has already prepared for us to do.

Discuss the way in which we come to share in the saving life of the Lord. By opening ourselves to God's message and following the way shown us by the Lord Jesus, we are saved from the path of sinfulness and will come to share fully in the life of the Father. This is the great gift of God to us. This is the promise of God's covenant for we who believe.

Then everyone could sing "If You Believe," with the appropriate motions. Conclude with a Repetition Movement Prayer, such as:

Father, God (*raise arms heavenward*)

you protect us. (*cross arms upon chest*)

Jesus, Lord (*make a sign of the cross*)

you have saved us. (*bend over, hands reaching the floor*)

Holy Spirit (*stand, placing hands folded upon head*)

you now guide us. (*extend hands, palms down, in front of self*)

By our faith (*fold hands in prayer*)

bring us to life everlasting. (*raise arms heavenward*)

Amen. (*bow head*)

CREATION CENTER

"I Believe" Poster

Materials Needed: poster board and a marking pen.

Before the celebration, take a large piece of paper or poster board. At the top write a title reading "I Believe..." Make two columns under the title as illustrated.

Invite the participants to write in the left-hand column a concluding statement to the "I Believe..." title. Next to their fill-in phrases, let each one put his/her name. For larger groups, two or three posters with this heading and format will help speed up the activity and avoid impatience among some of the participants.

SHARING CENTER

Read aloud the concluding phrases to the "I Believe" statements which were written by the participants at the Creation Center. Discuss the different professions of faith. Do we share the same beliefs? Have we demonstrated our common faith in God's ways?

Give the Witness Center assignment and conclude by singing "If You Believe."

WITNESS CENTER

The gestures and sounds which accompany the "If You Believe" song are common daily means of communicating. Let each be assigned as a daily reminder of our faith.

Monday — clapping hands
Tuesday — "Hooray"
Wednesday — "Yes"
Thursday — standing up (!)
Friday — "I do!"
Saturday — "Amen"

Every time the position or word is experienced on the assigned day, each participant should be reminded of his/her response to the Lord of salvation: "I Believe!"

The leader might give an example of this application before the dismissal by asking, "Do you all have your 'kidsletter'?" The participants will respond, "Yes." The leader could then ask, "What did you think of when you said, 'Yes'?" This might help the younger children to associate the words and actions of the lyrics "outside" of the context of the song.

WRITTEN ON THEIR

Jeremiah 31:31-34
Psalm 51
Hebrews 5:7-9
John 12:20-33

Jeremiah 31:31-34

Hebrews 5:7-9

Prayer is at the heart of the Christian's life. It is also a recurrent theme of the Church's teaching and devotion during the season of Lent. It is fitting that this celebration should focus upon the spirit of prayer as an essential dimension of the covenant we make with the Father.

The reading from the book of the prophet Jeremiah concludes our Lenten theme of covenant with the Father. Jeremiah writes of the new covenant written on the hearts of God's people.

GREETING CENTER

"Rejoice, Be Glad" or "Praise the Lord, Rejoice and Sing" should be sung when the participants are ready to celebrate.

Then review with the participants the many aspects of the covenant between God and his people which have been the themes of our Lenten center celebrations this year (fidelity, willingness, law of love, faith).

Repeat verse 1 and the refrain of "Rejoice, Be Glad!" or "Praise the Lord, Rejoice and Sing" after your review, and discuss with the participants the importance of our welcoming God's covenant into our heart, into our treasured way of life.

WORD CENTER

One of the participants could be asked to read aloud his passage from the prophet Jeremiah.

Jeremiah 31:31-34

The Lord says, "The time is coming when I will make a new covenant with the people of Israel and with the people of Judah. It will not be like the old covenant that I made with their ancestors when I took them by the hand and led them out of Egypt. Although I was like a husband to them they did not keep the covenant. The new covenant that I will make with the people of Israel will be this: I will put my law within them and write it on their hearts. I will be their God, and they will be my people. None of them will have to teach his fellow countrymen to know the Lord, because all will know me, from the least to the greatest. I will forgive their sins and I will no longer remember their wrongs. I, the Lord, have spoken."

Continue the discussion inaugurated at the Greeting Center. What is the covenant of the Lord? Why would the Lord make a new covenant as described in the book of Jeremiah? What (who) will be the new covenant, the new bond of fidelity between the Father and his chosen people? Help the participants realize that Jesus is the sign of the Father's covenant with us.

CREATION CENTER

Paper Hearts

Materials Needed: heart stencils, red construction paper, scissors, marking pens or crayons, and some safety pins or masking tape.

The reading from Jeremiah speaks of the image of the covenant of God being written on the hearts of God's people. We are God's people. In our hearts we treasure the covenant of our God. We love the Lord Jesus.

Distribute red construction paper to each participant. With prepared stencils, allow the participants to trace hearts about six-inches in size. Cut out with scissors.

If stencils have not been prepared, simply instruct the participants to fold a six-inch piece of the red construction paper and freely cut a half-heart starting on the folded edge. Open the fold for the symmetrical, free-hand heart.

With marking pens or crayons, write the name "Jesus" on the paper hearts and fasten them to the participants' clothing.

While the participants are busy making their hearts, all could sing "My Thankful Prayer" or "You Are My People."

HEARTS

PRAISE CENTER

The leader should talk with the participants about the symbol of the heart just made at the Creation Center. The heart is a symbol for our love, for our affection, for our most treasured care. Jesus is our fondest gift from the Father and the one bringing the new covenant of love which the Father makes with us, his chosen people.

This selection from the letter to the Hebrews could be read aloud.

Hebrews 5:7-9

In his life on earth Jesus made his prayers and requests with loud cries and tears to God, who could save him from death. Because he was humble and devoted, God heard him. But even though he was God's Son, he learned through his sufferings to be obedient. When he was made perfect, he became the source of eternal salvation for all those who obey him.

Jesus' example of praying to the Father must become part of our own lives as we continue to treasure all that Jesus did in our hearts. Our Father is always ready to hear our prayer, our petitions and our praise.

Sing "Call My Name."

Ask the participants to suggest titles with which we might address God in prayer. Remember that when we give a title to God, we use it analogously. For example, when we speak of God as Father or Lord we are making a comparison. In this example, we are saying that God is like a father or lord to us. If your first grade feminist speaks up and suggests we call God our "Mother," she could be right!

Then invite one of the participants to offer a prayer in the name of the group gathered here today.

SHARING CENTER

The Church has always encouraged an increased spirit of prayer during the Lenten season. Discuss with the participants the importance of praying to the Father as Jesus did. Prayer was written on the heart of Jesus; it was very dear to his way of living. The participants should be encouraged to live lovingly in their covenant with the Father, letting prayer be the source of strength to live in love as did Jesus.

Give the Witness Center activity assignment and conclude by singing "Sing A Song of Praise" or "Ballad of God's Love."

WITNESS CENTER

The participants should be instructed to take their paper hearts home and pin them onto the rainbows made on the first Sunday of Lent. These two symbols are reminders of our covenant with God. When they see the heart each day, they should be reminded to take a few moments to pray to our God as did Jesus, our treasured savior.

DON'T TEMPT ME!

Deuteronomy 26:4-10
Psalm 91
Romans 10:8-13
Luke 4:1-13

For the young person, the divinity of Jesus is such a marvelous and fascinating reality that it easily overshadows the fact of Jesus' humanity. Today's gospel passage places Jesus in a characteristically human situation: his temptation by the Devil in the desert. This gospel story provides an appropriate theme for our Lenten season as we ourselves concentrate upon ways to free our lives from the presence of the evil spirit and grow closer in our unity with the Spirit of God.

The Witness Center activity is an ancient religious practice which has been handed down through our tradition as a means of becoming more virtuous. It is a common Lenten practice among Christians which should be encouraged among the participants of this celebration.

GREETING CENTER

Begin this Lenten celebration with the "Promenade Song."

Discuss with the participants the human experience of being alone. You might ask such questions as:

1. Have you ever chosen to be alone? Why? Where were you or where did you go?
2. Were you ever left alone? On purpose? Accidentally?
3. How did you feel when no one was with you? Frightened? Peaceful?
4. Did you feel that God was with you? Or were you easily tempted by the devil?

WORD CENTER

Today's bible selection is a gospel story about Jesus. It tells of a time when Jesus was alone in the desert. Describe the desolation and barrenness of the desert for those who have never experienced a journey into the desert.

Luke 4:1-13

Jesus returned from the Jordan full of the Holy Spirit and was led by the Spirit into the desert, where he was tempted by the Devil for forty days. In all that time he ate nothing, so that he was hungry when it was over.

The Devil said to him, "If you are God's Son, order this stone to turn into bread."

But Jesus answered, "The scripture says, 'Man cannot live on bread alone.'"

Then the Devil took him up and showed him in a second all the kingdoms of the world. "I will give you all this power and all this wealth," the Devil told him. "It has all been handed over to me, and I can give it to anyone I choose. All this will be yours, then, if you worship me."

Jesus answered, "The scripture says, 'Worship the Lord your God and serve only him!'"

Then the Devil took him to Jerusalem and set him on the highest point of the Temple, and said to him, "If you are God's Son, throw yourself down from here. For the scripture says, 'God will order his angels to take care of you.' It also says, 'They will hold you up with their hands so that not even your feet will be hurt on the stones.'"

But Jesus answered, "The scripture says, 'Do not put the Lord your God to the test.'"

When the Devil finished tempting Jesus in every way, he left him for a while.

At the conclusion of the gospel reading, ask the participants about Jesus' temptation.

1. What happened to Jesus in the desert?
2. Did Jesus do as the Devil suggested?

If the participants suggest that Jesus could easily overcome the devil's temptings because of his divinity, be sure to remind them that Jesus was human, too, like us. How was Jesus able to turn from the devil's ways? Because of his never-ending faithfulness to the will of his Father.

PRAISE CENTER

Like Jesus, we are often tempted by the devil to do the wrong thing. Sometimes we are tempted when we are alone and sometimes even when we're with others. But unlike Jesus, we occasionally give in to the temptations of the devil and we sin against God.

Lead the participants in a simple litany of reconciliation allowing each to pray a phrase of repentance. After each phrase is prayed, all should join in the short refrain: "Lord, I Am Sorry" or "Prayer For Mercy." An example might be:

-for saying bad things about others,

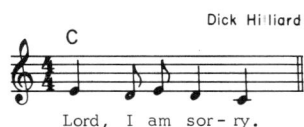

Dick Hilliard

Lord, I am sor-ry.

-hitting my brothers and sisters,

-for being late for sports practice,

-for playing longer than I was supposed to play,

Times when we're alone can be frequent occasions for temptations and loneliness. These times can become an opportunity for us to ask, "Where are you, God?"

As Christians we know that God is always and everywhere present to us. Conclude this Praise Center activity with a Repetition Movement Prayer to God for times when we're alone:

Loving Father, *(raise arms above head, pointing upward)*
when I am sad *(frown)*
and lonely, *(arms hugging self)*
let me know that you are with me. *(raise arms above head and bring down to a crisscrossed position upon chest)*
Put a smile on my face *(smile)*
and let me shout with joy *(cup hands at mouth)*
and sing praise to you. *(raise arms above head)*
Amen. *(bow heads)*

CREATION CENTER

Drawings
Materials Needed: paper and crayons.

Let the participants illustrate an occasion when they were not alone. Suggest, perhaps, an event like a birthday, a school party, a holiday or outing, or meal time. Encourage the inclusion of some sort of "good," such as smiles of happiness, in the illustration. Set a time limit so that this activity is not too prolonged.

SHARING CENTER

Allow each participant to describe briefly the illustration which they had drawn at the Creation Center. Hopefully many will have illustrated occasions when people shared food at a birthday party, on a holiday or at a meal. Highlight the role of food as a sign of celebration.

Then, repeat the opening verses of Luke's gospel proclaimed at the Word Center (Luke 4:1-2). Emphasize not the act of being tempted by the devil, but rather Jesus' fasting ("he ate nothing").

Discuss the meaning of fasting as an act of penance and prayer. Birthday parties, holidays and meals, as illustrated at the Creation Center, would not be the same without food.

Give the Witness Center assignment and conclude with a song such as "Thank You, God."

WITNESS CENTER

Suggest that each participant give up a favorite snack food during Lent as a form of fasting and prayer. Perhaps it will be gum for some, oatmeal cookies for others or peanut butter for a few. Whatever it is, let those "craving moments" be a time for us to say, "Thank you, God, for all your gifts to me!"

TAKE UP THE CROSS

Genesis 15:5-12, 17-18
Psalm 27
Philippians 3:17-4:1
Luke 9:28-36   Luke 9:23, 28-32, 34-36

The role of suffering in our lives can be mysterious to us unless we understand it as part of the promise of the resurrection. Jesus died on the cross to demonstrate that suffering can be transformed into new life.

Today's celebration allows us to hear the story of the Transfiguration of the Lord and gives us the opportunity to discuss the transformation which is promised to those who take up the cross of the Lord. The Witness Center activity encourages us to take active involvement in visiting the sick, aged and infirm, a practice which has marked Christian charity since the early church. Yes, Lord, we do believe you live and care for us!

For Parish Programs
and in the Religious Education Classroom
Before the celebration, the leaders should look over the Witness Center activity suggestions for one best suited to their situation.

GREETING CENTER

Repeat the short refrain, "Believe" (p. 97), several times as the opening song for today's celebration.

The leader should then ask the participants about their attempts at fasting since the last celebration. Did it cause them pain of any kind? Unhappiness? Hunger? Temptation? Ask them to describe the plight of the poor, especially the suffering they endure because of their hunger. Can their suffering be changed? How?

WORD CENTER

Scripture commentators doubt that the event of the Lord's transfiguration happened exactly as described in the gospel selection from Luke 9:28-36. It is believed, however, that the evangelists wrote of the transfiguration event as a prelude to understanding the meaning of the resurrection mystery. Thus, the story of the transfiguration of the Lord is a literary form which describes the triumph of transformed life through suffering and troubles.

The story of the Transfiguration of the Lord could be read aloud by the leader or one of the participants.
Luke 9:23, 28-32, 34-36

Jesus said to his disciples, "If anyone wants to come with me, he must forget himself, take up his cross everyday, and follow me.

About a week after he had said this, Jesus took Peter, John and James with him and went up a hill to pray. While he was praying, his face changed its appearance, and his clothes became dazzling white. Suddenly two men were there talking with him. They were Moses and Elijah, who appeared in heavenly glory and talked with Jesus about the way in which he would soon fulfill God's purpose by dying in Jerusalem. Peter and his companions were sound asleep, but they woke up and saw Jesus' glory and the two men who were standing with him.

While he was still speaking, a cloud appeared and covered them with its shadow; and the disciples were afraid as the cloud came over them. A voice said from the cloud, "This is my Son, whom I have chosen — listen to him!"

When the voice stopped, there was Jesus all alone. The disciples kept quiet about all this and told no one at that time anything they had seen.

Discuss with the participants Jesus' statement at the beginning of the passage. What does it mean to "take up the cross of the Lord?" This is an image we use which suggests that our sufferings and troubles are much like the pain which Jesus endured carrying the cross to Calvary. Jesus is teaching that we, too, must be willing to share in the pain of the world.

Allow time to sing "Carry The Cross" (p. 135).

But what happens to Jesus in the story of the Transfiguration? Jesus is transformed, made dazzling white, made fresh and bright when he speaks of his suffering and death. This should give us hope that we, too, will be made new, made better, because of the pains which we experience in our lives. Perhaps we won't recognize any change or improvement right away. But we are promised new life everlasting.

This is part of the mystery of suffering and part of the tale of the Transfiguration. We must heed the announcement in the gospel: "This is my Son, whom I have chosen — listen to him!" If we listen to Jesus, take up his cross and follow him, then we will share in eternal life.

OF THE LORD

CREATION CENTER

Sick Lists

Materials Needed: pencils and writing paper for each participant.

Distribute a pencil and sheet of paper to each participant. Each should be instructed to list their friends, relatives, and other people they know who are sick, lonely, troubled or suffering in any way. With smaller children, the leader could write a group list of names suggested by the participants. Ask the participants to also name the hospitals and rest homes in their area.

PRAISE CENTER

From its earliest beginnings, the church has always placed a special emphasis upon praying for the needs of the sick and infirm. Invite the participants to read the lists of friends and relatives which they compiled at the Creation Center. After every two or three participants have read their listings, all should sing "Father, Care" (p. 44).

Conclude with a Repetition Prayer, such as:

Father
fill our hearts
with love for one another.
Hear our prayers and petitions
for our relatives and friends.
Give them health
to do your will in love.
Amen.

SHARING CENTER

Ask the participants to describe a hospital, or a convalescent or retirement home. Help them to realize the value of visiting the sick and infirm and also of praying for their needs. Let them recall the names of the hospitals and rest homes which they announced at the Creation Center.

Give the Witness Center activity assignment and conclude with a song, such as "Thank You, God" or "Carry The Cross."

WITNESS CENTER

Families might make a special outing today or during the week to visit relatives or friends who are sick and unable to go out of doors.

School groups could arrange for a visit to a hospital or rest home during the week. They could sing songs for the patients or prepare an afternoon treat approved by the administrators.

All of us should be encouraged to pray daily for the care of the sick and suffering during the coming week. Let us also be grateful to God for blessing us with good health.

MERCY FIG-URES!

Exodus 3:1-8, 13-15
Psalm 103
1 Corinthians 10:1-6, 10-12
Luke 13:1-9   Luke 13:6-9

The parable of the barren fig tree is the bible story which lies at the root of today's celebration theme of the Father's mercy to us. A Scottish tradition is suggested as the Creation Center activity and will require some preparation of grocery items. Some of the recipes will be better appreciated if they are made a day in advance. Select the one which is most convenient for your group.

GREETING CENTER

"The Promenade Song" or "The Lord Blesses Me!" could be sung after the participants have settled for the start of today's celebration.

Ask the participants if any one has ever planted a tree, shrub, or flowering plant in a garden. If so, let them describe the preparation of soil and the care and cultivation which is necessary to help the plant take root and grow.

Then, ask if the plant prospered or died. If it died, ask the participants to describe the reasons for its death. What must be done to a dead plant? It must be removed!

If none of the participants can draw from their own experience to make this activity flow, simply create a story of a gardener who planted a tree that eventually died.

WORD CENTER

Materials needed: a fresh fig or picture of a fig.

Hold up a fig and ask the participants to name it, if they can. No doubt some of the participants will not be familiar with the fruit of the fig tree.

Then tell the Parable of the Unfruitful Fig Tree from the gospel.

Luke 13:6-9

Then Jesus told them this parable: "There was once a man who had a fig tree growing in his vineyard. He went looking for figs on it but found none. So he said to his gardener, 'Look, for three years I have been coming here looking for figs on this fig tree, and I haven't found any. Cut it down. Why should it go on using up the soil?' But the gardener answered, 'Leave it alone, sir, just one more year; I will dig around it and put in some fertilizer. Then if the tree bears figs next year, so much the better; if not, then you can have it cut down.'"

Some scripture commentators suggest that the three years mentioned in the parable refers to the time of Jesus' ministry. This is an hypothesis which makes for an interesting interpretation of the tale. All commentators agree, however, that this story told by Jesus is a tale of God's mercy, especially as symbolized in the digging and manuring of the tree. Jesus is teaching us that we are always given another chance in the sight of the Lord. We are never left to die.

Discuss this theme of the Father's mercy with the participants at the conclusion of the proclamation. We are like the fig tree planted in the soil of God's love. Should we refuse his care he will be ready to re-cultivate our love for Him. Jesus seems to indicate, however, that there might be a time when the fig tree must be removed — when it is completely rotted. Will we ever turn completely away from the Lord, becoming rotten in his sight? Can we be undeserving of his mercy?

PRAISE CENTER

With confidence in God's mercy, pray an Act of Contrition after sufficient silence for the participants to reflect upon their sinfulness.

Act of Contrition
Loving Father
I am sorry for my sins.
I am sorry for offending you.
You are deserving of all my love.
I promise, Father
with your help,
to sin no more
and to avoid all times of sin.
Amen.

Then sing ''Prayer of Mercy'' or ''Father, I Adore You'' at the conclusion of the prayer.

CREATION CENTER

In Scotland a Lenten custom has grown whereby fig pudding or cakes or candies are made to help children recall the parable of the barren fig tree. Today's bible reading suggests an appropriate observance of this Scottish Lenten tradition.

Choose a recipe which can be prepared by the participants. If time does not allow for complete preparation and serving, simply distribute fresh figs for all to eat later.

Fig Puffs
¾ cup dried figs, chopped
1 cup sifted flour
1½ teaspoons baking powder
¼ teaspoon baking soda
½ teaspoon salt
1 egg, well beaten
½ cup milk
¾ teaspoon grated lemon rind
1 tablespoon melted butter

Figs should be soaked overnight. When ready to use, drain thoroughly and chop or cut into small pieces. Sift dry ingredients together; combine beaten egg and milk and stir into dry mixture. Add chopped figs and grated lemon rind. Stir in the melted butter. Mix well. Drop by teaspoons into hot deep fat (360°) and fry until golden brown. Drain on absorbent paper. Serve with syrup. Serves 6.

Fig Candy
2 cups dried figs
½ pound dipping chocolate
2 cups cut nuts

Immerse figs in boiling water 10 minutes; dry thoroughly; clip stems; grind. Blend with nuts and pat into a thin square. Spread with half of melted chocolate, cool, turn square over and repeat. Cut into small pieces.

Fig Pudding
½ pound crystallized ginger
1½ pounds figs
2 cups sugar
5 cups water
½ teaspoon powdered ginger
½ ounce (1 tablespoon) granulated gelatin
½ cup cold water
whipped cream

Cut the crystallized ginger and figs into tiny pieces. Dissolve the granulated sugar in the water, and add the powdered ginger, the crystallized ginger and the figs. Place all in a double boiler and simmer slowly all day. The entire mass must form a soft pulp so that the ingredients will scarcely be recognized. Soften the gelatin in the cold water and stir into the mixture while hot. Serve ice cold with whipped cream.

SHARING CENTER

The Parable of the Unfruitful Fig Tree should be a reminder to us of the mercy which our loving Father gives to all who trust in him.

Celebrate this parable by feasting on the fresh figs (or eating the fig products later in the day as a snack or dessert).

Give the Witness Center activity assignment and sing ''Shepherd, Lead Me'' or ''My Thankful Prayer.''

WITNESS CENTER

If the participants can help water or hoe around a fig tree during the week, this would be a fitting reminder of the parable celebrated today. If it is not possible, simply encourage them to ask God for his mercy in their daily prayers during the week.

WELCOME BACK!

Joshua 5:9, 10-12
Psalm 34
2 Corinthians 5:17-21
Luke 15:1-3, 11-32   Luke 15:11-32

The gospel for today is the familiar story of the Lost Son returning to his loving Father. It provides us with the theme of our own need to return to the loving way of our Father because of our sinfulness.

The theme of returning home is also part of the centuries-old English Lenten custom of Mothering Sunday celebrated every fourth Sunday of the pre-Easter season. This custom becomes the Witness Center activity for this celebration and could allow for a touching family outing.

*For Parish Programs
and in the Religious Education Classroom*

Suggest that the participants request their parents to help them with the Witness Center activity as described. Where distance prohibits such an outing or when other circumstances prevent such an activity, suggest that the participants write to obtain their baptismal certificates from their "Mother Church."

In the Family Home

Families should make the Witness Center activity a special outing later in the day following this celebration, if possible.

GREETING CENTER

Begin this celebration with the song, "Shepherd, Lead Me."

Then ask the participants if they have ever been lost. Let them tell their stories in response to your question. Be sure to explore the emotions they might have felt while lost: fear? loneliness? happiness? freedom?

Then ask if anyone has ever deliberately left home, perhaps running away. If so, discuss this event and the feelings related to it before moving to the Word Center.

WORD CENTER

Materials Needed: puppet stage; backdrop; puppets of a father, two sons and a servant.

Prepare your puppet stage for the telling of the story of the Prodigal Son and the Loving Father from Luke's gospel 15:11-32. A simple landscape drawing would be an appropriate backdrop for the stage. Follow the directions written into the script. If some of the participants are selected to present this show, it might be easier if just the storyline is presented and they are allowed to tell the story in their own words and actions.

THE LOST SON — LOVING FATHER

(A puppet show telling of Luke 15:11-32.)

Narrator: *One time Jesus told this story.*

(Enter Father and sons.)

There was once a man who had two sons. The younger one said to him,

Younger Son: *Father, give me my share of the property now.*

Narrator: *So the man divided his property between his two sons. (Father distributes property deeds from pocket.)*

After a few days the younger son sold his part of the property and left home with the money. (Son begins to leave with a bag of money.)

(While moving toward the puppet stage wings he dances merrily, throwing coins.)

He went to a country far away, where he wasted his money in reckless living. He spent everything he had.

Then a severe famine spread over that country and he was left without a thing. (The son comes to an abrupt halt; he leaves crying.)

(He comes back on stage with a toy shovel in hand. The sound of pigs comes from backstage. He looks down at his feet, where the audience cannot see, to indicate the location of the pigs.)

So he went to work for one of the citizens of that country, who sent him out to his farm to take care of the pigs. He wished he could fill himself with the bean pods the pigs ate, but no one gave him anything to eat. At last he came to his senses and said,

Younger Son (stands): *All my father's hired workers have more than they can eat. And here I am about to starve! I will get up and go to my father and say, "Father, I have sinned against God and against you. I am no longer fit to be called your son; treat me as one of your hired workers."*

I WAS BAPTIZED AT ST MARK'S

Narrator: *So he got up and started back to his father. (He puts the shovel over his shoulder and exits.)*

(Enter Father, waving.)

He was still a long way from home when his father saw him. His heart was filled with pity, and he ran, threw his arms around his son, and kissed him. (Father greets son.)

Younger Son: *Father, I have sinned against God and against you. I am no longer fit to be called your son.*

Narrator: *But the father called to his servants.*

Father (speaks to offstage): *Hurry! Bring the best robe and put it on him. Put a ring on his finger and shoes on his feet. Then go and get the prize calf and kill it, and let us celebrate with a feast! For this son of mine was dead, but now he is alive; he was lost, but now he has been found.*

Narrator: *And the feasting began.*

(Father and son go offstage; make joyful sounds.)

(The older son enters.)

In the meantime the older son was out in the field. On his way back, when he came close to the house, he heard the music and dancing.

So he summoned one of the servants and asked him,

(Enter servant.)

Older Son: *What's going on?*

(The older son gets angry.)

Servant: *Your brother has come back home and your father has killed the prize calf because he got him back safe and sound. (The servant exits.)*

(Father greets the older son.)

Narrator: *The older son was so angry he would not go into the house; so his father came out and begged him to come in.*

But he spoke back to his father.

Older Son: *Look, all these years I have worked for you like a slave, and I have never disobeyed your orders. What have you given me? Not even a goat for me to have a feast with my friends! But this son of yours wasted all your property and when he comes back home you kill the prize calf for him!*

(Father puts his arm around his son.)

Father: *My son, you are always here with me, and everything I have is yours. But we had to celebrate and be happy, because your brother was dead, but now he is alive; he was lost, but now he has been found.*

At the conclusion of the story, ask the participants to tell who their favorite character is. Help them see the repentant heart of the prodigal son and the forgiving spirit of the loving father.

Jesus' parable is told to remind us that we, too, can repent and return to the open and trusting heart of our father. Our God is always ready to welcome us back to this home when we've lost our way.

PRAISE CENTER

The repentant spirit of reconciliation which pervades the season of Lent is captured perfectly in the story of the Prodigal Son and Loving Father. Let us be mindful in quiet prayer of our running away from the path of the Lord. Let us also be comforted knowing that our Father is ready to receive us back to himself. All we need do is ask for his mercy.

After sufficient quiet for individual recollection, everyone should sing together, "Bring Us Back."

SHARING CENTER

A charming custom originated in England, where, on the 4th Sunday of Lent, boys and girls who lived away from home were allowed to go back to the Mother Church in which they were baptized or brought up. They carried gifts with them to place in front of the altar. Before the Reformation it was a cherished festival, the one break in the rigors of Lent, a day on which games and feasting were permissible. In the outlying hamlets, parishioners of the local mission journeyed to the Mother Church of the parish to present their offerings and attend the Sunday Mass.

This is the fourth Sunday of Lent and the theme of the story of the Prodigal Son and Loving Father seems appropriate to the custom of Mothering Sunday. Explain this custom to the participants. To prepare them for a visit to the church in which they were baptized, gather at the Creation Center.

CREATION CENTER

Baptismal Record

Materials Needed: poster board and marking pen; or blackboard and chair.

On a large piece of poster paper or on a blackboard, list the name of each participant. Next to each name list the church or parish of that participant's baptism, if he/she is able to tell. If some do not know where they were baptized, list the city of their birth.

WITNESS CENTER

Today, or during the next week, each participant should be encouraged to visit the church of his/her baptism with his/her family according to the English custom of Mothering Sunday. The most special gift of all (ourselves) could be presented before the Lord upon the visit. When the family gathers in the sanctuary of the "Mother Church," all could say a prayer together or sing (or recite) "Keep Us Close."

DON'T BLAME ME!

Isaiah 43:16-21
Psalm 126
Philippians 3:8-14   Philippians 3:12-14
John 8:1-11   John 8:1-11

It is part of our human nature that makes it easy for us to point out the weaknesses of others and to neglect to examine our own failings. Lent is a time when we should make every effort to reform our lives.

The story of the woman caught in adultery is the central bible story for this celebration. It will help to understand the duty of the Christian when it it combined with St. Paul's image of the race to be won (in his letter to the Philippians).

Suggestion for Celebration:

The Creation Center activity might require more space than your room or home can provide. Consider alternative locations for this activity, if necessary.

GREETING CENTER

Sing "Be Happy!" when the participants have settled down for this celebration.

Then ask the participants if any of them has ever been caught in a group which was doing something wrong. Ask some to discuss the event or events in which they were caught. Who took the blame? Did some members of the group blame other members? Did everyone take responsibility for the wrongdoing? Was there a punishment given to the whole group? Or just to those who accepted the blame? Was it fair that not all in the group were punished?

WORD CENTER

The gospel story of the woman caught in adultery should be pantomimed spontaneously by the participants as it is read aloud by an adult. The word "sinning" has been substituted into the text for the term "adultery" so that the questions of younger children do not dominate this lesson.

Select participants to play the parts of Jesus, the woman, a crowd and some pharisees as the story is read aloud.

John 8:1-11

Jesus went to the Mount of Olives. Early the next morning he went back to the Temple. All the people gathered around him, and he sat down and began to teach them. The teachers of the Law and the Pharisees brought in a woman who had been caught sinning, and they made her stand before them all. "Teacher," they said to Jesus, "this woman was caught in the very act of sinning. In our Law Moses commanded that such a woman must be stoned to death. Now, what do you say?" Jesus bent over and wrote on the ground with his finger. As they stood there asking him questions, he straightened up and said to them, "Whichever one of you has committed no sin may throw the first stone at her." Then he bent over again and wrote on the ground. When they heard this, they all left, one by one, the older ones first. Jesus was left alone, with the woman still standing there. He straightened up and said to her, "Where are they? Is there no one left to condemn you?"

"No one, sir," she answered.

"Well, then," Jesus said, "I do not condemn you either. Go, but do not sin again."

Let the major actors describe the feelings they experienced as they played the parts of the woman, the spokesman of the pharisees and Jesus. Who is trying to blame whom? How does Jesus react to the situation? Does anyone admit to never having sinned? What instructions does Jesus give to the woman at the end of the story?

PRAISE CENTER

Jesus' teaching about blaming others for sin should be a harsh reminder to us all that we are to be more concerned with our own sinfulness and need for conversion than with casting judgment on others.

Mindful of the times when we have used people in order that we might look better in the eyes of others, let us pause and be sorry for our sins.

Sing "Prayer for Mercy" or "Bring Us Back" as a response to the silent prayer.

CREATION CENTER

Finish Lines

Materials Needed: rope, string or twine, and scissors.

Let the participants cut 2 or 3 six-foot lengths of small rope, string or twine.

Select 2 or 3 groups of participants for a racing contest. Let 2 participants in each group stretch the rope or string pieces as though for a finishing line. Pair the other participants for a race. When the racing contests are completed, gather at the Sharing Center.

SHARING CENTER

This selection from one of Paul's letters should be read aloud.

Philippians 3:12-14

I do not claim that I have already succeeded or have already become perfect. I keep striving to win the prize for which Christ Jesus has already won me to himself. Of course, my brothers, I really do not think that I have already won it; the one thing I do, however, is to forget what is behind me and do my best to reach what is ahead. So I run straight toward the goal in order to win the prize, which is God's call through Christ Jesus to the life above.

Let the participants compare their own racing contests to the image in Paul's letter. Help them to realize that it is more important for each of us to be concerned about how well we are running our race (how well we are preparing to win everlasting life by our love for others) than in placing blame on others or by pointing our others' sinfulness.

Give the Witness Center assignment and conclude by singing the "Ballad of God's Love" or "Let Me Lord."

WITNESS CENTER

Materials Needed: more rope, string or twine, and scissors.

Cut the strings or ropes into smaller lengths and distribute one to each of the participants. Ask them to place the string lengths at home in a location which they will notice every day. When they see the piece of rope or string, they should ask themselves, "How well am I running the Christian race?"

FINISH LINE

HOSANNA TO OUR KING!

Matthew 21:1-11
Mark 11:1-10
John 12:12-16
Luke 19:28-40   Luke 19:28-38

The Procession With Palms

The celebration of Palm Sunday is a favorite rite for many Christians. Its ritual before the Eucharistic celebration is rich in imagery and meaning. However, the focus of the day should be upon the reading of the passion narrative of our Lord.

This celebration highlights one of the events which took place at Jerusalem before Jesus' arrest. It is best celebrated before Palm Sunday itself, so that the central importance of the Passion reading may be preserved at Palm Sunday Mass. Alternative gospel tellings of the entry into Jerusalem are proclaimed in each cycle. The passage from Luke is selected for this Center Celebration.

*For Parish Programs
and in the Religious Education Classroom*

School and parish groups should be instructed the week before to bring olive branches or palm leaves to this celebration.

In the Family Home

Families should celebrate this event on the evening before Palm Sunday, when they might join the the larger community for the blessing of palms and reading of the Passion narrative at Mass. Pick palm or olive branches ahead of time for use during his celebration. Families will also enjoy the alternative Witness Center activity.

GREETING CENTER

Gather together with your tree branches. Teach the song "Hosanna" for use later at the Word Center. Explain that today's celebration is about Jesus' entry into Jerusalem. Ask the participants to describe this event in Jesus' life in their own words.

Then, select participants to dramatize the story which will be proclaimed at the Word Center. You'll need a Jesus, two disciples, two to play as a colt (use a sheet to drape over them), the colt's owner, and a crowd.

WORD CENTER

Read the passage from Luke's gospel to the participants. Sing "Hosanna" instead of reading the last verses of this story.

Luke 19:28-38

Jesus went on to Jerusalem ahead of his disciples. As he came near Bethphage and Bethany at the Mount of Olives, he sent two disciples ahead with these instructions: "Go to the village there ahead of you; as you go in, you will find a colt tied up that has never been ridden. Untie it and bring it here. If someone asks you why you are untying it, tell him that the Master needs it."

They went on their way and found everything just as Jesus had told them. As they were untying the colt, its owner said to them, "Why are you untying it?"

"The Master needs it," they answered, and they took the colt to Jesus. Then they threw their cloaks over the animal and helped Jesus get on. As he rode on, people spread their cloaks on the road.

When he came near Jerusalem, at the place where the road went down the Mount of Olives, the large crowd of his disciples began to thank God and praise him in loud voices for all the great things that they had seen: "Blessed be the king who comes in the name of the Lord!" (Sing "Hosanna!")

Lead the participants to the Creation Center to prepare for the dramatization of this gospel story.

CREATION CENTER

Player Masks

Materials Needed: butcher paper cut in 10-inch squares, scissors, crayons, masking tape, and a sheet for the colt.

Cut butcher paper into 10-inch squares. Let the participants draw the faces of the characters they will play in the Palm Sunday drama upon their 10-inch square. Even the crowd can draw faces for use as masks. Let the back-end of the colt make a tail to be taped to the sheet covering!

Explain the meaning associated with the use of palms and olive branches as the participants create their masks:

The gospel records that on Palm Sunday people took branches of palm trees and olive trees and went forth to meet Jesus. Jerusalem was filled with the largest crowd of the year because it was the occasion of the Passover celebration. In Matthew's gospel we are told that the happy people, many of whom knew Jesus because of his teachings, made a special event of His arrival, cheering and laying down palm branches for Him to ride over.

WORD CENTER

Return to the Word Center for the dramatization of the entry into Jerusalem. Let the participants tell the story as they play their parts with masks and tree branches. If necessary, help them recall the different events by referring to the gospel passage above.

After the dramatization, let the participants talk about the different characters in the story. How did each one act and feel!

PRAISE CENTER

Palm Sunday is a happy occasion for us and we should give glory to God for sending us his Son, Jesus, our savior and king.

All could pray the Glory to the Father and then sing "Glory to God."

Glory to the Father

Glory to the Father!
Glory to Jesus, His Son!
Glory to the Holy Spirit!
Glory to God forever and ever!
Amen.

SHARING CENTER

Many customs have grown through the years for celebrating the event of Jesus' entry into Jerusalem. One custom which developed early in the church's formation is the custom of bringing palm or olive branches to church for a blessing before the entrance procession. The custom has been altered in recent centuries as now the palms are usually received at church after the blessing. Ask the participants to bring the palm and olive branches they used today to the parish services for the priest's blessing.

Give the Witness Center assignment and sing "Hosanna!"

WITNESS CENTER

After the palms and olive branches are blessed at church on Palm Sunday, they should be placed at home, perhaps behind a crucifix or hung separately on a wall, as a reminder that Jesus is our savior and king. We should give him glory and praise!

Pax Cakes

Another custom which families might enjoy as a Witness Center activity is the tradition of the "Pax Cake." From the Latin word for peace, the Pax Cake originated in England among neighbors. People who had quarreled during the previous year met and ate the tiny Palm Sunday cakes together. They said, "Peace," to each other and tried to understand each other's problems. Originally the idea was that they did not want to go to their Easter Communion with anger or hatred in their hearts.

Pax cakes were small, individual cakes, much like our cupcakes. Invite your neighbors over for dessert on Palm Sunday evening. Why not have cupcakes?

HOSANNA!

"Hosanna!" was the cry of children in Jerusalem welcoming Jesus during his triumphant entry into the city. This is a lively processional song for celebration of Palm Sunday.

Dick Hilliard
arr. Rev. John H. Olivier, S.S.

Lively

Ho-san-na! Ho-san-na! Ho-san - na! Blest is he who comes as

king._____ Ho-san-na! Ho-san-na! Ho san - na! He comes in the name_____

___of the Lord._____ Give praise as we sing. Let our

voi-ces ring Ho- san - na! to the Lord._____ Give glo-ry

as we bring bran-ches for the king. Ho-san-na! to the Lord._____

Songs For Celebrating The Easter Triduum

Title/Composer	Modern Liturgy Vol:No	Gather 'Round Page	Gather 'Round, Too! Page	The Lord Blesses Me Page	My Heart is Happy
ALLELUIA Dick Hilliard				138	
CARRY THE CROSS Dick Hilliard				135	
EVERYBODY SING ALLELUIA Sr. Roberta McGrath	2:2	63			
FILL OUR NEED Dick Hilliard				131	
GLORY TO GOD Dick Hilliard					X
IF YOU BELIEVE Dick Hilliard					X
THE LORD BLESSES ME! Dick Hilliard	4:6		89	28	X
PRAISE THE LORD, ALLELUIA Paul F. Page	4:6		87		
PRAISE THE LORD, REJOICE AND SING Sr. Sheila Ann Dougherty	4:3		73		
PRAYER FOR MERCY Dick Hilliard				109	
SHEPHERD, LEAD ME Dick Hilliard					X
THIS IS THE DAY Dick Hilliard				139	

INTRODUCTION TO THE EASTER TRIDUUM

The ritual celebrations of the Easter Triduum, the three days before Easter Sunday, compose the high point of the Christian liturgical calendar. Beginning with the Mass of the Lord's Supper on the evening of Holy Thursday, the Church celebrates the Passover Feast of the Lord.

Each of the ceremonies of the Triduum is rich in symbol and message. Recalling the Israelite Exodus and the first Passover, Holy Thursday memorializes the last meal Jesus shared with his disciples, and presents for us the epitome of Jesus' preaching in the story of his washing the disciples' feet. Good Friday's solemn observance of the passion and death of our Lord calls us to ponder deeply the mystery of salvation. The Service of Light and the Liturgy of the Word on Holy Saturday evening prepare us for the Easter Vigil celebration of Christian baptism during which we renew our profession of faith in the joy of Easter Day: the Lord is risen!

The Center Celebrations for the Easter Triduum focus upon some of these deeply-rooted Christian themes and prepare young children and families for the most important community celebrations of the year.

May your prayerful gatherings lead you to recognize the Lord's blessing upon you in the Passover Feast of his death and resurrection.

OUR PASSOVER FESTIVAL

From the Mass of the Lord's Supper

Exodus 12:1-8, 11-14   Exodus 12:1, 3-4, 6-8, 11-14

Psalm 116   Psalm 116:12-14

1 Corinthians 11:23-26

John 13:1-15   John 13:1-5, 12-17

The Last Supper was a Passover meal in the Jewish tradition of Jesus' day. This center celebration adapts the Seder (Sá-dĕr) meal, the Passover dinner, into a remembrance of the festival celebrated by our Jewish forebears. It is prepared to help young children and families understand the roots of our eucharistic celebrations. Participation in the evening Mass of the Lord's Supper with the parish community would be most fitting after this center celebration.

For Parish Programs
and in the Religious Education Classroom

This celebration describes a Seder observance in the family home. It is easily adapted to classroom and parish program settings. Simply prepare your own table for the meal as suggested in the Praise Center activity.

In the Family Home

Families might choose to make this celebration of the Seder their evening meal on Holy Thursday. If so, increase the portions of food which comprise the Seder menu. It might also be fitting to invite a neighboring family or relatives to share this Seder event.

GREETING CENTER

Sing "Shepherd, Lead Me," especially verse 2, when the participants have come together to celebrate.

Then, ask one of the participants to read the account of the Passover described in the book of Exodus:

Exodus 12:1, 3-4, 6-8, 11-14

The Lord spoke to Moses and Aaron in Egypt:

"Give these instructions to the whole community of Israel: On the tenth day of this month each man must choose either a lamb or a young goat for his household. If his family is too small to eat a whole animal, he and his next-door neighbor may share an animal, in proportion to the number of people and the amount that each person can eat. Then, on the evening of the fourteenth day of the month, the whole community of Israel will kill the animals. The people are to take some of the blood and put it on the doorposts and above the doors of the houses in which the animals are to be eaten. That night the meat is to be roasted, and eaten with bitter herbs and with bread made without yeast. You are to eat it quickly, for you are to be dressed for travel, with your sandals on your feet and your walking stick in your hand. It is the Passover Festival to honor me, the Lord.

"On that night I will go through the land of Egypt, killing every firstborn male, both human and animal and punishing all the gods of Egypt. I am the Lord. The blood on the doorposts will be a sign to mark the houses in which you live. When I see the blood, I will pass over you and will not harm you when I punish the Egyptians. You must celebrate this day as a religious festival to remind you of what I, the Lord, have done. Celebrate it for all time to come."

An instruction on the meaning of the Passover Festival will help the participants to understand this event better.

Passover is the annual Jewish festival feast of freedom. Passover is a festival of loud rejoicing, which celebrates the time when the Lord freed the people of Israel from captivity in Egypt. It reminds us of the first Exodus when the Lord brought the Israelites out of Egypt, from slavery to freedom, from sadness to joy, from sorrow to feasting. Thus, the word "passover" means "deliverance" because in the story of the Exodus, the Lord "passed over" the homes marked with the blood of the lamb.

Passover is also known as the Feast of Unleavened Bread because the Israelites carried their bread dough, still unleavened, with them on their quick escape from Egypt.

The Passover Festival is celebrated by Jewish people in a meal called the "Seder," a word which means "order." At the Seder Meal, a special ritual order is observed. The meal includes, among other things, a roasted lamb (as a reminder of the blood which protected the Israelites) and unleavened bread, which the Jewish people call Matzoh.

CREATION CENTER

Let the participants prepare the unleavened bread now for later use during the Seder Meal at the Praise Center.

Matzoh Bread

2/3 cup boiling water
1/3 cup vegetable oil
1 tablespoon salt
1/2 teaspoon salt
1n1/2 cups matzoh meal
3 eggs

This recipe makes 5-7 small loaves, each serving 8-10 people. It should be reduced for smaller groups, or the remainder can be frozen for later use.

Mix the first four ingredients into a smooth liquid base. Add the matzoh meal and mix thoroughly. Add one egg at a time, beating well after each egg is added. Keep hands moistened with warm water when mixing. Roll the dough into 1" circles.

Bake on a greased cookie sheet at 400° for about 30 minutes until golden brown.

PRAISE CENTER

Let the dining room, or similar area, serve as the Praise Center for this celebration. Allow the participants to prepare their own setting at the table. Each setting should include:

plate;
knife, fork, spoon;
drinking glass;
small dish;
napkin;

Upon each plate should be placed small portions of:

Haroset: a combination of chopped nuts, diced apples, cinnamon, sugar and red wine, as a salad-type mixture.

Maror: a bitter herb, such as horseradish root or pieces of parsley.

Into the small dish pour *water mixed with salt.*

Prepare a pitcher of *wine or grape juice* to be poured during the meal into the glasses.

Participants should be selected to take these roles:

Leader/Father
Commentator/Adult
Mother

Place *seven candles,* unlighted, onto the table. Darken the room or center area and begin the Seder celebration.

The Passover Seder Meal

Commentator: Let us celebrate the saving acts of our Lord. Let us celebrate the Passover of the Lord, our God.

All sing verse 3 of "Fill Our Need."

Lighting of the Passover Candle:

(all should be seated) The **Mother** lights the candles on the table, leading a Repetition Prayer as she does so.

Blessed are you
Lord, God, of the universe.
Shine your blessing upon us
and save us from the darkness of sin.
You are the light
of all creation.

Blessing of the Feast:

The **Leader** prays this Repetition Prayer over the food of the meal:

Blessed are you
Lord, God of the universe.
You have saved us
from the darkness of sin.
Bless this feast
and celebrate with us
this sacred festival of the Passover.

Commentator: *Exodus 12:14*

The Lord says, "You must celebrate this day as a religious festival to remind you of what I, the Lord, have done. Celebrate it for all time to come."

Now let us drink the cup of holiness. We shall drink from the cup four times recalling the acts of the Lord during the Exodus: "I brought out... I saved... I delivered... I redeemed."

(The leader pours wine or juice into the glasses. Sing verse 2 of "Fill Our Need." Then, each drinks four times from the cup of holiness after the leader proposes this toast — all raise glasses.)

Leader/Father: Blessed are you, Lord, God of the universe. You have given us life and brought us to this festival of joy.

(Bring out the matzoh bread prepared at the Creation Center).

Commentator: Now let us eat of the bread of salvation. Let it remind us of the bread eaten by the Israelites in Egypt.

(Sing verse 1 of "Fill Our Need." Then everyone eats a small portion of the bread after the leader prays the blessing.)

Leader/Father: Blessed are you, Lord, God of the universe. You have given us freedom and brought us to this festival of joy.

(Then the marror and haroset are eaten between two pieces of matzoh, according to one ancient tradition. Another tradition of eating the marror and haroset is to dip it into salt water).

Commentator: Let us eat of the marror and the haroset. The marror symbolized the bitterness of the suffering of the Israelites in Egypt. The haroset reminds us of the mixture of the mortar used in the labor demanded by the Pharoah.

(All eat of the marror and haroset after the leader prays the blessing:)

Leader/Father: Blessed are you, Lord, God of the universe. You have brought us out of slavery to this festival of joy.

(Sing verse 3 of "Fill Our Need." Families could bring on a roasted lamb, lamb chops, or lamb stew to complete the Passover meal.)

Leader/Father:

Psalm 116:12-14

What can I offer the Lord for all his goodness to me? I will bring a wine offering to the Lord, to thank him for saving me.

In the assembly of all his people I will give him what I have promised.

Commentator: This is the Passover of the Lord. We have kept the feast. Let us rejoice and be glad!

WORD CENTER

When the participants are assembled at the Word Center, ask one to read this story of the Last Supper of the Lord.

John 13:1-5, 12-17

It was now the day before the Passover Festival. Jesus knew that the hour had come for him to leave this world and go to the Father. He had always loved those in the world who were his own, and he loved them to the very end.

Jesus and his disciples were at supper. The Devil had already put the thought of betraying Jesus into the heart of Judas, the son of Simon Iscariot. Jesus knew that the Father had given him complete power; he knew that he had come from God and was going to God. So he rose from the table, took off his outer garment, and tied a towel around his waist. Then he poured some water into a wash basin and began to wash the disciples' feet and dry them with the towel around his waist.

After Jesus had washed their feet, he put his outer garment back on and returned to this place at the table. "Do you understand what I have just done to you?" he asked. "You call me Teacher and Lord, and it is right that you do so, because that is what I am. I, your Lord and Teacher, have just washed your feet. You, then, should wash one another's feet. I have set an example for you, so that you will do just what I have done for you. I am telling you the truth; no slave is greater than his master, and no messenger is greater than the one who sent him. Now that you know this truth, how happy you will be if you put it into practice."

SHARING CENTER

Immediately following the Word Center proclamation, gather at the Sharing Center to discuss the meaning of John's account of the Last Supper. Be sure to emphasize that the meal celebrated by Jesus was the Passover meal such as we just celebrated.

Then discuss the imperative associated with Jesus' washing the disciples' feet. This an example given us by Jesus that we must love one another when we perform even the most degrading tasks and services.

Give the Witness Center activity assignment and conclude with a song, such as "Shepherd, Lead Me."

WITNESS CENTER

All the participants should be encouraged to join the parish community for the evening Mass of the Lord's Supper.

Perhaps each participant could perform some simple act of love during the next day for a member of his/her family. Polish Mom's or Dad's shoes for Easter? Cut flowers for the Easter table? Help prepare the Easter dinner? Make the bed for a brother or sister? What suggestions do the participants have?

FILL OUR NEED

This is a song of offering during the preparation of the eucharistic gifts. When the verses are sung in reverse order, it is also a prayerful blessing for use during a Passover Meal.

Dick Hilliard
arr. Rev. John H. Olivier, S.S.

Prayerfully

1. Wheat made bread, _____ we of-fer, Lord. _____ May
2. Grapes made wine, _____ we of-fer, Lord. _____ May
3. This sac-red meal, _____ we of-fer, Lord. _____ May

1. it be-come our strength and core. Food to fill
2. it be-come our strength and core. Drink to fill
3. it be-come our strength and core. Gifts to fill

1. our bod - ies, no. But love to fill our
2. our bod - ies, no. But love to fill our
3. our bod - ies, no. But love to fill our

1. hearts to grow. We are your peo-ple, Lord, come
2. hearts to grow. We are your peo-ple, Lord, come
3. hearts to grow. We are your peo-ple, Lord, come

1. sat - is - fy our hun - gry soul. Come a-mong us, here, O Lord,
2. sat - is - fy our thirst - ing soul. Come a-mong us, here, O Lord,
3. sat - is - fy our long - ing soul. Come a-mong us, here, O Lord,

1. Bless this bread, to fill our need.
2. Bless this drink, to fill our need.
3. Bless this meal, to fill our need.

LET US CARRY THE

Isaiah 52:13-53:12
Psalm 31
Hebrews 4:14-16, 5:7-9
John 18:1-19:42

John 18:28-31, 38b-40,
19:1-2a, 16, 16b-17, l8, 19,
23a, 25, 28-30, 31, 38, 41-42

The Passion of the Lord forms part of the Word Service of the Good Friday liturgy. This Center Celebration helps young participants understand some of the meaning which we have given to the story of the Passion by combining the Word Center and Praise Center activities as though they were "stations of the cross."

At each Word Center "station" you will need to select (before every reading) a narrator and someone to play the part, as indicated, of Jesus or Mary. Alternate the roles among the participants during the various "stations."

The Word Center-to-Praise Center format is suggested so that the participants might sense the physical movement of the way of the Lord's journey to the hill of Calvary.

In the Family Home

Check the baking project at the Creation Center activity. This could be an enjoyable family endeavor.

GREETING CENTER

Because this center celebration commemorates the Passion of the Lord, do not begin with a song. The mood should be solemn. If possible, remove distracting decorations from the center celebration area.

The leader should ask the participants these, or similar questions:

1. What does it mean to be condemned to death?
2. Why are people sometimes sentenced to death?
3. How is the death sentence sometimes carried out?
4. Why was Jesus punished by death on a cross?

After the participants have shared their responses to these questions, the leader should summarize their answers. Then, ask this final question:

5. How do you think Jesus felt when he was arrested and sentenced to die?

Let the participants give their ideas of Jesus' emotions. Some possible responses might be:

- disappointed in the people he loved;
- lonely and sad;
- hated and persecuted;
- confused;

Announce to the participants that this celebration will offer reminders of the pain and suffering which our Lord endured on his way to Calvary as we pray in response to the gospel passion.

Move to the Word Center as everyone sings "Carry the Cross."

WORD CENTER

Each time the participants gather at the Word Center during this celebration, they should be seated, except for the Narrator and Jesus or Mary.

Jesus should stand with arms at his side and head bowed down innocently.

John 18:28-31, 38b-40

Narrator: *Early in the morning Jesus was taken from Caiaphas' house to the governor's palace. The Jewish authorities did not go inside the palace, for they wanted to keep themselves ritually clean, in order to be able to eat the Passover meal. So Pilate went outside to them and asked, "What do you accuse this man of?"*

Their answer was, "We would not have brought him to you if he had not committed a crime."

Pilate said to them, "Then you yourselves take him and try him according to your own law."

They replied, "We are not allowed to put anyone to death."

Then Pilate went back outside to the people and said to them, "I cannot find any reason to condemn him. But according to the custom you have. I always set free a prisoner for you during the Passover. Do you want me to set free for you the king of the Jews?"

They answered him with a shout, "No, not him! We want Barabbas! (Barabbas was a bandit.)

PRAISE CENTER

The participants should stand with arms at their sides and heads bowed down. Lead this Repetition Prayer:

> Dear Father,
> do not let me punish others
> or blame others
> for things they do not do.
> Help me accept the blame
> and punishment
> for my own actions
> and my own words
> when they are wrong.

Everyone should sing "Carry the Cross" as they return to the Word Center.

CROSS

WORD CENTER

Materials Needed: a short piece of rope.

Jesus should stand with hands tied below his waist.

John 19:2-2a, 16
Narrator: *Then Pilate took Jesus and had him whipped. The soldiers made a crown of thorny branches and put it on his head.*

Then Pilate handed Jesus over to them to be crucified.

PRAISE CENTER

The participants should stand with hands clenched below the waist. Lead this Repetition Prayer:

>Dear Father,
>do not let me persecute others.
>Help me walk hand in hand
>with others in love.

Everyone should sing "Carry the Cross" as they return to the Word Center.

WORD CENTER

Jesus should stand slumped in pain.

John 19:16b-17, 10
Narrator: *So they took charge of Jesus. He went out, carrying his cross, and came to the "The Place of the Skull," as it is called. (In Hebrew it is called "Golgotha.") Pilate wrote a notice and had it put on the cross. "Jesus of Nazareth, the King of the Jews," is what he wrote.*

PRAISE CENTER

The participants should stand bent over in pain. Lead this Repetition Prayer:

>Dear Father,
>I offer you my sufferings.
>Help me to free others of pain
>and bring them happiness.

Everyone should sing "Carry the Cross" as they return to the Word Center.

WORD CENTER

Jesus should lie face up on the floor with arms outstretched, as though crucified.

John 19:18
Narrator: *There they crucified him; and they also crucified two other men, one on each side, with Jesus between them.*

PRAISE CENTER

The participants should lie on the floor with arms outstretched as though crucified. Lead this Repetition Prayer:

>Dear Father,
>give me courage
>when others don't like me.
>Help me like all people
>and never be unkind.

Everyone should sing "Carry the Cross" as they return to the Word Center.

WORD CENTER

Mary, the mother of Jesus, should stand with hands covering her face.

John 19:25
Narrator: *Standing close to Jesus' cross were his mother, his mother's sister, Mary the wife of Clopas, and Mary Magdelen. Jesus saw his mother and the disciple he loved standing there; so he said to his mother, "He is your son."*

Then he said to the disciple, "She is your mother." From that time the disciple took her to live in his home.

PRAISE CENTER

The participants should cover their faces with their hands, as though in tears. Lead this Repetition Prayer:

>Dear Father,
>I love my family very much.
>Please protect them
>from being hurt by others.
>Help me show my love
>to my parents,
>to my brothers,
>and to my sisters.

Everyone should sing "Carry the Cross" as they return to the Word Center.

WORD CENTER

Jesus should lie upon the floor, face up and stiffly, as though a corpse.

John 19:38, 41-42
Narrator: *After this, Joseph, who was from the town of Arimathea, asked Pilate if he could take Jesus' body. (Joseph was a follower of Jesus, but in secret, because he was afraid of the Jewish authorities.) Pilate told him he could have the body, so Joseph went and took it away.*

There was a garden in the place where Jesus had been put to death, and in it there was a new tomb where no one had ever been buried. Since it was the day before the Sabbath and because the tomb was close by, they placed Jesus' body there.

PRAISE CENTER

The participants should lie upon the floor, face up, and stiffly, as a corpse. Lead this Repetition Prayer:

> Dear Father,
> when I die
> take me home with you
> and with my Lord, Jesus.
> Help me prepare everyday
> to share eternal life with you.

Sing "Carry the Cross" as a conclusion to this activity.

CREATION CENTER

Wooden Twig Crosses

Materials Needed: two tree twigs for each participant, twine or string.

Fasten the twigs with twine to form small crosses. Younger participants will need help in tying a knot.

OR

Hot Cross Buns

Eating hot cross buns is one of the few Good Friday customs that has taken root in North America. While the symbol of the hot cross buns may be older than Christianity itself, these breads have become connected with the day on which the cakes are traditionally eaten. Once they were made at home by English housewives who rose at dawn to have them ready for the family breakfast, or by bakers who worked through the night, and then roamed the streets in the early hours with their cries of "Hot Cross Buns! One a penny, two a penny, Hot Cross Buns!"

Today the buns cost more to make than a penny, but they are an old custom which most families would enjoy restoring. Decorated with a deeply cut cross, they are meant to remind us of the crucifixion of the savior who rises from the death of the cross to the joy of the resurrection.

1 cake yeast
¼ cup warm water
1 cup scalded milk
¾ teaspoon salt
½ cup sugar
½ cup shortening
4½ cups sifted flour
3 egg yolks
plain frosting
1 cup raisins (if desired)

Soften yeast in water. Add scalded milk to salt, sugar and shortening. When lukewarm add yeast and 1½ cups flour. Beat well and let rise until very light. Add egg yolks and remaining flour. Knead lightly and let rise until doubled in bulk. Roll out dough to 1-inch thickness and cut into rounds. Place 1 inch apart on greased baking sheets and let rise. Glaze the surface of each bun with a little egg white diluted with water. With a sharp knife cut a cross on top of each bun. Bake in hot oven (400°) about 20 minutes. Just before removing from the oven, brush with sugar and water. Fill the cross with a plain frosting. A cup of raisins may be added to the dough if desired. Makes 2½ dozen.

SHARING CENTER

The story of the passion and death of Jesus is a tale which should remind us of the ways in which we bring pain and suffering to others. It might also be a model to us of how bravely we should accept the suffering in our lives. Discuss these simple lessons with the participants.

Then ask the participants to tell of their least favorite episode in the passion story. Help them to explain their reasons.

Then, give the Witness Center activity assignment and conclude by singing "Carry the Cross."

WITNESS CENTER

The participants should be encouraged to place their wooden twig crosses on a wall at home. Let these be reminders to them that Jesus died to save us and bring us out of our sinful ways. The cross should be a reminder, also, that we must be sorry for our sins so that we might share with Jesus the hope of the crucifixion: eternal life in the resurrection. Let us carry the cross of the Lord!

OR

Reheat the Hot Cross Buns for Holy Saturday morning breakfast. Let the decoration of the cross remind us that we must carry the cross of the Lord so that we, too, might share in the hope of the resurrection.

CARRY THE CROSS

This melody is a Lenten song to guide the follower to Calvary. Children enjoy it as an accompaniment to the Stations of the Cross. It is also appropriate during times of suffering and struggle.

March tempo
Capo 3: Play D

Dick Hilliard
arr. Rev. John H. Olivier, S.S.

Car-ry the cross___ of the Lord.___ Car-ry the cross of the

Lord like me!___ Car-ry the cross___ of the Lord.___

Car-ry it high for ev-'ry - one to see.___ see.___

THE PASSOVER LIGHT

Genesis 1:1-2:2
Psalm 104
Genesis 22:1-18
Psalm 16
Exodus 14:15-15:1
Exodus 15:1-6, 17-18
Isaiah 54:5-14
Psalm 30
Isaiah 55:1-11
Isaiah 12:2-6
Baruch 3:9-15, 32-4:4
Psalm 19
Ezekiel 36:16-28
Psalm 41
Romans 6:3-11   Romans 6:3-4, 6-10
Psalm 118
Matthew 28:1-10 or
Mark 16:1-8 or
Luke 24:1-12   Luke 24:1-12

The story of the Christian Passover culminates in the triumphant retelling of the Resurrection of Christ Jesus. These center activities should be celebrated after sunset so that the light of the candle flames can convey its richest symbolic message. The activities are carefully linked together to unravel the many messages which children and families must come to understand as their own celebration of the Easter event.

The Old Testament and Epistle readings are the same for the Years A, B, and C. During this celebration, one Old Testament selection is told in song and one Epistle is selected as a reading. Three different gospel accounts of the Resurrection are suggested, one for each year. The gospel of Luke is chosen here for its simplicity.

GREETING CENTER

Materials Needed: 1 large candle, a candle holder and some matches.

When the participants have come together for this celebration of the Easter mystery, begin by reviewing the events of Holy Thursday and Good Friday. Then ask these questions, ''What is so special about this evening? Why is this night different from every other night?''

Let the participants give their responses, helping them to realize that this is the night on which we recall that the Lord saved the Israelites during the first Passover. This is also the night that we rejoice and give thanks to God for saving us through the resurrection of Jesus. By his death and resurrection, Jesus has passed over from the darkness of sin to be the light of life. This is our Passover Feast!

Move to the Praise Center with the single lighted candle as your only source of light.

PRAISE CENTER

When everyone is quiet, lead a litany of forgiveness, in words such as these:

We are God's chosen people.
We have been given special responsibilities.
Let us be sorry for the times we have disappointed the Lord by not caring for all of creation.

Forgive us our sins, Lord, as we pray:

(Sing response 1 of ''Prayer for Mercy.'')

Keep us as your chosen people, Lord, as we pray:

(Sing response 2 of ''Prayer for Mercy.'')

Lead us to eternal life, Lord, as we pray:

(Sing response 3 or ''Prayer for Mercy.'')

Conclude with this simple Repetition Prayer, following the directions as indicated:

God, our Father
We do not like
the darkness of sin. *(extinguish candle)*

We want to follow you. *(in darkness)*

We want to live in your ways.
We want to live with Christ,
the Light of the World. *(relight the candle)*

Pause briefly, in silence, before moving to the Word Center.

WORD CENTER

A participant should be selected to read this passage by candlelight:

Romans 6:3-4, 6-10

For surely you know that when we were baptized into union with Christ Jesus, we were baptized into union with his death. By our baptism, then, we were buried with him and shared his death, in order that, just as Christ was raised from death by the glorious power of the Father, so also we might live a new life.

And we know that our old being has been put to death with Christ on his cross, in order that the power of the sinful self might be destroyed, so that we should no longer be the slaves of sin. For when a person dies, he is set free from the power of sin. Since we have died with Christ, we believe that we will also live with him. For we know that Christ has been raised from death and will never die again — death will no longer rule over him. And so, because he died, sin has no power over him; and now he lives his life in fellowship with God.

The participants should be reminded of their baptism. At baptism we are welcomed into the Christian community because we choose to follow Christ. With the Lord's help, we promise to put sin to death, to destroy its presence in our lives, to bury it out of sight. In this way, we die from a sinful life. Through baptism we rise from death to a life of love, peace and joy in Christ.

Ask the participants to renew their baptismal promises by singing "If You Believe."

CREATION CENTER

Easter Tapers

Materials Needed: candle tapers, cake-size paper plates, and scissors, if desired.

Each participant should prepare small paper plates to fit through a candle taper. Punch a hole in each plate's center and slide a candle through the hole.

WORD CENTER

When the participants return to the Word Center, only the large candle should still be lighted at this point. The participants should quietly listen to this reading of the gospel.

Luke 24:1-12

Very early on Sunday morning the women went to the tomb, carrying the spices they had prepared. They found the stone rolled away from the entrance to the tomb, so they went in; but they did not find the body of the Lord Jesus. They stood there puzzled about this, when suddenly two men in bright shining clothes stood by them. Full of fear, the women bowed down to the ground, as the men said to them, "Why are you looking among the dead for one who is alive? He is not here; he has been raised."

Interrupt the reading by singing "Alleluia" several times. Light the participants' candle tapers as everyone sings.

Then continue the reading of the Resurrection story:

"Remember what he said to you while he was in Galilee: 'The Son of Man must be handed over to sinful men, be crucified, and three days later rise to life.'"

Then the women remembered his words, returned from the tomb, and told all these things to the eleven disciples and all the rest. The women were Mary Magdalene, Joanna, and Mary the Mother of James; they told these things to the apostles. But the apostles thought that what the women said was nonsense, and they did not believe them. But Peter got up and ran to the tomb; he bent down and saw the grave cloths but nothing else. Then he went back home amazed at what had happened.

The Lord is risen!
He has passed over from death to life!
He has passed over from darkness to light!
This is our Passover Feast!
The Light of the World is with us!
Sing "Alleluia" again several times.

SHARING CENTER

Invite the participants to explain, in their own words, what this night means to them. Then, summarize the center activities in words similar to these:

We were once chosen by God. We were given special responsibilites. We disappointed God and lived in the darkness of sin.

By the death and resurrection of the Lord, we are once again chosen by God to be his special people. He has brought us over from the darkness of sin to the light of loving ways.

By our baptismal promises we have chosen to pass over with the Lord from sin to life. We, too, must be lights destroying the darkness of evil ways by our good actions.

Let us give praise and glory to our God for his marvelous acts of salvation.

Sing "This Is The Day" (p. 139), "Glory To God" or "Praise the Lord, Rejoice and Sing." Give the Witness Center activity assignment.

WITNESS CENTER

The participants should place their candles on the dining room table as the centerpiece for Easter dinner. Let the candles remind us that if we keep our baptismal promises we, too, will rise to everlasting life with Christ, our risen Lord.

ALLELUIA

This simple alleluia verse should be sung slowly at first, then repeated several times, each time growing faster. It is appropriate as a greeting to the gospel or as a proclamation during the Easter season.

Dick Hilliard
arr. Rev. John H. Olivier, S.S.

Grow faster each time

Al - le-lu - ia! Al - le-lu - ia! Al - le-lu - ia! Al - le-lu - ia! Al - le-lu - ia! ia! Al - le-lu - ia! Al - le-lu - ia! Al - le-lu - ia!

THIS IS THE DAY

The celebration of Easter was the occasion for writing this song. It is a song of gladness and Easter joy, particularly appropriate as a processional.

Psalm 118:24
Lively

Dick Hilliard
arr. Rev. John H. Olivier, S.S.

This is the day that the Lord has made. Let us re-

joice and be glad! Say Al-le, Al-le. Sing Al-le-lu-ia.

Shout Al-le-lu! This is the day God has made.

THIS IS THE LORD'S DAY

Acts 10:37-43
Psalm 118
Colossians 3:1-4 or
1 Corinthians 5:6-8
John 20:1-9

Acts 10:37-43
Psalm 118:1, 4, 15, 17, 21, 24, 26-27

The joy of Easter dawns with the rising of the sun. Children will no doubt be up early to find the gifts left by the Easter bunny. When they have finished their Easter hunt, if this is their custom, bring them together for this celebration so that the true meaning and message of the Resurrection is part of the holyday celebration in your home.

Bring the children to Mass on Easter so that the gladness of the Easter ritual is shared by all.

For Parish Programs
and in the Religious Education Classroom

This is a simple family celebration. In classroom or program settings it can be easily adapted for proper enjoyment and meaning.

GREETING CENTER

Gather early in the morning for this celebration and sing a song of praise such as "Glory to God," "Sing Praise" or "Sing A Song of Praise."

Then, tell the story of the resurrection in your own words. It might be enjoyable to allow the story to be a Chain Tale: someone starts the story, then the next participant adds to the tale, then the next, and so on, until the Resurrection of Jesus is retold in its fullest dimension.

WORD CENTER

Select one of the participants to proclaim this reading from the Acts of the Apostles:

Acts 10:37-43

You know of the great event that took place throughout the land of Israel, beginning in Galilee after John preached his message of baptism. You know about Jesus of Nazareth and how God poured out on him the Holy Spirit and power. He went everywhere, doing good and healing all who were under the power of the Devil, for God was with him. We are witnesses of everything that he did in the land of Israel and in Jerusalem. Then they put him to death by nailing him to a cross. But God raised him from death three days later and caused him to appear, not to everyone, but only to the witnesses that God had already chose, that is, to us who ate and drank with him after he rose from death. And he commanded us to preach the gospel to the people and to testify that he is the one whom God has appointed Judge of the living and the dead. All the prophets spoke about him, saying that everyone who believes in him will have his sins forgiven through the power of his name.

At the conclusion of the proclamation, let the participants suggest possible ways in which we might respond to Peter's statement, "He commanded us to preach the gospel."

Move to the Creation Center for the making of a symbol which will help us to "preach the gospel," explained later as the Witness Center activity.

CREATION CENTER

Easter Eggs

Materials Needed: hard-boiled eggs, bowls for dyes, and tongs for dipping eggs.

The custom of coloring Easter eggs does have a religious significance for Christians. An egg has the appearance of being dead, still, lifeless. But, in fact, when the shell is broken, its appearance is transformed. It indeed has life inside. It nourishes and gives strength.

Originally hard-boiled eggs were painted as gifts for friends and relatives. Many countries have special customs attached to the Easter egg.

Hard boil enough eggs for all the participants before this celebration. Prepare packaged egg dyes.

Let the participants decorate the eggs with the colored dyes. Then set them aside to dry.

A song of Easter joy, such as "Alleluia," "Everybody Sing Alleluia," or "Praise the Lord, Alleluia," might be sung while performing this egg-coloring activity.

PRAISE CENTER

Assemble at the Praise Center to pray in thanksgiving to God for the joy of Easter.

Sing "This Is The Day" between the verses of the psalm, as indicated. Select different participants to read the verses of the psalm aloud in prayer.

Psalm 118:1, 4, 15, 17, 21, 24, 26-27

Give thanks to the Lord,
  because he is good,
  and his love is eternal.
Let all who worship him say,
  "His love is eternal."

Sing "This Is The Day."

Listen to the glad shouts of
  victory in the tents of God's people.
"The Lord's mighty power has done it!"
I will not die; instead I will live
  and proclaim what the Lord has done.

Sing "This Is The Day."

I praise you, Lord, because you heard me,
  because you have given me victory.
This is the day of the Lord's victory;
  let us be happy, let us celebrate!

Sing "This Is The Day."

May God bless the one who
  comes in the name of the Lord!
From the Temple of the Lord
  we bless you.

Sing "This Is The Day."

The Lord is God; he has been good to us.
With branches in your hands,
  start the festival
  and march around the altar.

Sing "This Is The Day."

SHARING CENTER

Summarize today's Center Celebration in words such as these:

  This is the day the Lord has made.
  We should rejoice and be glad.

  Let us proclaim this day to all people.
  Let us preach the good news of Easter.

  The Lord has blessed us with the gift of eternal life.

Give the Witness Center assignment and conclude with a song such as "The Lord Blesses Me!" or "This Is The Day."

WITNESS CENTER

Today's New Testament reading summons us to preach the gospel of the Lord. He is risen!

Each participant should take a colored Easter egg from the Creation Center activity and present it to a friend. As the egg is presented, be sure to explain its significance. In this way we proclaim the gospel of the Lord. He is risen!

In Poland and Russia it has been a custom for young children to bring a basket of eggs to their parish priest for a blessing on Easter Sunday before distribution to friends and relatives. This might be a custom which some families would like to continue. How about yours?

WE'VE GOT THE SPIRIT

PENTECOST SUNDAY

To omit the Feast of Pentecost from this book would be to suggest that the Christian observance of Easter is complete without a celebration of the Spirit's presence in the life of the post-resurrection Church. Easter is given its fullest significance with the subsequent celebration of the Holy Spirit on Pentecost. It is the presence of the Spirit in our lives that allows us to profess with firmness of faith that "Jesus Christ is Lord" and he is risen!

Songs For Celebrating Pentecost

My Heart is Happy				
The Lord Blesses Me Page				
Gather 'Round, Too! Page				
Gather 'Round Page				
Modern Liturgy Vol:No				
Title/Composer				
GLORY TO GOD Dick Hilliard				X
IF YOU BELIEVE Dick Hilliard				X
PEACE Dick Hilliard				X
RED BALLOON Paulette Davis	1:7	45		
WE'VE GOT THE SPIRIT Dick Hilliard and Beverly Hilliard				X

Acts 2:1-11
Psalm 104
1 Corinthians 12:3-7, 12-13
John 20:19-23

Acts 2:1-12

John 20:19-23

This celebration begins with a balloon activity which is explained more fully as the other center activites progress. The story of Pentecost forms the basis of the first Word Center event. The gift of peace is the focus of attention at a second Word Center activity which is followed by a sharing of peace and a celebration of the Spirit's variety of gifts.

We've got the Spirit of God! Let's not lose it! Let's celebrate!

GREETING CENTER

Materials Needed: balloons, one for each participant; strips of string for each balloon, and one straight pin.

As the participants come together for this feast's celebration, distribute a deflated balloon to each child. When everyone is settled, "Glory to God" could be sung enthusiastically as the opening song.

When the song is ended, the participants should be asked these, or similar, questions about their balloons:

1. What are we supposed to do with balloons? — blow them up!
2. Why are we supposed to inflate balloons? — so we can use them, play with them, etc.
3. Can't we just leave them deflated? — then they aren't useful! — they're dead!

A few minutes could be allowed for each of the participants to inflate their balloons. Younger children might need help with this task, and most children will require assistance with the tying of the end! Let the balloons be the object of a brief period of play.

"Red Balloon" could be sung during this time of play.

After a few moments, one of the leaders should purposely pop one or two of the participants' balloons with a straight pin. When everyone's attention is captured, all should reassemble for a continuation of the discussion just interrupted. These, or similar, questions could be asked:

1. What happened to the popped balloons? — they lost their air.
2. Can they be used again? — no!
3. What should we do about this? — replace the popped balloons with new ones.

New balloons should be inflated to replace the popped ones. Then, with strips of string, each participant's balloon should be tied closely to his/her wrist before moving on to the Word Center. (Because of the Sharing Center activity, be sure that the balloons are tied with a bow. No knots, please!)

WORD CENTER

This exciting tale of the first Pentecost could be introduced in words like these:

> Our balloons can't do very much when they aren't inflated. They seem to be dead and good for nothing until they're filled with air. Then they can do all kinds of amazing things!

> Let's listen to this story from the book of the Acts of the Apostles. It's a story about the disciples who one day were filled with something so powerful that they began to do astonishing things!

Acts 2:1-12

When the day of Pentecost came, all the believers were gathered together in one place. Suddenly there was a noise from the sky which sounded like a strong wind blowing, and it filled the whole house where they were sitting. Then they saw what looked like tongues of fire which spread out and touched each person there. They were all filled with the Holy Spirit and began to talk in other languages, as the Spirit enabled them to speak.

There were Jews living in Jerusalem, religious men who had come from every country in the world. When they heard this noise, a large crowd gathered. They were all excited, because each one of them heard the believers talking in his own language. In amazement and wonder they exclaimed, "These people who are talking like this are Galileans! How is it, then, that all of us hear them speaking in our own native languages? We are from Pathia, Media, and Elam; from Mesopotamia, Judea, and Cappadocia; from Pontus and Asia, from Phrygia and Pamphylia, from Egypt and the regions of Libya near Cyrene. Some of us are from Rome, both Jews and Gentiles converted to Judaism, and some of us are from Crete and Arabia — yet all of us hear them speaking in our own languages about the great things that God had done!" Amazed and confused, they kept asking each other, "What does this mean?"

At the conclusion of the Pentecost story, questions, such as these, could be asked about the reading:

1. What filled the believers? — the Holy Spirit.
2. What amazing thing did they do when the Holy Spirit filled them? — they spoke in tongues and everyone understood.
3. Some of them asked, "What does this mean?" What do you think this means? — the Holy Spirit continues to fill the hearts of believers and helps us do amazing things.

The leader might then summarize the importance of the Pentecost event in a way similar to this:

> Our balloons need air to give them power to do amazing things like bounce and float and fall and hang. Without air, balloons are without life!

> We need the Holy Spirit to give us power to do amazing things like have faith and to love and teach and live in peace. Without the Spirit we are without life in Christ!

PRAISE CENTER

This praying activity could be introduced in words like these:

> When a balloon pops and loses its air, it is useless. It has to be thrown away and a whole new balloon has to be inflated.

> We're not balloons, though! If ever we decide to stop believing in Jesus or try to lose our faith, do you know what happens to us? Do you think we lose the life of the Holy Spirit? Well, it might seem like it to us for a while. But Jesus promised us that the Holy Spirit remains with us always, giving us power to have faith and love and live in peace. Unlike the air in a popped balloon, the Holy Spirit never leaves us. We can feel the power of the Holy Spirit in us whenever we are loving and hoping and patient and courageous and living in peace. It's the Holy Spirit that helps us do all these amazing things!

Everyone could then participate in a Chain Prayer of petition to the Holy Spirit. Each child should repeat the petitions announced by the previous participant. An example might be:

Participant 1: Holy Spirit, help us love.

Participant 2: Holy Spirit, help us love and bring peace to everyone.

Participant 3: Holy Spirit, help us love, bring peace to everyone and be patient.

Participant 4: Holy Spirit, help us love, bring peace to everyone, be patient, and recognize your amazing gifts, etc...

"We've Got the Spirit" would be an appropriate song to sing as a conclusion to this Praise Center activity.

WORD CENTER

The participants should return to the Word Center to hear this proclamation of the gospel for Pentecost. One of the participants could be selected to read this passage. (At the conclusion of the reading, the participants could be divided into two groups, each group preparing a short dramatization of Jesus' appearance to the disciples for the other group.)

John 20:19-23

It was late that Sunday evening, and the disciples were gathered together behind locked doors, because they were afraid of the Jewish authorities. Then Jesus came and stood among them. "Peace be with you," he said. After saying this, he showed them his hands and his side. The disciples were filled with joy at seeing the Lord. Jesus said to them again, "Peace be with you. As the Father sent me, so I send you." Then he breathed on them and said, "Receive the Holy Spirit. If you forgive people's sins, they are forgiven; if you do not forgive them, they are not forgiven."

A short discussion about Jesus' final gift of peace and the Holy Spirit might be appropriate following this reading or group dramatization.

CREATION CENTER

Peace Balloons

Materials Needed: crayons or marking pens, construction paper (8½" X 5½"), and glue or tape.

On paper cut to the size indicated, each participant should print the word "PEACE." With a small amount of glue or a piece of tape, the "peace signs" should be attached to each participant's balloon (still fastened to his/her wrist).

During this project everyone could sing "If You Believe," with special emphasis on the third verse.

SHARING CENTER

The participants should be reminded of the celebration's gospel story in which Jesus appeared to the disciples and said, "Peace be with you."

Everyone should be invited to make the same blessing of "Peace be with you" upon their family and friends and new acquaintances and even during this celebration! The participants should make two lines, side by side, then face a partner. As everyone sings "Peace," then an exchange of the "Peace Balloons" could be made by simply unfastening the strings from their wrists.

The Witness Center activity assignment should be given before concluding with a song of the Spirit, such as "Glory to God" or "We've Got the Spirit."

WITNESS CENTER

The Holy Spirit is the source of a variety of gifts and powers in the lives of Christian people. The participants should discuss with their parents the different gifts of the Holy Spirit, perhaps concentrating on one gift each day during the coming week. They could write the "gift of the day" on a piece of paper, attach it to the string of their balloon (to be hung in their bedrooms) and seek to "find" that gift in other Christians during each particular day.

1 Corinthians 12:4-11 gives a partial listing of the Spirit's gifts. This passage could be given as a reference in the "kidsletter" or distributed on a separate sheet as an aid to the parents.

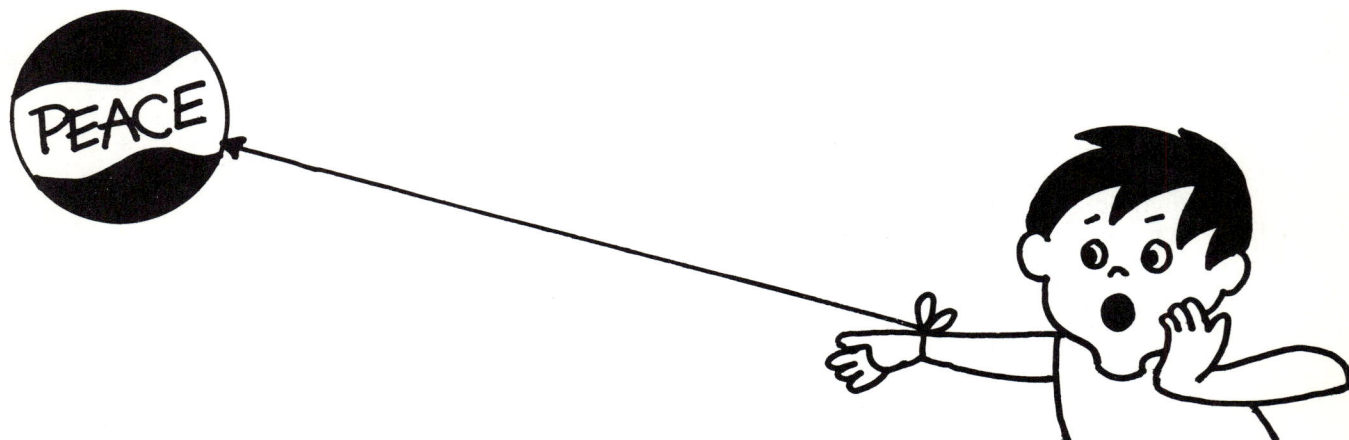

APPENDICES

Appendix I:

CALENDAR TABLE OF LITURGICAL SEASONS AND FEASTS
(for determining dates of celebrations and cycles of readings)

YEAR	CYCLE	FIRST SUNDAY OF ADVENT	ASH WEDNESDAY	EASTER
1977-1978	A	27 Nov 77	8 Feb 78	26 Mar 78
1978-1979	B	3 Dec 78	28 Feb 79	15 Apr 79
1979-1980	C	2 Dec 79	20 Feb 80	6 Apr 80
1980-1981	A	30 Nov 80	4 Mar 81	19 Apr 81
1981-1982	B	29 Nov 81	24 Feb 82	11 Apr 82
1982-1983	C	28 Nov 82	16 Feb 83	3 Apr 83
1983-1984	A	27 Nov 83	7 Mar 84	22 Apr 84
1984-1985	B	2 Dec 84	20 Feb 85	7 Apr 85
1985-1986	C	1 Dec 85	12 Feb 86	30 Mar 86
1986-1987	A	30 Nov 86	4 Mar 87	19 Apr 87
1987-1988	B	29 Nov 87	17 Feb 88	3 Apr 88
1988-1989	C	27 Nov 88	8 Feb 89	26 Mar 89
1989-1990	A	3 Dec 89	28 Feb 90	15 Apr 90

Center — A center is an area in a room or house designated for a particular activity during a celebration of God's Word. Each center is given a title (i.e. Greeting, Word, Praise, Creation, Sharing, Witness) which reveals the general kind of activity to be performed in this area by the participants in the celebration.

The purpose of a center is to demonstrate the varied components of Christian worship. When combined, centers form an integrated celebration for participants who are eager to hear the Word of the Lord and respond to its calling.

Chain Prayer — A Chain Prayer is a multiple series of petitions which several persons join together as one continuous offering to the Father. A Chain Prayer begins when one person announces his/her petition before the group assembled to pray. It continues when another person repeats this same petition and adds an additional petition. Another person adds his/her petition after repeating those which have gone before, and so on. No person should contribute more than one link in the prayer.

The purpose of a Chain Prayer is to help the petitioners realize the infinite needs of those who rely on the help of the Lord, whose unceasing love pours forth countless blessings upon his creation. A Chain Prayer ends when everyone in the praying group has offered his/her link in the series of petitions.

Chain Tale — A chain tale is one story to which several story tellers contribute fact or fiction.

If it is a factual telling, one person begins the story until he/she has deviated from the truth. Another person continues the tale until he/she has also deleted important information. Anyone can continue the storytelling, as long as the truth or sequence of fact is announced. The chain tale ends when all the facts are revealed.

If the story is fictional, each person contributes to the tale's development according to his/her imagination within a determined time span, such as 30 or 60 seconds each. Each story teller is to contribute to the tale, in turn, only once.

The purpose of a chain tale is to involve all persons of the group in one continuous story-telling adventure. It is often used to retell Scripture passages, testing the memory of the listeners.

Kidsletter — A Kidsletter is a written summary statement of activities performed during a Center Celebration. It is most often written by teachers or coordinators of parish Center Celebration programs for the parents of children participating in the celebrations. It is often written in language which would suggest it was authored as a narrative by the children sharing in the celebration. Hence, a ''kids' letter.'' (See Appendix III.)

The purpose of a Kidsletter is to inform parents of the activities shared, to stimulate discussion between parent and child about the Center Celebration, and to encourage parents' challenging children to perform the Witness Center activity at home as suggested during each celebration.

Movement Prayer — A Movement Prayer seeks to visualize through simple physical gesture the words of a prayer offered in praise, thanksgiving, or petition to the Lord. Those participating in the prayer mirror the bodily movements of the prayer's leader. The purpose of a Movement Prayer is to fully engage the praying person in the spirit of the prayer through total bodily involvement.

When first attempted, Movement Prayers are usually combined with a Repetition Prayer. With practice, Movement Prayers can be more touching when the gestures are spontaneous interpretations of the phrases of the prayer by each participant. In its most sophisticated form, a Movement Prayer can employ simple bodily gesture without the aid of the spoken word.

Repetition Prayer — A Repetition Prayer is a verse prayer in which the words of the leader are repeated at phrased intervals by other participants. The leader pauses after each spoken phrase to allow the other participants to repeat the words as though these were their own prayers.

The purpose of a Repetition Prayer is to provide a model of prayerful attitude and wording for participants learning to pray. It is an attempt to demonstrate the reverence, versatility and spontaneity with which prayer is composed. Repetition Prayers are most frequently used with young children or whenever the leader desires to involve the entire gathering in the speaking of a prayer.

Secret Message — A Secret Message is a whispered communication spoken quietly into the ear of another person. It has a chained effect in that once it is received it is to be immediately transmitted in similar fashion to the next participant until everyone has received the Secret Message. Each participant is to whisper the Secret Message only once, and is never to repeat it, even if it was not entirely heard by the recipient. The Secret Message is announced to the group by the last receiver, and is most often distorted in some fashion from its original composition.

The purpose of a Secret Message is to emphasize some essential or important lesson which the leader desires the participants to grasp. (It is often a clever means of restoring order to a restless group of participants!)

Secret Message Prayer — A Secret Message Prayer is a short, concise petition or statement of praise or thanksgiving to the Lord transmitted from one participant to the next as in the method of a simple Secret Message. Its purpose is to intensify the emotion of a prayer among the participants. A Secret Message Prayer differs from a simple Secret Message in that it is never announced aloud to the group. It remains written only on the hearts of the participants.

Spontaneous Prayer — A Spontaneous Prayer is a petition of praise, thanksgiving or need presented to the Lord without preparatory formulation. It is composed on the spot by the leader or a participant in his/her own words.

The purpose of a Spontaneous Prayer is to capture the emotion or sentiment of the participants at a particular moment and to place that feeling before the Lord. Spontaneous Prayer is the kind of prayer with which most people come to be comfortable. It takes courage at first to pray spontaneously with others, but, with practice, it will come more easily.

Appendix III: THE KIDSLETTER

The Kidsletter has been designed by teachers and adult leaders of Center Celebrations in which children participate without the company of their parents. It is a printed summary of the many center activities shared during a Center Celebration distributed to the participants at the close of the celebration for delivery to their parents. Kidsletters are written in an effort to involve and encourage parents in discussion with their children about the theme, lesson and activities of the Center Celebration.

As the Kidsletter concept has developed, it has been found most effective when it is written in words suggestive of a child's authorship. In this way the printed communication of the Kidsletter to parents is received at home as though the child were giving a short account of his/her involvement in the Center Celebration conducted at school or church.

Kidsletters have particular significance when parents not only read the informative statement of shared activities, but when they actively assist their children in the Witness Center activity assignment between Center Celebrations. Thus, the gospel's message, emphasized in the center activities, becomes fully integrated into the lives of children when the family shares in responding to its summons to action.

Kidsletters can become an enjoyable feature of Center Celebrations conducted in schools and parish programs. Written and duplicated in preparation for the Center Celebration, Kidsletters are an effective means of communication between celebration leaders and the parents of celebration participants.

The style and format of Kidsletters will vary according to each leader. The following Kidsletter is prepared as an example based upon the First Celebration beginning on page 26.

A SAMPLE KIDSLETTER

Date: September 15
Theme: "Getting To Know You"

GREETING CENTER

What a surprise to walk into our Center Celebration room today and find it filled with so much color and activity! All us kids huddled around the Greeting Center waiting anxiously for our kids' celebration to begin. Then all of a sudden, without any warning, we heard "Howdy, Friends" (that's our new song written just for kids!). We all took our turns singing our names to one another, and just as you might expect, some of us goofed! But that's all the goofin' around we had time for today!

WORD CENTER

Did you know that the bible is full of God's Word? We found that out today as we listened to a story about creation. We pretended that we were the very first people God loved, so we gave names to lots of animals who made noises like "roar!" and "chirp" and "meow." Can you guess who made these strange sounds today?

PRAISE CENTER

We gathered together to pray to God at the Praise Center. Did you know that God has lots of names, too? I know a few of his names. Would you like to hear them?

Then we sang a song called "Call My Name" and learned that God wants us to call his name whenever we pray. What name do you call when you pray to God?

CREATION CENTER

We're gonna be making lots of special things at the Creation Center this year. Today we drew names from a hat and made name tags for each other. Guess who drew my name?

SHARING CENTER

Do you know who I am in God's eye? (It's a really simple answer. But, if you need help, I can tell you!) We sang this funny song called "Who Am I In God's Eye?" and gave our name tags to our new friends. I bet you can't guess who got the name tag that I made!

WITNESS CENTER

The Witness Center takes place at home. That' right! So, please help me after every Center Celebration with my Witness Center activity. This week's activity sounds simple...Will you help me find out the meaning of the word "Christian"?

INDICES

INDEX OF CREATION CENTER ACTIVITIES

Advent Calendars	32
Advent Wreath	59
Balloons	70
Balloons, Peace	144
Baptismal Records	121
Baptismal Stoles, Paper	87
Buttons, Good News	55
Calendars, Advent	32
Candle Holders	100
Cards, Christmas Greeting	44
Cards, Christmas Wreath	44
Cards, Petition	81
Clay Creatures	47
Crosses, Wooden Twig	134
Drawings	115
Drawings, Family	77
Easter Eggs	141
Easter Tapers	137
Fig Treats	119
Finish Lines	123
Hearts, Paper	113
Hearts, Pocket	83
Holy Water Cans	99
Hope Chests	103
Hot Cross Buns	134
Jesse Tree Ornaments	35
Love Circles	109
Masks, Player	125
Masks, Sack	39
Matzoh Bread	129
Megaphones	66
Mobiles, Star	85
Name Tags	27
Offering Cans	107
Ornaments, Creation	93
Ornaments, Jesse Tree	35
Peace Balloons	144
Peace Grams	57
Petition Cards	81
Posters, "I Believe"	111
Prayer Jars	91
Pretzels	95
Puppets, Paper Bag Prophets	39
Rainbows, Paper	105
Sick Lists	117
Signs, Paper Road	62
Star Mobiles	85
Stoles, Paper	87
Tapers, Easter	137
"Things To Do" Lists	51
Tree, Creation	93
Tree, Jesse	35
Wreath, Advent	59
Wreath, Christmas Card	44

INDEX OF FOOD RECIPES

Fig Candy	119
Fig Pudding	119
Fig Puffs	119
Hot Cross Buns	134
Matzoh Bread	129
Pax Cakes	125
Pretzels	95

INDEX OF GAMES FOR CELEBRATION

Hide-and-Go-Seek	30
Mystery Persons	77
Noah's Song Game	104
Racing Contest	123
Secret Message Game	56, 84
We Doubt It	96
Wishing Game	102

INDEX OF PUPPET SHOWS BASED ON SCRIPTURAL TALES

Abraham's Sacrifice (Genesis 22)	106
Believe (John 4:5-42)	97
The Garden of Eden (Genesis 2 and 3)	92
The Lost Son and Loving Father (Luke 15:11-32)	120
The Song of Isaiah (Isaiah 61)	53

INDEX OF SHORT STORIES

Disaster at the Damascus Zoo	68
Wilbur in the Wilderness	64

INDEX OF SONGS AND REFRAINS

Alleluia	138
An Advent Wreath Song	61
Carry the Cross	135
Fill Our Need	131
Follow the Star	88
Hosanna!	126
Keep Us Close	75
The Lord Blesses Me!	28

This Is The Day 139
Today is Born Our Savior 74

Believe 97
Come, Lord 102
Father, Care 44
Prayer for Mercy 109

INDEX OF STORIES AND FAMILIAR PER-
SONALITIES OF SCRIPTURE

Abraham, Call of 35, 94
Abraham and Isaac 106
Adam and Eve 35, 92
Annunciation of Mary 56
Creation 26, 92
Elizabeth 69
King David, Call of 36
Gabriel, the angel 56
Herod the King 84
Holy Family's Flight into Egypt 76
Holy Spirit's Descent 143
Isaiah 36, 39, 50, 53
Jesus, Childhood of 76, 78, 80
Jesus, Entry into Jerusalem 124
Jesus, Family Lineage 34
Jesus, Finding in the Temple 80
Jesus, Infancy of 43, 72, 82, 84
Jesus, Last Supper 130
Jesus, Passion of 132
Jesus, Presentation in the Temple 78
Jesus, Resurrection 137
Jesus, Temptation in the Desert 114
Jesus, Transfiguration of 116
John the Baptist 36, 40, 50, 62, 86
Jonah and the Whale 36
Joseph, Betrothal to Mary 36
Lazarus, Raising of 102
The Magi 84
Mary, Annunciation of 36
Mary, Betrothal to Joseph 56
Mary, Mother of God 82
Mary and Martha 102
Moses 35
Nicodemus 110
Noah's Ark 31, 35, 104
Parables of Jesus: Barren Fig Tree 118
Parables of Jesus: Prodigal Son and Loving Father 120
Passover, Jewish 128
Pentecost 142
Pilate 132
Psalm 23 101
Samaritan Woman 97

St. Paul 42
Ten Commandments 108
Three Kings 84
Visitation 69

INDEX OF TRADITIONAL AND CULTURAL
CUSTOMS

Advent Calendars 32
Advent Wreath 59
Almsgiving 107
Christmas Candle 73
Christmas Cards 44
Easter Eggs 141
Family Dedication 79
Fasting 115
Hope Chests 103
Hot Cross Buns 134
Jesse Tree 35
Mothering Sunday 121
Pax Cakes 125
The Pretzel 95
Seder Passover Meal 128
Stations of the Cross 132

INDEX OF TRADITIONAL PRAYERS ADAPTED FOR
USE WITH CHILDREN

Apostle's Creed 87
Act of Contrition 118
Act of Faith 98
Act of Hope 103
Glory to the Father 125
Hail Mary 57, 83
Lord's Prayer 91
Stations of the Cross 132

INDEX OF THEMES FOR CELEBRATION

Acquaintance 26
Almsgiving 106
Ancestry of Jesus 34
Angels 56
Baptism 86, 96, 120, 136
Being Alone 114
Being Lost 62, 64, 120
Belief . . . . See Faith
Blame 122
Blessing from the Lord 52, 104
Christian, (meaning of name) 34

Community 26, 96, 100, 114
Covenant 104-113
Creation of Man 46
Creation of World 92
Cross of Christ . . . . . 116, 132 See also Sacrifices
Darkness . . . . See Light
Death 132
Death and Life 140
Devil 114
Expectation 64
Expected, The Least 68
Faith 86, 96, 110, 142
Family Life 76-81
Family of Jesus . . . . . 34, See also Family Life
Forgiveness . . . . See Reconciliation
Freedom 128
Gifts from God
    92, 142, See also Blessings from the Lord
Good News, Announcing 64
Good News, Receiving 52
Guilt . . . . See Blame
Hope 102
Human Weakness 122
Jesse Tree 34
Jesus, Baptism of 86
Jesus, Birth of 72
Jesus, Death of 132
Jesus, Humanity/Divinity of 114
Jesus, Kingship of 124
Jesus, Pointing to 84
Jesus, Preparing for 30, 50
Jesus, Resurrection of 136, 140, 142
Law . . . . See Rules
Least Expected 68
Life (Resurrection) 140, 142
Light/Darkness 72, 100, 140
Loneliness 114
Lost . . . . See Being Lost
Love, God's 46, 104, 112, 118
Love, Family 76-81
Love, of Neighbor
    108, (See the Witness Center Activities)
Mary, Mother of God 82
Meal, Seder 128
Mercy of God 118-121
Messengers (Angels) 110
Mothers 82
Names, God's 26, 112
Names, Human 26, 34, 86, 78
Passover, Christian 136
Passover, Jewish 128
Patience 38
Peace . . . . 124, 142, See also Reconciliation

People, Chosen . . . 92-99, 112, 136, See also Covenant
Personhood 92
Poor, concern for 106
Prayer . . 90, 94, 112, (See the Praise Center activities)
Preparation for the Lord 30, 50
Promises, of God 58, 102, 104, 110
Promises, of People 58, 104
Reconciliation . . 76, 90, 100, 108-111, 114, 120, 136
Rules 108
Sacrifices 106, 114
Secrets 84
Seder Meal 128
Service, Christian . . See the Witness Center activities
Sin . . . . See Reconciliation
Sorrow . . . . See Reconciliation
Suffering . . . . 116, 132, See also Sacrifices
Surprise 68
Temptation 114
Thanksgiving 82, 92
Trust 96, 102
Vocation 82, 92-103
Waiting 96
Weakness 122
Willingness . . . . See Vocation

INDEX OF CENTER CELEBRATION THEME TITLES

As Clay in God's Hands 46
Be Patient 38
Believe the Way of Salvation 110
A Colorful Covenant 104
Come Before the Lord 78
Don't Blame Me! 122
Don't Tempt Me! 114
The Family of Jesus 34
Follow the Star! 84
Getting to Know You! 26
The Gift of Faith 108
God Keeps His Promises! 58
Grace and Peace Be Yours 42
Growing in God's Favor 80
A Heart Filled With Treasures 82
Holy Ones, Pray! 94
Hope in God's Life 102
Hosanna To Our King 124
I'm Gonna Be An Angel 56
Jesus Christ is Born! 72
Let Us Carry the Cross 132
Let Us Pray 90
Light the Way of Love 100
The Lord Chooses Me 52
The Lord Comes To Us 30
Love God, Love All 108

Mercy Fig-ures! 118
Our Life Together 76
Our Passover Festival 128
The Passover Light 136
Proclaim This Faith 86
Rejoice! The Lord Is Coming! 64
Take Up the Cross of the Lord 114
This is the Lord's Day 140
This Way to the Savior 62
Very Special Persons 92
Welcome Back 120
We've Got Things to Do 50
What A Sacrifice 106
What A Surprise 68
Written on Their Hearts 112